"With an impressive mastery of the pri... detailed yet accessible account of the liturgical contexts that shaped the exegesis of one late tenth-century English monk, Ælfric of Eynsham. By close analysis of four Old English homilies on the gospel of Matthew, Olsen contributes to a growing body of scholarship that takes Ælfric seriously as an original theologian, not just a compiler of patristic authorities. Approaching Ælfric's writings from the vantage point of a New Testament scholar, moreover, Dr. Olsen is well placed to observe some broader tendencies in Ælfric's hermeneutics that previous scholars have missed."

> —Christopher A. Jones
> Professor, Department of English
> Ohio State University

"Derek A. Olsen has broken new ground in the field of biblical studies. For years Christians serious about the foundations of their faith have pleaded for the kind of work Olsen has produced, but theologians and biblical scholars have typically responded either by merely nodding silently or, at most, by quoting a handful of patristic and medieval writers in their explorations and commentaries. Olsen's thesis, carefully researched and elegantly and clearly written, is nothing less than the one and only substantial sequel to Jean Leclercq's *The Love of Learning and the Desire for God*. Monastic men and women reading the first two chapters will have an experience of self-discovery: 'So this is what monastic culture is all about.'"

> —Mark A. Scott, OCSO, SSL
> Abbot
> New Melleray Abbey

"*Reading Matthew with Monks* invites contemporary students of the Bible to read Matthew in conversation with Benedictine monks of medieval England. The surprising result of this generative conversation is that, at the same time that contemporary readers learn much *about* the liturgically framed reading practices of the monks, we may actually learn more *from them* about how to expand and deepen our own reading practices."

> —Gail R. O'Day
> Dean and Professor of New Testament and Preaching
> Wake Forest University School of Divinity

"In *Reading Matthew with Monks*, Derek Olsen invites us into a conversation with the communion of saints, both living and dead. This communal reading across time and space is grounded in careful scholarship—medieval and modern—while bringing alive the faith experiences of those who, then and now, read and perform the Scriptures. In particular, Olsen demonstrates the central but much neglected role that liturgy played in early medieval monastic interpretive communities. In restoring that performative context for reading Scripture, he corrects the misguided modern notion that early medieval Europe lacked a commentary tradition but was merely derivative. Indeed, Olsen succeeds in taking one prolific Anglo-Saxon homiletic writer, Ælfric of Eynsham, and makes him the equal of modern biblical scholars brought into the dialogue on select passages of the Gospel of Matthew, including the paradigmatic Beatitudes from Jesus' Sermon on the Mount. The exciting challenge of this book is the invitation to continue the conversation."

> —Karen Louise Jolly
> Professor of History, University of Hawai'i Mānoa
> Author of *The Community of St. Cuthbert in the Late Tenth Century*

"Derek Olsen's study of biblical interpretation at the hands of the medieval monk Ælfric of Eynsham strikes just the right balance. He suggests that today's serious work with biblical texts is competent to answer certain questions and then shows how alternative approaches enrich how we engage those texts spiritually and theologically. He drills down into the interpretive sensibilities and practices of a single monk yet contextualizes that work so that we are challenged by them. Whether read as an expanded chapter in the history of biblical interpretation or as an exemplar on how theological interpreters might learn from premodern readings of Scripture, this is a welcome contribution."

> —Joel B. Green
> Dean of the School of Theology
> Fuller Theological Seminary

"*Reading Matthew with Monks* introduces us modern readers into this distinct culture of medieval liturgy and teaches us to catch the voice and the thoughts of those monks who not only read but truly strove to live the Gospel."

> —Wim Verbaal
> Latin Language and Literature
> University of Ghent, Belgium

Reading Matthew with Monks

Liturgical Interpretation in Anglo-Saxon England

Derek A. Olsen

Foreword by
Luke Timothy Johnson

A Michael Glazier Book

LITURGICAL PRESS
Collegeville, Minnesota

www.litpress.org

A Michael Glazier Book published by Liturgical Press

Cover design by Jodi Hendrickson. Illustration from the Historisches Archiv der Stadt Köln, HAStK 7010 147, f. 7v-8r. Photo by the Hill Museum & Manuscript Library. Used by permission.

1	2	3	4	5	6	7	8	9

Library of Congress Cataloging-in-Publication Data

Olson, Derek A.
    Reading Matthew with monks : liturgical interpretation in Anglo-Saxon England / Derek A. Olson ; Foreword by Luke Timothy Johnson.
        pages   cm
    "A Michael Glazier book."
    Includes bibliographical references.
    ISBN 978-0-8146-8317-0 — ISBN 978-0-8146-8342-2 (ebook)
    1. Bible. Matthew—Sermons.   2. Bible—Criticism, interpretation, etc.—History.   3. Aelfric, Abbot of Eynsham.   I. Johnson, Luke Timothy, writer of foreword.   II. Title.

BS2575.54.O47   2015
226.2'060942—dc23   2014043815

Contents

Foreword

Luke Timothy Johnson

In this superb study of medieval liturgical interpretation of the Gospel of Matthew, Derek Olsen makes an important contribution to a growing movement among biblical scholars, namely, paying serious attention to the history of interpretation. This movement, I am convinced, is more than a fad driven by boredom and frustration at the meager yield of obsessive historical criticism of Scripture or the hunger for less trampled territory to explore. It is inspired by the simple conviction that the world that shaped the Bible—so sedulously examined by historical critics—is ultimately less interesting and significant than the world that the Bible shapes. Scripture imagines a world that centuries of believers have entered and, through embodied practices, made their own. Biblical scholars are beginning to appreciate that the history of interpretation is of genuine significance even for their traditional task of exegesis: the way in which scriptural texts were used and understood within the tradition not only tells us about the perceptions of interpreters but also reveals the rich polyvalence of the texts themselves. How passages *were* understood helps show how they *can* be understood.

Although the patristic interpretation of Scripture has long been analyzed and applauded, medieval interpretation continues to be widely regarded as derivative and undistinguished. This, despite Henri de Lubac's universally admired study, *Medieval Exegesis*. Indeed, the massive size and apparent comprehensiveness of de Lubac's work may have encouraged the sense that all other investigators would find among medieval interpreters would be what de Lubac had already discovered. But while de Lubac pointed the way to an appreciation of medieval interpretation, by no means did he exhaust the subject, especially since he paid relatively little attention to the true center of interpretive creativity in the Middle Ages, the liturgy.

Building on the seminal work of Jean Leclercq on monastic culture (*The Love of Learning and the Desire for God*) and on William Flynn's groundbreaking analysis of a single interpretive community (*Medieval Music as Exegesis*), Olsen sets out to re-create in minute detail the liturgical context within which the sermons of Ælfric—a key figure in the Benedictine revival in tenth-century England—were delivered. Thanks to his astonishing reconstruction of the entire monastic *ordo*, we are able to read Ælfric's sermons on Matthew, translated by Olsen from the Old English, not as isolated literary productions, but as moments within a living cycle of reflection on Scripture throughout the monastic day. This historical contextualization is by itself a major accomplishment, all the more impressive because carried out not by a professional medievalist but by a New Testament scholar.

It is as a New Testament scholar, indeed, that Olsen brings something genuinely original to the study of medieval monastic interpretation. First, he provides a careful comparison between the respective reading cultures of contemporary historical critics of the New Testament and monastic interpreters like Ælfric; the present-day world of academic analysis has different premises but shares many of the practices of the monks: both monks and academics, for example, make extensive use of earlier authorities in constructing their own interpretations. Second, he shows in detail how contemporary commentators interpret selected passages in Matthew, comparing them to interpretations of the same passages in Ælfric's sermons. By comparing social settings, interpretive practices, and specific readings, Olsen creates the possibility of conversation between critical and so-called precritical exegesis, a conversation that does not in the least slight the contributions of modern readers but sharpens an appreciation for the monastic interpretive tradition.

Despite the evenhandedness of his approach, readers of Olsen's work will, I think, be impressed by how much more "scriptural" was the world of medieval monks, compared to our own. The contemporary exegetes whom Olsen analyzes are all believers and all dedicated to the church.

But because their discourse is shaped by the conventions of the academic guild more than by the tropes of worship, their engagement with the text seems detached and merely descriptive, whereas the words of Ælfric serve to advance the goal of the entire monastic enterprise, which was (and remains) the transformation of life according to the mind of Christ. One can only hope that this fine study, having shown the way, will encourage similar studies of individual interpreters, especially those who, like Ælfric, are deeply shaped by the liturgy.

Acknowledgments

This work began life as a dissertation for Emory University's graduate division of religion, Department of New Testament. It evolved under the direction of my committee, Gail O'Day, Michael Brown, James Morey, Charles Hackett, and my director, Luke Timothy Johnson. I owe them all a great debt for their assistance.

In the five years since I defended the original dissertation, much valuable work has been published in the many and various fields on which it touches. My attempts to keep myself up to date on this expanding body of literature were made possible through the dedication of the interlibrary loan department of Baltimore's Enoch Pratt Free Library, and especially the wonderful folks at the Light Street Branch.

Thanks also are due to Liturgical Press and Hans Christoffersen for taking a chance on this work. Patrick McGowan's editing saved me from countless infelicities of wording and grammar.

There have been, over the years, countless people who have supported this work intellectually, emotionally, spiritually, and financially—to all of you I owe my deepest gratitude. Special acknowledgment goes to my long-suffering and beloved wife, Meredith Kefauver Olsen, and our wonderful daughters, Greta and Hannah, who sacrificed the most; to my advisor and mentor, Luke Timothy Johnson, without whom this never would have gotten off the ground, let alone completed; and to the congregations and clergy of St. Mary the Virgin, Times Square, and the Cathedral of St. Philip, Atlanta, who stood by us and gave us strength in the darkest hours.

Abbreviations

ÆCHom I (Pref)[1]	Preface to the first cycle of Ælfric's *Catholic Homilies* as edited in Peter Clemoes, *Ælfric's Catholic Homilies: The First Series, Text*, Early English Text Society, supplementary series 17 (Oxford: Oxford University Press, 1997), 174–77.
ÆCHom I, 1	Homily *De initio creaturae* in the first cycle of Ælfric's *Catholic Homilies* as edited in Peter Clemoes, *Ælfric's Catholic Homilies: The First Series, Text*, Early English Text Society, supplementary series 17 (Oxford: Oxford University Press, 1997), 178–89.
ÆCHom I, 8	Homily for the Third Sunday after Epiphany in the first cycle of Ælfric's *Catholic Homilies* as edited in Peter Clemoes, *Ælfric's Catholic Homilies: The First Series, Text*, Early English Text Society, supplementary series 17 (Oxford: Oxford University Press, 1997), 241–48.
ÆCHom I, 8 (App)	Appendix to the Homily for the Third Sunday after Epiphany in the first cycle of Ælfric's *Catholic Homilies* as edited in Peter Clemoes, *Ælfric's Catholic Homilies: The First Series, Text*, Early English Text Society, supplementary series 17 (Oxford: Oxford University Press, 1997), 553.

[1] These and all other titles of Old English texts follow the standards established by the *Dictionary of Old English* which can be found online at: http://www.doe.utoronto.ca/st/index.html. Accessed November 7, 2014.

ÆCHom I, 11   Homily for the First Sunday in Lent in the first cycle of Ælfric's *Catholic Homilies* as edited in Peter Clemoes, *Ælfric's Catholic Homilies: The First Series, Text*, Early English Text Society, supplementary series 17 (Oxford: Oxford University Press, 1997), 266–74.

ÆCHom I, 13   Homily for the feast of the Annunciation in the first cycle of Ælfric's *Catholic Homilies* as edited in Peter Clemoes, *Ælfric's Catholic Homilies: The First Series, Text*, Early English Text Society, supplementary series 17 (Oxford: Oxford University Press, 1997), 281–89.

ÆCHom I, 36   Homily for the feast of All Saints in the first cycle of Ælfric's *Catholic Homilies* as edited in Peter Clemoes, *Ælfric's Catholic Homilies: The First Series, Text*, Early English Text Society, supplementary series 17 (Oxford: Oxford University Press, 1997), 486–96.

ÆCHom II, 1   Homily for Christmas in the second cycle of Ælfric's *Catholic Homilies* as edited in Malcolm Godden, *Ælfric's Catholic Homilies: The Second Series, Text*, Early English Text Society, supplementary series 5 (London: Oxford University Press, 1979), 3–11.

ÆCHom II, 44   Homily for the Common of Virgins in the second cycle of Ælfric's *Catholic Homilies* as edited in Malcolm Godden, *Ælfric's Catholic Homilies: The Second Series, Text*, Early English Text Society, supplementary series 5 (London: Oxford University Press, 1979), 327–34.

ÆHex   Ælfric's *Hexameron* as edited in Samuel J. Crawford, *Exameron Anglice or The Old English Hexameron*, Bib. ags. Prosa 10 (Hamburg: H. Grand, 1921 [repr. Darmstadt, 1968]), 33–74.

ÆHom 12   Ælfric's sermon *De sancta Trinitate et de festis diebus per annum* as edited in; John C. Pope, *Homilies of Ælfric: A Supplementary Collection*, 2 vols., Early English Text Society 259, 260 (London: Oxford University Press, 1967–1968), 1:463–72.

ÆLet 4
(SigeweardB)

Ælfric's *Letter to Sigeweard* as edited in Samuel J. Crawford, *The Old English Version of the Heptateuch*, Early English Text Society 160 (London: Oxford Univeristy Press, 1922 [repr. with additions by N. R. Ker, 1969]), 18–33, 39–51.

ÆLet 6
(Wulfgeat)

Ælfric's *Letter to Wulfgeat* as edited in Bruno Assmann, *Angelsächsische Homilien und Heiligenleben*, Bib. ags. Prosa 3 (Kassel: G. H. Wigand, 1889 [repr. with intro. by P. Clemoes, Darmstadt, 1964]), 1–12.

ÆLS (Memory
of Saints)

Sermon on the Memory of the Saints in Ælfric's *Lives of the Saints*, edited in Walter W. Skeat, *Ælfric's Lives of Saints*, 4 vols., Early English Text Society 76, 82, 94, 114 (London: Oxford University Press, 1881–1900 [repr. in 2 vols., 1966]), 1:336–62.

CAO

René-Jean Hesbert, *Corpus Antiphonalium Officii*. 6 vols. (Rome: Herder, 1963ff.).

De Doc. Chr.

Augustine, *On Christian Doctrine*, trans. D. W. Robertson, Jr. (Upper Saddle River, NJ: Prentice-Hall, 1958).

LME

Ælfric's *Letter to the Monks at Eynsham* as edited in Christopher A. Jones, *Ælfric's Letter to the Monks at Eynsham* (Cambridge: Cambridge University Press, 1998).

OR

Ordines Romani as edited in Michel Andrieu, ed., *Les Ordines romani du haut moyen âge*. 5 Vols., *Spicilegium Sacrum Lovaniense* 11, 23, 24, 28, 29 (Louvain, 1931–1961).

PL

Jean-Paul Migne, ed., *Patrologia Latina* (Paris 1844–1855), with supplementary volumes.

RB

Rule of St Benedict as edited in Timothy Fry, ed., *RB 1980: The Rule of Saint Benedict in Latin and English with Notes* (Collegeville, MN: Liturgical Press, 1981).

RC   *Regularis Concordia* as edited in Thomas Symons,
                *Regularis Concordia Anglicae Nationis Monachorum
                Sanctimonialiumque. The Monastic Agreement of the
                Monks and Nuns of the English Nation* (London:
                Nelson, 1953).

Introduction

Hermeneutics and Reading Cultures

Christians are people who read the Bible as a foundational religious text. The choice of a text, however, raises just as many questions as it solves—if not more. Although this simple assertion answers the question of *what* to read, solving what inevitably leads to the questions of *how* and *why*. The question of how a text is read involves the way in which a reader engages the text, what methods are brought to bear on it, and what assumptions are granted with regard to it. How a text is read has a dramatic effect on what that reader will take away. Why a text is read injects an orientation into the reading process by raising the question of the ultimate goal of reading. Once a goal is on the table, certain kinds of readings or methods of reading can be judged to be helpful, unhelpful, or indifferent to achieving the goal.

All of these questions about reading—what, how, why—fall within the study of hermeneutics, the science of interpreting texts and making meaning from them. Hermeneutics are like theology: everyone has one whether they realize it or not. The more aware readers are about their hermeneutics, the more clearly they can align their reading practices with their reading goals.

One of the great advances in hermeneutical theory in the last few decades is the increasing recognition that these three main questions—what, how, and why we read—are inextricably connected with the

1

question of *with whom* we read. Readers do not exist in isolation; reading is a communal activity. No matter how alone we may seem to be when we sit down with a text, we read embedded within cultures and microcultures that shape our assumptions, methods, and models of reading and interpreting. The communities within which we read bring their own hermeneutics to the table. Our readings, therefore, are done in the context of our reading communities, and our hermeneutics are learned within the communities within which we read.

When Christians sit down to read the Bible, their default hermeneutical system is probably going to be defined by the faith community that formed them. In acts of worship, in hearing sermons, while receiving religious instruction, and in the words, thoughts, and themes of prayers, hermeneutical fundamentals ingrain themselves into a congregation. From these experiences, believers are taught how to regard the Bible, how to understand the Bible, what kind of respect is owed to it, as well as the Bible's central themes as understood by that faith community. Of course, exactly what these are vary quite differently from church to church!

But Christians do not only read in church. They read within their broader culture as well, sometimes within other specialized fields or microcultures. In our school years students are taught to read different texts in different ways: a novel is not read in the same way as a poem, an encyclopedia, or lab instructions. We learn to take certain kinds of texts more seriously than others; we realize that our reading strategies must shift in response to the purpose for which we read. As a result, readers in modern society become members of a variety of overlapping reading cultures. Usually these different cultures reinforce one another. Sometimes, though, the reading strategies of one culture will clash with another.

Divinity students entering seminary will often come with a warning from home ringing in their ears: "Don't let them take away your Jesus!" In a very real way, this admonition relates directly to the negotiation of hermeneutics. To phrase it another way, the students' faith communities recognize that the students will be immersed in a new reading culture—and that the methods of biblical interpretation taught at seminary may be at odds with their own. The concern is that the students will return having absorbed the hermeneutics of the academic study of Scripture and will no longer be able to relate—or participate—with the hermeneutics of the community who brought them to faith in the first place.

Whether they realize it or not, these students are being confronted with a series of options about how they will negotiate the encounter between differing reading communities with differing hermeneutics. Some try to make this encounter an all-or-nothing "either/or" between the new and old ways of reading, either turning their backs on their formative communities or plunging dogged through coursework determined that they will complete the required classes without learning a thing or being changed in any way. Others, though, find a middle ground, a more inclusive "both/and" position that allows them to retain the spiritual richness they received from their nurturing community but also enables them to engage the intellectual rigor of the academic approach. The key to finding the middle ground lays in identifying and understanding the fundamentals of hermeneutics—the why and the how of the different reading communities—and grasping where these fundamentals come into conflict with one another and where they may be of mutual benefit.

Indeed biblical scholarship has, in recent decades, begun this same process of negotiation itself. By listening to readers outside of the modern academic microculture, it is finding new approaches into biblical texts through the eyes of others. It has been enriched by a growing plurality of voices representing interpretive communities from around the globe. While African, African-American, Latino, feminist, womanist, queer, and liberation perspectives have challenged the more traditional academic reading strategies, these challenges and critiques have not always taken the form of condemnations. Strong advocates of the new readings insist that they neither displace nor replace one another. Brian Blount, in the conclusion to his groundbreaking *Cultural Interpretation*, states:

> The biblical text harbors a vast potential of meaning. A researcher's questions codetermine his or her final conclusions regarding which segment of that potential meaning to access. It is not necessarily the case that a new meaning is placed in the text, but that meaning may be interpersonally and therefore contextually extracted from it. For this reason we come to the conclusion that the fullest possible meaning can be achieved only by drawing from the variety of interpretations, not understanding them as alternatives, but as providing a complementary range of meanings. Encouraged by Enrique Dussel, we conclude that an analectical engagement that precipitates a recognition and appreciation for the different kinds of sociolinguistically

determined evaluations can push us beyond the boundaries that attempt to place limits on the possibilities for text meaning.[1]

The questions that researchers bring to any text inevitably shape what they find in the text. Different motivations for reading the text, different notions of what will be found in the texts, and different methods for interpreting the text inevitably yield different results—but they are not necessarily antithetical to other readings. Instead, different communities can choose to learn from one another; by seeing the text through the eyes of others, their own reading can be improved.

Much of the fruitful work in conversation with other cultures has occurred across ethnic and socioeconomic lines. Primarily, though, the voices heard in such conversations have been contemporary ones. In the present project, I lay the foundations for a conversation that is historical. I make the preliminary introductions in order to begin a conversation between interpreters of the modern American academic microculture and an interpreter from the early medieval monastic microculture.

THE EARLY MEDIEVAL MONASTIC MICROCULTURE

In looking for conversation partners, the early medieval monastic microculture stands out because of its steadfast dedication to Scripture. The goal of monastic life was to conform as perfectly as possible to the life commanded by Scripture. In particular, it attempted to exemplify the New Testament command to be formed into the mind of Christ through obedience to the commands in the gospels and imitation of the Christ found there. For monastics, this quest was not occasional or seasonal but formed the bedrock of their very existence. Monastic life was preeminently the embodiment of the Gospel discipline.

To speak of anything "monastic," however, is to speak with the broadest of strokes. Christian monasticism as a movement spans some seventeen centuries, is found on all inhabited continents, and takes a wide range of forms under a multitude of rules distributed throughout Protestant,

---

[1] Brian K. Blount, *Cultural Interpretation: Reorienting New Testament Criticism* (Minneapolis, MN: Fortress Press, 1995), 176.

Catholic, and Orthodox Christianity. Tremendous variation has existed throughout these various times and places. Rather than speak in generalities, I focus here on one particular monastic author from an identifiable time and place with a sizeable and representative corpus of interpretation to draw from: Ælfric of Eynsham, monk, priest, and sometime abbot of Eynsham, who flourished around the end of the first millennium.[2]

Since postmodernism has raised academic discussions of objectivity and subjectivity, some modern scholars—especially those with faith commitments—have begun discussing the difference between academic reading strategies and ecclesially shaped readings; that is, readings that begin from a premise of faith are often guided by doctrinal commitments and are intended for communities of faith. There is no question that the monastic readers under discussion here are doing ecclesially shaped readings; however, the ecclesial shape alone is not the most significant aspect of these readings. The Benedictine life lived at the end of the early medieval period is a distinctive culture in its own right: a religious culture, a literary culture, that sought to form itself around Scripture, particularly Scripture enacted liturgically in a way not seen within Western Christianity before or after. It is ecclesially shaped, but its significance extends far beyond this single factor.

Within the monastic milieu, Ælfric occupies a unique position. He inhabited this Benedictine culture thoroughly and, more than that, chronicled its methods and hermeneutics to a degree virtually unparalleled. The difference between Ælfric and other authors of his time—the German monk and teacher Hrabanus Maurus comes to mind—is Ælfric's deep drive to communicate his way of life intertwined with his way of reading to the larger world. Hrabanus Maurus's vast corpus is in Latin: written by a monk, for monks. Ælfric's work, with a few exceptions, was in Old English: written by a monk but for the edification of an entire nation.

After centuries of Viking attacks, ecclesial life in tenth-century Anglo-Saxon England received a boost from the Benedictine Revival, a cultural movement spearheaded by three monastic bishops—Dunstan, archbishop

---

[2] As a result of my historical focus, verbs relating to monastics will be in the past tense. Let the reader not forget that for thousands of monastics around the world, many of the disciplines and methods described are not historical but part of their everyday lives.

of Canterbury; Æthelwold, bishop of Winchester; and Oswald, bishop of Worcester—who sought to restore national culture through a renewal of English monastic houses. Following the Continental reforms of Benedict of Aniane, an eighth-century Frankish reformer, they championed a strict Benedictine monasticism that emphasized fidelity to the Rule of Benedict. The vast majority of Anglo-Saxon materials extant are the products of the scriptoria from houses founded by these reformers.

The greatest figure of the second generation of the Benedictine Revival is Ælfric of Eynsham. The scarce biographical data that survives is gleaned from his own writings.[3] He entered the Old Minster at Winchester under Æthelwold around 970 and was a priest at Cernel in 987. He became abbot of the monastery at Eynsham in 1005 and probably died around 1010.

Ælfric's particular contribution to the Revival was a vast literary production aimed not at the intellectual giants of the day but at the literate nobles[4] who served as his patrons, the semiliterate monastic and secular clergy of the day, and their parishioners. Eschewing Latin for all but his most learned works, Ælfric wrote in the Old English vernacular in a rhythmic alliterative prose style reminiscent of the vernacular poetic tradition. He is consistently hailed as one of the greatest vernacular stylists of the Anglo-Saxon period by modern scholars. Indeed, the survival of his corpus is due not to the intellectual novelty of his works but rather their stylistic excellence.

When compared to other figures of his age, the scope of his writings is enormous. Angus Cameron, in preparation for the *Dictionary of the Old English Corpus*, identified 203 discrete pieces written by Ælfric in Old English, ranging from brief notes to lengthy treatises. Of these, 166 are homilies, sermons, or substantive additions to sermons. The bulk of these are gathered into two cycles that follow the church year—the *Catholic Homilies*, series 1 (*CH* I) and series 2 (*CH* II)—that contain forty items each. Another identifiable set is the *Lives of the Saints*, which also—according to Ælfric's preface—contains forty items.[5] These three collections

---

[3] In particular, his preface to his translation of Genesis and the prefaces to the two cycles of *Catholic Homilies* contain limited autobiographical material.

[4] The ealdorman Æthelweard, for instance, could not only read and write his native tongue but also wrote a Latin chronicle that has survived to the present.

[5] Displaying a difference between medieval and modern numbering conventions—and the capriciousness of scribes in a manuscript culture—Cameron identifies

were written relatively early in Ælfric's career while he was a simple monk and mass-priest at Cerne Abbey. The rest of the sermons were written throughout Ælfric's career as he reenvisioned his project from a set of cycles to a single complete Temporale cycle.[6]

The thirty-nine nonhomiletic materials in Ælfric's Old English writings and a small number of Latin works not accounted for in Cameron's list consist of a variety of texts, from a grammar, to Old Testament translations, to the earliest introduction to the Scriptures in English, to treatises on doctrinal topics. Ælfric did not simply write or translate at random, though. He was working toward a particular end. If the monastic bishops attempted to restore English culture by promoting rigorous monastic practice, Ælfric sought to restore it by giving the clergy, both monastic and secular,[7] access to comprehensive catechetical texts in their native language in order for them to more perfectly nurture their congregants. In addition to being the greatest prose stylist, Ælfric was, without a doubt, the greatest Christian educator of his age. He took great pains to present the intellectual and theological treasures of the church to both clergy and laity as clearly and directly as possible. He was constantly attentive to the risk of heresy on one hand and the danger of knowledge without adequate formation on the other.

Because of the ecclesial circumstances of the Benedictine Revival and the survival of Ælfric's corpus, he becomes a useful object for study. Rather than speaking in generalities gleaned from various authors separated by centuries and vast distances, Ælfric's situation allows us to engage him as a discrete author working within an identifiable embodied

---

thirty-four discrete items in the LS apart from the preface; see Angus Cameron, "A List of Old English Texts," in *A Plan for the Dictionary of Old English*, ed. Roberta Frank and Angus Cameron (Toronto: University of Toronto Press, 1973), 70–76.

[6] This term will be explained later when we discuss the monastic liturgical calendar.

[7] While the reformers would have preferred for all clergy to be monks, this was impractical as well as impossible. Thus, a distinction is made in the writings of the period between the monastic and secular—nonmonastic—clergy. For a useful discussion of the interaction between monastic establishments, minsters, and the secular priesthood, see Karen Jolly's sociological study of clerical dynamics, *Popular Religion in Late Saxon England: Elf Charms in Context* (Chapel Hill: University of North Carolina Press, 1996).

community whose educational and liturgical practices can be accurately described even if they are not entirely recoverable.

CONSIDERING THE SUITABILITY OF MONASTIC READING

Let us consider Ælfric and the early medieval monastic microculture to determine whether they will provide suitable conversation partners. I draw on Ælfric's own works, as well as the main stream of Western monasticism located chiefly in the Rule of Benedict and the writings of John Cassian.

A first criterion would be whether there is serious engagement with the New Testament text. Monastic life was an attempt to embody the commands of Scripture as completely as possible, and this emphasis appears through monastic writings. The alphabetical collection of the *Apothegmata Patrum* records a saying of Antony the Great (†ca. 356)—considered the founder of monasticism:

> Someone asked Abba Antony, "What must one do in order to please God?" The old man replied, "Pay attention to what I tell you: whoever you may be, always have God before your eyes; whatever you do, do it according to the testimony of the Holy Scriptures; in whatever place you live, do not easily leave it. Keep these three precepts and you will be saved."[8]

Whether this was spoken by Antony or not is immaterial, for this counsel is reiterated countless times in countless ways through monastic literature: from the *Institutes* and *Conferences* of John Cassian, through the eponymous Rule of Benedict of Nursia, through the *Commentary on the Rule of Benedict* and the *Diadem of Monks* by Smaragdus of Saint-Mihel.

The Rule of Benedict concludes by directing its readers away from itself and toward Scripture and the interpretations of it by the church fathers:

---

[8] *The Sayings of the Desert Fathers: The Alphabetical Collection*, trans. Benedicta Ward, Cistercian Studies 59, rev. ed. (Kalamazoo, MI: Cistercian Publications, 1984), 2.

> For anyone hastening on to the perfection of monastic life, there are the teachings of the holy Fathers, the observance of which will lead him to the very heights of perfection. What page, what passage of the books of the Old and New Testaments is not the truest of guides for human life? What book of the holy catholic Fathers does not resoundingly summon us along the true way to reach the Creator? (RB 73.3-4)

This general statement is given concrete expression in chapter 4, the longest chapter of the Rule. Entitled "The Tools for Good Works," it is a dizzying deployment of scriptural and scripturally based commands that begins with Jesus' summary of the Law and moves through seventy-four commands focusing on behavior and monastic decorum.

The context in which these seventy-four commands are to be lived out, according to Benedict, is balanced between three fundamental activities: liturgical prayer consisting primarily of scriptural materials, especially the psalms; holy reading, which consists of reading, meditating on, and memorizing Scripture and the catholic Fathers; and manual labor. The first two are explicitly focused on the Scriptures; monastic sources indicate that the third is as well. John Cassian defines the goal of sacred reading as gaining the ability for constant meditation on the Scriptures whether reading or not: "Hence the successive books of Holy Scripture must be diligently committed to memory and ceaselessly reviewed."[9] For the monastic who has memorized large swathes of Scripture that are recalled during manual labor, the activities of daily work are just as much a potential location for insights into Holy Scripture as reading in the monastic cell.

A second criterion is difference—does the microculture offer a genuinely different way of reading? While Ælfric participates within many of the same categories as the majority of interpreters informing the academy—he is a white European Christian male—his tenth-century Anglo-Saxon macroculture is entirely different. Ælfric lived within a completely different worldview where the incessant Viking raids afflicting

[9] John Cassian, *Conferences* 14.10.4, trans. Boniface Ramsey, Ancient Christian Writers 57 (Mahwah, NJ: Paulist Press, 1997), 514. Unless otherwise indicated, all citations from the *Conferences* will come from this edition.

England are considered as the immediate harbinger of the Antichrist. His microculture was also quite different; his interpretive strategies and purposes are not those of the modern academy and the dominant historical-critical paradigm. Specific differences will be discussed in detail throughout the study.

A third criterion is points of contact. Given differences between the two microcultures, are there enough similarities and points of contact to allow engagement to occur? Despite the many and very real differences between Ælfric and modern interpreters, there are a number of significant parallels between early medieval monastic culture and modern academic culture that will be described in the course of chapter 1. On the most basic level, however, both Ælfric and the modern interpreters choose a reasoned written discourse as the primary means for spreading their insights into the Scriptures, producing texts that can be analyzed and compared with one another. While Ælfric's primary literary form is the sermon, and orality is clearly an important aspect of preaching, Ælfric consciously wrote and maintained a written body of sermons that could be used by the clergy who could not (or possibly should not, in his opinion) produce their own. His Latin prefaces to the *Catholic Homilies* clearly indicate that he hoped his sermons would be copied and circulated to ensure orthodox preaching in England.

A fourth criterion is breadth of scope—do we have enough information on how the microculture engaged the biblical text to make the effort worthwhile? In this respect, Ælfric is ideal. While we do have collections of materials from various authors in the early medieval period, rarely is there such a broad and coherent body of materials as we have from Ælfric. He is the author of the first introduction to the Bible in English and a number of catechetical treatises that give us a clear sense of how he conceptualized the Christian faith and the place of the New Testament within it. Between the *Catholic Homilies* and the supplemental homilies Ælfric wrote later in life, he wrote exegetical works on over 150 distinct New Testament pericopes, the majority being gospel passages, with occasional epistle texts included as well. Furthermore, he produced a Latin customary, a document that describes how a monastic rule will be interpreted and kept within his abbey. It gives important details on how Ælfric expected monastic life to function, and documents the environment he created for himself and his fellow monastics.

A fifth criterion is a cross-cultural approach—how much of the interpretive work "goes without saying" and how much of it is described to allow an outsider to grasp what is going on? Here, Ælfric once again proves ideal. While he certainly did not write in order to engage later academics, Ælfric very much understood his overall catechetical program in cross-cultural terms. He was attempting to transmit the learned knowledge of the early medieval monastic microculture to broader Anglo-Saxon culture, to those who lacked both the leisure and the capacity to access truth from the Latin texts of Scripture and earlier Latin interpretation of Scripture. Indeed, this is the stated purpose of his *Catholic Homilies*:

> Then it came to my mind, I believe through God's gift, that I should turn this book from the Latin tongue into the English language, not through boldness on account of great learning, but because I saw and heard great heresies in many English books that unlearned men through their ignorance thought to be great wisdom. And it saddened me that they did not have the gospel lore in their writing except only the men who knew Latin and except for the books that we have that King Alfred wisely turned from Latin into English.[10]

In addition to his homilies, Ælfric's catechetical letters and biblical paraphrases, prepared for literate nobles, testify to a desire to communicate outside of his microculture and to share his grasp of Christian doctrine and biblical teaching with the wider culture. This very drive to communicate makes Ælfric an ideal ambassador from his culture to ours.

RECONSIDERING EARLY MEDIEVAL READING

In constructing its self-identity, the academy went through a process of rejecting certain forms of dogmatically driven reading that it saw as

---

[10] Preface to the first cycle of Ælfric's *Catholic Homilies*, in *Ælfric's Catholic Homilies: The First Series, Text*, ed. Peter Clemoes, Early English Text Society, supplementary series 17 (Oxford: Oxford University Press, 1997), lines 47–57, pp. 174–77, here 176. The mention of King Alfred (†899) refers to his translation project where Gregory the Great's *Dialogues* and *Pastoral Care*, the *Consolation of Philosophy* of Boethius, Orosius's *History of the World*, Augustine's *Soliloquies*, and Bede's *Ecclesastical History of the English People* were translated into English by the king and his circle.

limiting critical approaches to the New Testament text. Early medieval monastic readings clearly fall into this category; in order for the field to advance, these readings and their limitations had to be left behind. The process of stripping such limitations, however, has left behind prejudices. The thousand years or so of the medieval period between the end of Late Antiquity and the beginning of the Renaissance receive only scant treatment in the histories of interpretation found among critical biblical scholars. Even within treatments that mention so-called "precritical interpretation," the early medieval monastic milieu is slighted.

Most New Testament surveys of the history of interpretation either begin with the Protestant Reformation or jump fairly quickly from the fourth century over to the Reformation. Those that do not tend to equate "medieval" with "scholastic." For example, Robert Grant devotes a chapter in his survey to the medieval interpretation of the Bible but focuses entirely on scholastic interpretation. He locates interpretation within the genres of *catena* and glosses. There is no discussion of monastic interpretation as distinct from scholasticism. Grant's brief survey transmits a surface impression of an unbroken allegorical commentary tradition located in the schools from the patristic period to the Reformation.[11]

Aside from such broad surveys, two classic works within the field of biblical studies focus specifically on medieval exegesis, Beryl Smalley's important *Study of the Bible in the Middle Ages*[12] and Henri de Lubac's *Exégèse médiévale*.[13] Smalley primarily focuses on scholastic interpretation, allotting only a partial chapter to postpatristic, prescholastic interpretation.[14] Her description of the period following the Carolingian Revival is striking: noting a dearth of commentaries for a century and a quarter, she calls this period "a dramatic pause in the history of Bible

[11] Robert M. Grant with David Tracy, *A Short History of the Interpretation of the Bible*, 2nd ed. (Philadelphia: Fortress Press, 1984), 83–84.

[12] Beryl Smalley, *Study of the Bible in the Middle Ages*, 3rd ed. (Notre Dame, IN: University of Notre Dame Press, 1983).

[13] Henri de Lubac, *Exégèse médiévale: Les quatre sens de l'écriture*, 2 vols. (Paris: Abier, 1959–1961). Published in English as *Medieval Exegesis: The Four Senses of Scripture*, trans. Mark Sebanc, 4 vols. (Grand Rapids, MI: Eerdmans, 1998–2009).

[14] Section 1 (The Carolingian Revival) in chapter 2 (Monastic and Cathedral Schools) addresses the specific period and environment under consideration here.

studies."[15] Smalley explains it thus: "The real reason was a shift of interest. The Cluniac and other tenth-century religious reformers emphasized the liturgy at the expense of study. As the offices multiplied, *lectio divina* moved out of the cloister into the choir."[16] Thus, Smalley interprets the lack of commentaries and the increase in liturgies as a sign of a hiatus in "Bible studies" rather than a redirection of exegetical work. Ælfric receives only two brief mentions.[17] Out of the mass of medieval materials, moreover, Smalley has selected one genre—the commentary—as the locus of biblical interpretation. While she accurately notes a shift in interest as a result of the Cluniac reforms of Benedictine practice, she does not consider that the liturgical productions of these monastic houses might be biblical interpretation as well; she labors under the assumption that liturgical materials must not involve biblical interpretation and vice versa. In doing so, she established a prejudice inherited by the next several generations of scholars who equally dismissed material other than commentaries as something other than biblical interpretation.

Henri de Lubac's work on medieval exegesis is one of the great accomplishments of twentieth-century Roman Catholic scholarship. Encyclopedic in character, his study cites the majority of extant medieval sources and categorizes their treatments of the Scriptures into one of the four dominant senses. His is a massive and erudite work that sketches a grand narrative from Origen through the medieval period. His goal is to provide a foundation for a theological return to spiritual exegesis, historically located as a challenge to a dogmatic Thomism that tended to ignore the very patristic and medieval sources on whom Thomas Aquinas relied. Therefore, de Lubac is interested in establishing the theological validity of the multiple senses of Scripture and is focused on them as theologically interpretive categories. With such a goal, de Lubac necessarily works programmatically. As a result, he does not show how specific readers read within specific contexts; he cannot address the variety of interpretive contexts within which interpretation occurred; and, he ends up glossing over the fundamental distinctions between interpretations located in scholastic debate or monastic homilies.

[15] Smalley, *Study of the Bible*, 44.
[16] Ibid., 44–45.
[17] Ibid., 147, 244.

Ælfric is mentioned once in de Lubac's work. He appears as an example of the orators who "scarcely do more than plagiarize [Gregory the Great]."[18] It is only fair to contextualize this remark, however, as part of an encomium to the enduring greatness and influence of Gregory. Immediately before this quotation, de Lubac correctly identifies the often-overlooked debt that Western homiletics owes to Gregory: "Through his *Regula pastoralis*, Gregory, along with Augustine and Rabanus Maurus, is the master of the art of preaching; through his other works he is the principal source of preaching itself, as well as spirituality."[19] Thus, de Lubac's remark (which will be addressed later in this study) casts more glory on Gregory than shame on Ælfric.

Overall, the interpretive practices of the early medieval monastic microculture have been ignored by earlier biblical scholarship. First, they have been rejected on paradigmatic grounds; they represent the "old" way of doing things that prevent an intellectually rigorous study of the New Testament documents. Second, they have been overshadowed by interpretive movements both before and after it: by patristic reading on the one hand and scholastic reading on the other. Third, they have been dismissed on grounds of genre; if biblical interpretation appears exclusively in commentaries and commentaries are lacking from the period, substantive interpretive work must not have occurred. Fourth, on the occasions when they have been considered, they have primarily been dismissed as plagiaristic of patristic readings. As a result, much work remains to be done on what the early medieval monastic interpretive practices actually were and whether the modern charges stand up to examination.

A shift, however, is taking place. In recent years, a number of calls have been put forth to reexamine the promise and potential of exegesis from before the advent of critical study in the eighteenth century. A number of biblical scholars have called for greater attention to premodern methods. Most of the calls, however, have been general and programmatic in nature. In particular, the work of engaging and understanding early medieval interpretations in their specificity still remains to be done. While biblical scholars have not yet conducted this work, valuable contributions to this larger project have been made by scholars in other fields.

[18] De Lubac, *Medieval Exegesis*, 2:120.
[19] Ibid.

Positive Assessments of Early Medieval Monastic Reading

An influential study that addresses this topic from a more positive perspective approaches it culturally rather than exegetically. Jean Leclercq's *The Love of Learning and the Desire for God: A Study of Monastic Culture* is a masterful work that gathers together a lifetime of reflection and study within a monastic milieu. Leclercq succinctly summarizes the results of his study thus:

> The principal literary sources of monastic culture may be reduced to three: The Holy Scripture, the patristic tradition, and classical literature. The liturgy, which will be treated later, is the medium through which the Bible and the patristic tradition are received, and it is the liturgy that gives unity to all the manifestations of monastic culture.[20]

Leclercq's success in describing monastic exegesis is rooted in the scope of his study; he is not attempting to examine only the methods and literary production of monastic scriptural reading. Instead, he sets it broadly within a study of the overall purpose of monastic existence. Thus, he discusses the study of grammar as the essential background from which exegesis proceeds, he discusses the models for exegesis as represented by the patristic tradition, and he discusses the various literary forms that the monastics preferred and ultimately relates all of these to the liturgy, which is at the heart of monastic practice and experience.

For Leclercq, the monastic culture is characterized by a tension between the two elements found in his title. He writes:

> The content of monastic culture has seemed to be symbolized, synthesized, by these two words: grammar and spirituality. On the one hand, learning is necessary if one is to approach God and to express what is perceived of Him; on the other hand, literature must be continually transcended and elevated in the striving to attain eternal life.[21]

---

[20] Jean Leclercq, *The Love of Learning and the Desire for God: A Study of Monastic Culture*, trans. Catharine Misrahi (New York: Fordham University Press, 1982), 71.
[21] Ibid., 53.

Learning gives monastics the keys to begin the search for God in the Scriptures and the liturgy, but learning for its own sake is not the monastic goal. Instead, "the one end of the monastic life is the search for God."[22] Exegesis plays a crucial role because it is therefore "entirely oriented toward life, and not toward abstract knowledge."[23] Leclercq continually illustrates and delineates this monastic approach in contrast to the scholastics:

> The scholastic *lectio* [reading] takes the direction of the *quaestio* [question] and the *disputatio* [disputation]. The reader puts questions to the text and then questions himself on the subject matter: *quaeri solet*. The monastic *lectio* [reading] is oriented toward the *meditatio* [meditation] and the *oratio* [prayer]. The objective of the first is science and knowledge; of the second, wisdom and appreciation. In the monastery, the *lectio divina* [meditative reading of Scripture], which begins with grammar, terminates in compunction, the desire for heaven.[24]

Reading creates a theology rooted in experience. "Monastic speculation is the outgrowth of the practice of monastic life, the living of the spiritual life which is the meditation on Holy Scripture. It is biblical experience inseparable from liturgical experience."[25] The purpose of monastic reading is to form the community into a lived and experienced scriptural pattern where the desire for God takes pride of place.

While the scope of his work enables Leclercq to appropriately situate monastic reading within monastic life, it also does not allow him the space within this slim volume to demonstrate the processes of which he speaks. He states clearly in his preface that the book is "a series of lectures given to young monks"[26] as "an introductory work and therefore not intended for specialists, for already well-informed scholars."[27] Rather: "Its purpose is not to offer a synthesis that would be premature, nor to provide

---

[22] Ibid., 18.
[23] Ibid., 17.
[24] Ibid., 72.
[25] Ibid., 213.
[26] Ibid., vii.
[27] Ibid.

a bibliography which can be found elsewhere, but to draw attention to subjects for further investigation and to suggest partial and provisional solutions."[28] He does not, in a word, so much demonstrate as assert. Nevertheless, the vision that he presents has been found compelling and his seminal work is more often considered to be the last word on the subject than a tentative first word.

A few scholars have taken up the call to build on this foundation. As far as exegesis is concerned, one great successor of Leclercq's work is William T. Flynn's *Medieval Music as Medieval Exegesis.*[29] Beginning with the synthetic vision of Leclercq, Flynn presents a dense and close-knit explication of the study of grammar, rhetoric, and ornamented language, the application of these arts to the teaching and composition of eleventh-century musical forms—especially the emerging chant genres of tropes, prose, and sequences—and Scripture interpretation within the liturgy. Ultimately, he examines a single liturgical manuscript, the Autun Troper, and demonstrates through a careful analysis of the Christmas and Easter Masses how the liturgies of these feasts explicate the biblical texts appointed through juxtaposition and exposition in the texts and music of the interpretive musical genres.

Flynn validates Leclercq's assertions concerning the liturgy as the ultimate locus of biblical interpretation and demonstrates how liturgy is interpretive. Leclercq's synthesis follows an educational trajectory moving from the formative sources of monastic culture, Scripture, the patristic inheritance, and grammar, and ends at its products in theology and ultimately liturgy. Flynn takes a similar route and demonstrates how monastic and clerical formation is formation for the liturgy and how the music portions of the liturgy in turn have a formative, mystagogical effect:

> All of the [musical] tropes are "tropological" not because they explain what the choir should do about their faith but because they help them actually do it. For the principal participants, the choir, these liturgies could be expected to continue to reveal their riches as the clerics, monks, and nuns probed the mysteries of advanced

---

[28] Ibid.

[29] William T. Flynn, *Medieval Music as Medieval Exegesis* (Lanham, MD: Scarecrow, 1999), 1ff.

latin grammar and applied this knowledge to their daily celebrations. . . . In short, eleventh-century liturgies engaged the participants at their varying levels of expertise, opening the treasury of the sacred page in ways that could be appreciated by all.[30]

Music and the liturgy was the practice at the heart of the canons' common life. Furthermore, the liturgy was therefore a means of teaching exegesis and an exegetical product in its own right.

Flynn's work, then, examines the liturgy as both the fruit of exegetical process and as a means of formation into the process. His particular area of interest is the new compositional genres that appeared in the liturgy shortly before the end of the first millennium—the prose, trope, and sequence. He demonstrates their development from grammatical study, the study at the heart of monastic biblical exegesis, then demonstrates how these liturgical forms continue and enrich biblical understanding within the liturgies.

Susan Boynton and Diane Reilly's *The Practice of the Bible in the Middle Ages* contains several essays that directly engage early medieval monastic reading practices. Susan Boynton's essay, "The Bible and the Liturgy" does a wonderful job of introducing readers to how the Bible and the liturgy interacted in the early medieval period. In particular, her final paragraph neatly summarizes the situation:

In the Middle Ages, the words of the Bible were most often experienced through the chants and readings of the liturgy. Just as the written Bible was frequently accompanied by glosses and commentary, likewise the performance of Scripture was a form of interpretation: biblical texts were fragmented, altered, and combined with other texts in ways that reflected traditions of biblical hermeneutics. The ensuing juxtapositions in turn provoked new interpretations. The liturgy shaped the understanding of biblical exegesis because it rendered audible, in real time, the relationships between the different parts of the Bible; even those few who used the Bible as a written book frequently heard and uttered its words in the context of worship services. Thus, liturgical performance was the single most important factor influencing the reception of the Bible in the Middle Ages.[31]

[30] Flynn, *Medieval Music*, 245.

[31] Susan Boynton, "The Bible and the Liturgy," in *The Practice of the Bible in the Middle Ages: Production, Reception, and Performance in Western Christianity*, ed. Susan Boynton and Diane Reilly (New York: Columbia University Press, 2011).

I will examine much of what she identifies here in greater detail in chapter 2.

The chapter that follows, "When the Monks Were the Book," builds on Boynton's work and focuses specifically on the monastic reading environment. Isabelle Cochelin describes the place of the Scriptures in early medieval monastic life, discussing the holy reading and the liturgical practices of the monastic communities. Having established the importance of the Scriptures to monastic life, she suggests that the monastic liturgies, particularly those of Holy Week, served as a performative embodiment of the scriptural accounts, bringing the sacred histories to life before the laity who were unable to read the biblical text for themselves.

The work that directly addresses Ælfric as an interpreter of Scripture is a brief eleven-page essay by Paul Szarmach, one of the great contemporary experts on Old English homiletical literature. Szarmach begins by noting the dearth of similar studies:

> When there is literary interest in Ælfric, it is in his style. Aside from studies of style and Milton McC. Gatch's important interpretive study emphasizing Ælfric's eschatology, the study of Ælfric remains broadly philological, i.e., showing an interest in manuscripts and sources, not at all in hermeneutics. In short, the study of Ælfric's exegesis is still at a nascent stage and often emerges as an adjunct to studies with other objectives in mind.[32]

Szarmach presents this short study as a first word toward a larger appreciation of Ælfric as an exegete.

Szarmach's study opens by examining Ælfric's own reflections on the art of biblical interpretation. A central simile appears in Ælfric's homily on the five loaves and two fishes; Ælfric draws a distinction between a man who sees a fair painting and praises it and a man who reads fair characters and praises their author—having not only appreciated the form of the letters but also having understood the message they sought to convey. So it is with the miracle. It is not enough to look at it and wonder;

---

[32] Paul E. Szarmach, "Ælfric as Exegete: Approaches and Examples in the Study of the *Sermones Catholici*," in *Hermeneutics and Medieval Culture*, ed. H. Damico and P. Gallacher (Albany: State University of New York Press, 1989), 237–47, here 238.

profitable engagement requires an understanding of its spiritual significance to give God due praise for what has occurred.[33] Szarmach detects
here a preference for binary understandings, finding terms or concepts
like "words and images, ignorance and understanding, understanding
and reaction" in which Ælfric finds a "complementary unity."[34] That is,
Ælfric identifies dualities, then embraces the "both/and" rather than the
"either/or." Szarmach continues:

> Ælfric's habit of mind is to find such [binary] pairing. When it
> comes to the important pair "understanding and reaction," the
> grounds change from the text to the audience. This shift of focus
> or emphasis explains how in other expositions the moral sense of
> scripture is a natural development; there is a habit of mind that
> enables Ælfric to move from analysis of text to moral application
> for the audience.[35]

The movement from the text to a moral application is a natural mode for
Ælfric.

From this point, Szarmach notes three major factors that help him
characterize Ælfric's exegesis. The first is a recognition of a basic fact
about interpretation and meaning within Ælfric's milieu. Modern
interpreters often regard interpretation as a movement to a typological
or allegorical level. Drawing on the work of Thomas D. Hill,[36] Szarmach
notes that "all too often Anglo-Saxonists think that exegesis is
allegory."[37] Instead, Szarmach demonstrates from both Augustine and
Ælfric that "explanation of what is the literal sense is part of a long
tradition"; historical and geographical references have to be explained
and possible contradictions with other texts must be resolved (typically
harmonized) before any deeper levels of the text can be sought. When,

---

[33] Ibid. Szarmach does not mention the source of Ælfric's reflection, but Bede is
similarly reflective on how readers/hearers should find meaning in Christ's miracles
in his treatment of a similar feeding story in John 6:1-14 (Bede *Hom* 2.2).

[34] Szarmach, "Ælfric as Exegete," 239.

[35] Ibid.

[36] Thomas D. Hill, "Literary History and Old English Poetry: The Case of *Christ
I, II, III*," in *Sources of Anglo-Saxon Culture*, ed. Paul E. Szarmach, Studies in Medieval
Culture 20 (Kalamazoo, MI: The Medieval Institute, 1986), 3–22.

[37] Szarmach, "Ælfric as Exegete," 240.

how, and why the literal sense has to be clarified is part of the exegetical task as well.

The second factor to consider concerns what Ælfric learned from the early medieval homiliary tradition.[38] Szarmach reminds his readers that Ælfric did not just take material from the patristic excerpts he found there; he also learned exegetical method from these texts. The exegetical methods of Bede, Gregory, and Augustine—though sharing broad similarities—are different, and Szarmach suggests that Ælfric's facility in adapting and assimilating the distinct styles of patristic authors accounts for some of the interest in Ælfric's style.

The third factor that Szarmach identifies is "the narrative impulse."[39] While Ælfric's second cycle of *Catholic Homilies* contains a more narrative character than the first, Szarmach points beyond this observation to the notion that Ælfric understands the Bible "primarily as story, secondarily as text for analysis."[40] Szarmach notes that the sermon for Palm Sunday illustrates the point; Ælfric deftly weaves a harmony of the gospels to concisely convey an orthodox Passion of his own creation: "The effect of the Palm Sunday homily is the effect of a narrative, shaped and formed to stand as a sequence of events in time. Ælfric has made narrative sense of his varied sources."[41] When faced with complexities on the literal level, Ælfric's instinct is to tell the story within the text as clearly as possible.

Szarmach ends his brief study with a cogent appeal to his fellow scholars:

> Anglo-Saxonists must unburden themselves from antecedent scholarship that either blatantly or subtly brings with it assumptions that are invalid for the late tenth century. A self-conscious and proper historicism can help establish a context for discussion. With this context, which must take into imaginative account Ælfric's use of sources, the development of early medieval theology, and the valid meaning of early medieval exegesis, it will be possible to assess more accurately Ælfric's role as medieval "father" and to move on to related cultural issues such as Ælfric's audience, the problem of rendering the Christian message

---

[38] I take up the shape and scope of this tradition at the end of chap. 1.
[39] Szarmach, "Ælfric as Exegete," 241.
[40] Ibid.
[41] Ibid., 243.

to it (a new form of the *translatio* question, it would appear), and even perhaps a new definition of Christian literature. The new view of Ælfric that will thus result will have to account for issues of Christian genres and styles as well.[42]

Thus, Szarmach's study itself is fundamentally another programmatic essay, but one from a veteran scholar of Anglo-Saxon literature, especially homiletics.

Ælfric is a Benedictine Revival–era preacher. Szarmach insists that Ælfric and his exegesis be read in terms of his late tenth-century setting and the forces that produced it. Leclercq, Flynn, and Boynton signal that the fundamental paradigm for early medieval monastic biblical interpretation is the liturgy. An early medieval monastic sermon, therefore, should not be treated as an independent or acontextual text—a freestanding document in the same way that a biblical commentary can be—but is rightly considered when located securely within the context of early medieval monastic liturgies and their interpretive practices.

Building a Conversation, Selecting Texts

To begin the conversation-building process, I consider first what biblical texts might be used to focus the conversation. Recalling again a fundamental criterion, the texts selected must be engaged by both sets of conversation partners. Since modern commentaries cover every verse of the biblical text, Ælfric's corpus becomes the limiting factor. His sermons follow closely the gospel readings appointed by the early medieval church calendar. Of the seventy-five surviving witnesses to gospel lectionaries from the span of the Anglo-Saxon period in England, 457 readings are from Matthew, 391 from Luke, 234 from John, and 155 from Mark. Looking at Ælfric's sermons in the *Catholic Homilies*, the ratios are similar; of the eighty items, twenty-eight are from Matthew, twenty-four from Luke, twenty-three from John, and five from Mark. Based on lectionary statistics, Matthew emerges as the favorite gospel. More importantly, however, Matthew is the gospel most focused on the notion of constructing a community around the life, death, and resurrection of Jesus.

[42] Ibid., 244.

For the early and medieval church, Matthew was the first gospel, both in terms of its canonical position and its importance to the growth and formation of Christian communities. Matthew was the most commented on and most frequently cited of the gospels in the patristic period, and the Sermon on the Mount was the most frequently cited pericope of Scripture. Liturgically, Matthew became the dominant text cited in both liturgies and lectionaries of the West. Two features of the text in particular enabled Matthew to achieve this status: first, the completeness of its account of the life, death, and resurrection of Jesus gave Christian communities identity through the birth, deeds, and death of their founder; second, the ecclesial usefulness of its catechetical collections of dominical sayings made it a teaching resource *par excellence.*

In addition, the Western church took the communal references within the text seriously. Under the influence of texts like the Acts of the Apostles, Eusebius's *Ecclesiastical History*, and Jerome's *Chronicon*, the church assumed direct continuity between the community of the apostles and that of their own day. The polity of the Western church was mapped onto the Matthean text so thoroughly that Peter's confession (Matt 16) became a central text undergirding arguments for the primacy of the bishop of Rome. Both the communal and the formational aspects of the gospel were embraced to the fullest. Since the early medieval monastic microculture privileged both community and lifelong formation into the example of Jesus, an examination of how Ælfric read Matthew is a natural choice.

With twenty-eight available sermons on Matthean texts, we have a sizeable sample from which to choose. I have chosen to focus on four texts that represent four major literary forms appearing within Matthew: a mythological narrative (Matt 4:1-11), a dominical teaching (Matt 5:1-12), a set of healing miracles (Matt 8:1-13), and a parable (Matt 25:1-13). Surveying a range of materials will enable us to examine what interpretive strategies are used for the different forms, and whether strategies change with the form under consideration or are uniform throughout.

Selecting Conversation Partners

To represent the modern academic microculture's side of the conversation, I have chosen four recent commentaries on Matthew: Ulrich Luz's work (translated by James Crouch) for the Hermeneia series,[43] W. D. Davies and Dale Allison's work for the International Critical Commentary series,[44] Douglas Hare's work for the Interpretation series,[45] and Eugene Boring's portion for the New Interpreter's Bible commentary.[46] Of the central literary genres produced by the modern academy—commentaries, monographs, and scholarly articles—the commentary best presents the exegetical perspectives and outlooks of representative scholars that will address all four selected pericopes. All of these commentaries have been selected from recognized series that represent the mainstream of modern biblical interpretation.

The first two are recognized scholarly commentaries that are written specifically for the modern academic microculture—these are works by the academy for the academy. Luz's commentary stands squarely within the European commentary tradition. His approach is a combination of literary and historical methods that are characterized by his two major working hypotheses: first, that "the Gospel of Matthew tells the story of Jesus' activity in Israel" which is a story of conflict between Jesus and the Jewish leaders, embedded in which is the story of Jesus' relationship with his disciples;[47] second, "the experiences of the Matthean church are reflected in the Matthean Jesus story," which is a two-level drama where the conflict-story of Jesus is understood as an allegory for the situation of the Matthean community.[48] Davies and Allison present a textually focused commentary that discusses lexical and grammatical issues and particularly focuses on textual or thematic parallels in contemporary Jewish and Greco-Roman literature.

---

[43] Ulrich Luz, *Matthew 1–7: A Continental Commentary*, trans. Wilhelm C. Linss, Hermeneia (Minneapolis, MN: Fortress Press, 1992); Ulrich Luz, *Matthew 8–20: A Commentary on the Gospel of Matthew*, trans. James E. Crouch, Hermeneia (Minneapolis, MN: Fortress Press, 2001); Ulrich Luz, *Matthew 21–28*, trans. James E. Crouch, Hermeneia (Minneapolis, MN: Fortress Press, 2005).

[44] W. D. Davies and Dale C. Allison, *A Critical and Exegetical Commentary on the Gospel According to Saint Matthew*, 3 vols., International Critical Commentary 26 (London/New York: T & T Clark International, 2004).

[45] Douglas Hare, *Matthew*, Interpretation (Minneapolis, MN: Fortress Press, 1995).

[46] M. Eugene Boring, "Matthew," in *The New Interpreter's Bible: Matthew-Mark*, ed. Leander E. Keck, vol. 8 (Nashville, TN: Abingdon, 1995), 87–506.

[47] Luz, *Matthew 1–7*, 11.

[48] Ibid.

The last two are, like Ælfric's work, cross-cultural. They are intended to mediate the findings of the modern academic endeavor to confessionally Christian microcultures, particularly for the work of teaching and preaching—these are works by the academy for broader Christian audiences.[49] Hare's approach is generally literary. He is not explicit about his methods but uses a combination of narrative readings, literary parallels, and clarifications of the historical context as the basis of his exegesis. Boring also uses these tools but is more explicit in his use of a narrative approach as a framing device. He identifies a chiastic structure that is rooted in conflict—similar to Luz—but Boring emphasizes that the central conflict is apocalyptic in nature. Thus, while drawing on the same kinds of literary, historical, and rhetorical methods as the rest, he gives a prominent place to Matthew's own theological perspective in his work.[50]

The Aim of the Conversation

The purpose of this conversation is twofold: first, to clarify the primary interpretive contexts and methods of the early medieval monastic microculture; second, to assess its usefulness as a foil for modern academic readings. In other words, through the conversation model, I hope to identify interpretive strengths and weaknesses of both conversation partners so as to assess what areas of potential meaning within the biblical text early medieval methods identify more clearly than modern, and to show what early medieval monastic methods and results have to offer modern scholarship. At the same time, I acknowledge the ways that modern methods represent significant insights on their own terms. Furthermore, I explore the fruitfulness of early medieval conversation partners as aids in moving beyond modern critical impasses. As outsiders in modern critical debates, Ælfric and his sources may provide alternative approaches or perspectives that open interpretive possibilities where modern interpreters are locked in disagreement.

[49] While it could be both possible and interesting to look at sermons on Matthew by modern academics, this would be at cross-purposes with our project. Due to the faith commitments required and the differing context of proclamation, these texts would misrepresent the explicitly nonconfessional character of the modern academy's exegetical project.

[50] More attention will be given to these modern commentaries in chap. 1.

The point is not to judge between the interpretive projects of the two microcultures and to declare one superior, the other inferior. Rather, I hope to show how these older methods may help us access more complete interpretive possibilities inherent in the Matthean text and how Matthew has served in the past as a catalyst for the formation of intentional Christian communities.

The Shape of the Conversation

Moving forward, chapter 1 will be an examination of the commonalities between the modern academic microculture and the early medieval monastic microculture. This chapter will explore three fundamental characteristics that are central to both cultures: mimesis, literary focus, and critical conversations.

Chapter 2 will examine the fundamental differences between the two cultures. Because the modern context is much better known, I shall focus here on the primary interpretive context of the early medieval monastic microculture, the monastic liturgy, and the interpretive forces this context exerts upon the discursive interpretation found in monastic preaching.

Once the pertinent features of the two microcultures have been investigated, I can address the Matthean texts themselves. Chapter 3 treats Matthew 4:1-11 and Matthew 5:1-12; chapter 4 treats Matthew 8:1-13 and Matthew 25:1-13. For each passage, I examine the interpretations of the four modern interpreters, then consider Ælfric's text and the liturgical context that informs it. Then, I put the modern and medieval into dialogue with one another, assessing the areas of strength for the various interpreters and suggesting how Ælfric's early medieval monastic interpretation may contribute to the modern academic interpretive project. The Conclusion will offer a brief summary of my findings and present a concluding statement of what Ælfric and other early medieval monastic interpreters might have to offer the modern students of the Scriptures.

Chapter 1

How Monastic Living Shaped Reading

INTRODUCTION

In his classic study of monastic culture, Jean Leclercq summarizes his synthesis in a compact paragraph: "The principal literary sources of monastic culture may be reduced to three: Holy Scripture, the patristic tradition, and classical literature. The liturgy . . . is the medium through which the Bible and the patristic tradition are received, and it is the liturgy that gives unity to all the manifestations of monastic culture."[1] Gathering up these sources and moving beyond the solely literary, monastic culture can be characterized as mimetic, literary, and liturgical. Individually these marks are not unique to monastic culture—indeed, modern biblical scholarship is also characterized by the first two marks—but the ways it embodies these marks and the ends it pursues by this embodiment give this culture its unique character. In order to appreciate both the continuities and the discontinuities between the two profoundly literary cultures of early medieval monasticism and modern New Testament scholarship, it

---

[1] Jean Leclercq, *The Love of Learning and the Desire for God: A Study of Monastic Culture*, trans. Catharine Misrahi (New York: Fordham University Press, 1982), 71.

is worth examining how the medieval monastic microculture has embodied mimetic and literary qualities, and how such qualities build on and reinforce one another. Both also operate within a critical conversation—a conversation with special rules, resources, and patrons solemnly invoked. The final monastic dimension, the liturgical, serves as a point of entry into the key differences between the early medieval monastic and modern academic cultures.

THE MIMETIC CHARACTER OF MONASTIC LIFE

Mimesis in Early Medieval Monastic Culture

Tucked in the midst of Ælfric's *Lives of the Saints* stands a text for general use. Like the other writings, it bears the marks of a homily—including a brief scriptural passage—but was probably intended more for private reading than for public proclamation. Unlike the others, which focus on particular deeds of particular saints or which address particular liturgical occasions, this work is general enough to serve as an introduction to the whole set. In fact, Godden has suggested that it did originally function in this fashion and that its current placement—sixteenth in the collection—is a dislocation from an original initial position.

This work, titled "Sermon on the Memory of the Saints," contains a survey of sanctity. The first half presents examples. It begins by touching on various heroes of the Old Testament and identifying the virtues that made them stand out. Turning to the New Testament, Ælfric discusses John the Baptist, Christ himself, then the apostles and disciples. A discussion of the various kinds of postbiblical confessors rounds out this half. An exhortation concerning the evils of the present time and imminence of the Antichrist segues into the second half. This half is a formal explication of the three theological virtues, the eight chief sins and their remedies, and the eight chief virtues. A concluding exhortation encourages the cultivation of the virtues as primary weapons against the devil and sin.

This work communicates the early medieval monastic concept of mimesis—formation through imitation. First, it presents human exemplars for imitation drawn primarily from the Bible and secondarily from the history of the church. Preeminent among these is Christ himself. Second, it draws out—implying induction through juxtaposition—the specific moral lessons that the holy histories teach, the specific virtues cultivated by the saints, and the corresponding vices they overcame. It identifies who is to be modeled and the specific qualities of what is to be modeled. Furthermore, it also locates the *telos*—why these are to be modeled. Saints are not just examples; they embody the goal.

The "Sermon on the Memory of the Saints" is clearly not an exegetical work. Nevertheless, a passage of Scripture, Revelation 1:8 stands at the head of the work and provides a starting place. Playing off the multiple senses of the words "beginning" and "end," Ælfric translates the passage from the Vulgate into Old English, then uses it as a point of departure:

> *Ego sum Alfa et W. Initium et finis dicit Dominus Deus qui est et qui erat et qui venturus est omnipotens.* That is in English: I am the beginning and the end says the Lord God who was and who is and who is coming, the Almighty (God). There is one Almighty God, ever existing in three natures, who shaped all things. Now, we have our beginning through him because he shaped us when we were not and afterward redeemed us when we were lost. Now we should take great care that our life may be structured so our end might end in God who came to us at our beginning.[2]

By using "beginning" both as a temporal marker and as a source, Ælfric can make "end" serve as a final temporal marker and as a *telos*. The anagogical use of these temporal terms sets up an eternal aim for his audience. The next sentence clarifies how his hearers should strive for this goal: "We may take good examples, first from the holy patriarchs who pleased God in their lives and also from the holy ones who followed the Savior."[3] The exhortation that lies at the end of the piece ties the systematic exposition of the virtues into this overarching anagogical scheme as Ælfric notes in a concluding line: "We may, through God's help, overcome these evil vices through struggle if we fight bravely and [may] have in the end the eternal glory forever with God himself if we toil here and now."[4]

---

[2] "Sermon on the Memory of the Saints," in *Ælfric's Lives of the Saints: Being a Set of Sermons on Saints' Days Formerly Observed by the English Church*, ed. Walter W. Skeat, vol. 1, Early English Text Society 82 (London: Oxford University Press, 1881–1900 [repr. in 2 vols., 1966]), lines 1–8, p. 336. Hereafter ÆLS (Memory of Saints). All Old English translations are mine.

[3] ÆLS (Memory of Saints), lines 9–12.

[4] ÆLS (Memory of Saints), lines 378–81.

Mimesis for Ælfric, then, is a lifelong process through which monastics pattern themselves after Christ, his forbearers and saints, and cultivate the virtues through which they will attain to the eternal joys of God's presence. Imbedded in "Memory of the Saints" are the monastic values that place a premium on personal modeling and which spawned a literature of example that quickly became foundational for the spread of monasticism and the monastic ethos.

Personal Mimesis and the Monastic Community

The core legislative documents of the Western monastic movement construct a community grounded in imitation and mutual correction for the purpose of fulfilling the commands of Scripture and thus embodying the virtues of Christ. Legislative documents like the works of John Cassian, the *Rule of Columban*, and the Rule of Benedict should be understood less as distinct legislative documents but instead vehicles for the transmission of a common body of teaching:

> The various rules were merely so many individual expressions of the tradition. All the ancient monks considered their real rule, in the sense of the ultimate determinant of their lives, to be not some product of human effort but the Word of God himself as contained in the Scriptures. Monasticism was simply a form of the Christian life itself, and hence it drew its inspiration from divine revelation.[5]

The Rule of Benedict became normative in early medieval Europe through its adoption at synods in Aachen chaired by St. Benedict of Aniane in 816 and 817 and subsequently achieved authoritative status throughout the Carolingian Empire. Benedict of Aniane's writings clarify that the Rule's normativity comes not from the inherent superiority of its legislation above other competing rules but rather because it most clearly exemplified the common tradition.[6] Therefore the legislative work of John Cassian, the

---

[5] Claude Peifer, "The Rule of St. Benedict," in *RB 1980: The Rule of St. Benedict in English and Latin with Notes*, ed. Timothy Fry (Collegeville, MN: Liturgical Press, 1980), 65–112, here 85.

[6] Claude Peifer, "The Rule in History," in *RB 1980: The Rule of St. Benedict in English and Latin with Notes*, ed. Timothy Fry (Collegeville, MN: Liturgical Press, 1980), 113–51, here 121–22.

Institutes (and the *Conferences* to a lesser degree), and the Rule of Benedict are mutual witnesses of a common way of life handed down by monastic communities and bolstered by documents of legislation and exhortation.

John Cassian was, with Evagrius of Pontus, the main figure responsible for the transmission of the monastic tradition from the East to the West. Probably a native of the Balkans, John and his comrade Germanus journeyed to Bethlehem in the last quarter of the fourth century to join a monastery. Itching to see the roots of monasticism for themselves, they left the monastery and made two successive journeys to the monastic motherland, Egypt. Later ordained a deacon by St. John Chrysostom and exiled from the East for supporting the controversial patriarch, he settled in Gaul around 410, founding monastic communities and writing of his experiences for the benefit of the nascent monastic movement there.

The *Institutes*, composed between 419 and 426, are the closest that Cassian produced to a Rule. A monastic Rule:

> normally includes, on the one hand, theoretical spiritual teaching and, on the other, practical regulations to govern the daily life of the monastery by determining the time and measure of food, sleep, and liturgical prayer, relationships with the outside, authority structures, etc. These two elements may be combined in quite different proportions. Some rules contain chiefly spiritual doctrine, some consist almost exclusively of practical regulations; others combine both.[7]

Of the twelve books of the *Institutes*, the first four are chiefly practical, detailing the minutiae of Egyptian monastic practice; the later eight are spiritual instruction on the eight chief vices and their remedies.

In both sections, Cassian constantly appeals to the principle of imitation and describes its practical application. Men seeking admission to a monastery must first serve a year under the elder who oversees the hospitality of guests, learning the basics of humility, obedience, and service, then are turned over to an elder who oversees ten junior monks to be taught the alphabet of virtues, "first syllables in the direction of perfection."[8] The

[7] Peifer, "Rule of St. Benedict," in *RB 1980*, 85.
[8] John Cassian, *Institutes.* 4.7-9, trans. Boniface Ramsey, Ancient Christian Writers 58 (New York: Newman Press, 2000), 81, 82. Unless otherwise indicated, all citations from the *Institutes* will come from this edition.

junior monks remain under the authority of the elders, ever learning from them the virtues, chiefly discretion, obedience, and humility. These monks are exhorted to observe all their seniors, not just those placed over them, but the community as a whole. Just a few ought to be selected as particular models for imitation while the novice advances:

> In order to attain more easily to [virtue], you should seek out, while you live in the community, examples of a perfect life that are worthy of imitation; they will come from a few, and indeed from one or two, but not from the many. For, beyond the fact that a life that has been scrutinized and refined is found in few, there is a question of utility to be considered—that a person is more carefully schooled and formed for the perfection of this chosen orientation (namely, the cenobitic life) by the example of one.[9]

Once monks have reached a more advanced level, Cassian commends advice attributed to St. Antony, the Father of Egyptian—and therefore all—monasticism:

> For it is an ancient and admirable saying of the blessed Antony to the effect that when a monk, after having opted for the cenobium, is striving to the heights of a still loftier perfection, has seized upon the consideration of discretion and is already able to rely on his own judgment and to come to the pinnacle of the anchorite life, he must not seek all the kinds of virtue from one person, however outstanding he may be. For there is one adorned with the flowers of knowledge, another who is more strongly fortified by the practice of discretion, another who is solidly founded in patience, one who excels in the virtue of humility and another in that of abstinence, while still another is decked with the grace of simplicity, this one surpasses the others by his zeal for magnanimity, that one by mercy, another one by vigils, yet another by silence, and still another by toil. Therefore the monk who, like a most prudent bee, is desirous of storing up spiritual honey must suck the flower of a particular virtue from those who possess it most intimately, and he must lay it up carefully in the vessel of his heart. He must not begrudge a person for what he has less of, but he must contemplate and eagerly gather

[9] Ibid., 100.

up only the virtuousness that he possesses. For if we want to obtain all of them from a single individual, either examples will be hard to find, or, indeed, there will be none that would be suitable for us to imitate. The reason for this is that, although we see that Christ has not yet been made "all in all" (to cite the words of the Apostle), we can nonetheless in this fashion find him partly in all. For it is said of him that "by God's doing he was made for us wisdom, righteousness, holiness, and redemption." Inasmuch, therefore, as there is wisdom in one, righteousness in another, holiness in another, meekness in another, chastity in another, and humility in another, Christ is now divided among each of the holy ones, member by member. But when we are all assembled together in the unity of faith and virtue, he appears as "the perfect man," completing the fullness of his body in the joining together and in the characteristics of the individual members.[10]

For Cassian, then, the practice of virtue is not fundamentally the cultivation of self-improvement. Rather, as monastics grow in virtue, they grow into the fullness of Christ and as constituent members of the Body of Christ—they contribute to the eschatological consummation when Christ will be all in all. The quest for virtue is the quest to more fully and completely participate in the life and redemptive work of the risen Lord.

St. Benedict in his Rule works along the same lines. The three Benedictine vows, obedience, stability, and conversion of life, are designed to construct an environment in which long-term mimesis is made possible. Benedict makes clear in a number of ways that the first two are prerequisites for the third, demonstrating this most eloquently in his opening chapter. Clearly adapting *Conferences* 18.4-8, Benedict describes cenobites by describing what they are not—neither sarabaites nor gyrovagues. The first of these sorts of monks live without an abbot and thus without obedience: "Their law is what they like to do, whatever strikes their fancy. Anything they believe in and choose, they call holy; anything they dislike, they consider forbidden" (RB 1.7-8).[11] As a result, "with no experience

---

[10] Ibid., 118–19.

[11] All quotations from the Rule of Benedict are from *RB 1980: The Rule of St. Benedict in English and Latin with Notes*, ed. Timothy Fry (Collegeville, MN: Liturgical Press, 1981).

to guide them, no rule to try them, as gold is tested in a furnace, [they] have a character as soft as lead" (RB 1.6). The second sort have no stability. Rather they "spend their entire lives drifting from region to region, staying as guests for three of four days in different monasteries. Always on the move, they never settle down, and are slaves to their own wills and gross appetites. In every way they are worse than sarabaites" (RB 1.10-11). Without these two vows, conversion of life is impossible. Mimesis is a process that requires time, discipline, and the external controls of a Rule and an abbot to curb the destructive impulses of self-will.

Instead, Benedict constructs the abbot as both the head of the community and the linchpin of the chain of command that stretches from heaven to earth. On the one hand, "He is believed to hold the place of Christ in the monastery since he is addressed by a title of Christ" (RB 2.2). Being in the place of Christ, his word commands obedience no matter how absurd or impossible his orders appear; the monastics are bound to "carry out the superior's order as promptly as if the command came from God himself" (RB 5.4). This commanded obedience gives no opportunity for tyranny as the abbot himself is also one set under authority:

> Therefore the abbot must never teach or decree or command anything that would deviate from the Lord's instructions. On the contrary, everything he teaches and commands should, like the leaven of divine justice, permeate the minds of his disciples. . . . Furthermore, anyone who receives the name of abbot is to lead his disciples by a twofold teaching: he must point out to them all that is good and holy more by example than by words, but demonstrating God's instructions to the stubborn and dull by a living example. (RB 2.4-5, 11-12)

Standing in the place of Christ means, therefore, that the abbot must provide the preeminent example of holiness in both words and works for the community. As Christ, he is responsible for the charges put into his trust: "Let the abbot always remember that at the fearful judgment of God, not only his teaching but also his disciples' obedience will come under scrutiny" (RB 2.6).

Monastic legislation puts a premium on human example. At each step of the journey, monastics have those above them who model the virtues that will lead them into the mind of Christ. Observation of monastic superiors is constantly exhorted throughout the tradition; it is the experience of living with good guides that forms the cenobites, making them the strongest kind of monk, ultimately giving them the spiritual strength and training in order that some may reach the goal of being strong enough to live alone as anchorites.

Literary Aspects of Mimesis

This monastic emphasis on imitation led to particular attention to texts about people and their deeds. Scripture was mined for its positive and negative examples, extending an interpretive tradition that has its roots in Scripture itself, exemplified by the book of Sirach 44–50 and the letter to the Hebrews 11. An array of scriptural notables fill the pages of Benedict, Cassian, and Ælfric: Abel, Enoch, Judas, Gehazi, Elijah, Josiah, Judith, Ananias and Sapphira, functioning as examples and counterexamples for monastics striving to grow into the stature of the great exemplar, Christ himself.

The search for exemplars, however, was not the only way that early medieval monastics sought to imitate the Scriptures. Benedict is clear that the monastic life is an embodiment of what Scripture enjoins: "What page, what passage of the inspired books of the Old and New Testaments is not the truest of guides for the human life?" The Prologue of the Rule adapts the wisdom form of a father's exhortation to his son; it is an impressive deployment of Scripture that includes a line-by-line run through a portion of Psalm 34 and another through the beginning of Psalm 15. This scriptural pastiche is placed as a cry in the mouth of Christ calling the prospective monk into his service through the embodiment of the Scriptures. After concluding with the parable of the builders on sand and rock from the end of the Sermon on the Mount, Benedict summarizes his exhortation: "With this conclusion, the Lord waits for us daily to translate into action, as we should, his holy teachings" (RB Prol. 35). These teachings are further enumerated in the fourth chapter, "Tools for Good Works."[12]

In addition to Scripture, monasticism was nurtured and spread through the developing art form of Christian hagiography. Athanasius's *Life of St. Antony* had an incalculable effect on the growth of monasticism. In the

---

[12] This chapter of the Rule was discussed above in the introduction.

West, four other lives quickly grounded both the shape of monasticism and the conventions of the hagiographical genre: Jerome's *Lives* of Malchus, Hilaron, and Paul of Thebes, and—especially central to the growth of Gaulish monasticism—Sulpicius Severus's *Life of St. Martin*. Lives of saints became an enormously popular form of literature. Lapidge reports that "C. W. Jones once estimated that some 600 [saints' lives] survive from the period before 900."[13]

These lives fulfill two important functions in the monastic milieu. First, they present examples of virtue and saintliness for imitation. Second, they continually remind their readers and hearers of the end result of such imitation—they record the miracles performed by God through the saint before and after death. Through their power of efficacious intercession on behalf of the living, the glorified saints extend divine power into the world of the living, participating in and advancing the eschatological consummation in a manner different but not ultimately dissimilar from Cassian's vision of Christ made complete in his Body.

Some modern readers seeking historical data or the flavor of local medieval life from saints' lives are sorely disappointed to find generic and stereotyped *topoi* repeated throughout the genre. The same kind of miracles keep happening; the same sort of events occur in their lives. They impart little data for historical use. In order to accomplish the mimetic and theological functions, the genre followed certain prescribed conventions, conventions that seem strange to us now. The tradition provides a basic template:

> the saint is born of noble stock; his birth is accompanied by miraculous portents; as a youth he excels at learning and reveals that he is destined for saintly activity; he turns from secular to holy life (often forsaking his family) and so proceeds through the various ecclesiastical grades; he reveals his sanctity while still on earth by performing various miracles; eventually he sees his death approaching and, after instructing his disciples or followers, dies calmly; after his death many miracles occur at his tomb. Of course any number of variants

[13] Michael Lapidge, "The Saintly Life in Anglo-Saxon England," in *The Cambridge Companion to Old English Literature*, ed. Malcolm Godden and Michael Lapidge (Cambridge: Cambridge University Press, 1986), 243–63, 253.

is possible within these basic frameworks; but the framework itself is invariable.[14]

As a body of literature, these lives had a specific use in the community; during Chapter,[15] the head of the community would read from the life of the saint on the day before his or her veneration that the monks might meditate on the virtues of the saint throughout the coming feast. During the Night Office on the feast, the life—or a different version thereof—would be read as the main reading for one of the nocturns. Thus, the presence of a life for any given saint remembered in the community's liturgical kalendar[16] was not optional—they were ecclesially necessary documents. As a result, the framework could be utilized even for saints about whom the hagiographer had only the most scant information: "An anonymous monk of Whitby wished to honor with a vita the pope responsible for the conversion of the English; knowing little about Gregory the Great or miracles associated with him, however, he must ask his readers' indulgence if he simply praises the saint extravagantly, randomly assembling passages from Scripture, references to Gregory's writings, and some absurd fables."[17] Thus, working from the basic framework and resorting to a handful of stock *topoi*, a saint's life could be easily assembled for any one of the some three hundred post-biblical saints venerated in an average Anglo-Saxon institution that

[14] Ibid., 253. The outline for a *passio* or death by martyrdom is equally stereotyped, but by this point in the life of the Western church, few martyrs were being made, Boniface and other northern missionaries being exceptions.

[15] See the section on the daily round in chap. 2.

[16] This is a standard technical term that serves to distinguish a liturgical listing of occasions to be observed from the more standard use of the term. As medieval months were reckoned according to the Roman system of counting down to the kalends, nones, and ides, most kalendars begin with the word "kalends" in a large, brightly colored, distinctive script indicating the first day (the kalends) of the month of January.

[17] Rachel S. Anderson, "Saints' Legends," in *A History of Old English Literature*, ed. R. D. Fulk and Christopher M. Cain (Maldon, MA: Blackwell, 2005), 87–105, 90. The particular life mentioned is found in Betram Colgrave, ed. and trans., *The Earliest Life of Gregory the Great* (Lawrence: University of Kansas Press, 1968).

would satisfy the liturgical and mimetic requirements of the genre while frustrating historians of a later age.[18]

The mention of Scripture in the above life of Gregory the Great is significant. The construction of sanctity was an important function of these works and that construction had to conform to expectations: "It was the overall intention of any hagiographer to demonstrate that his saintly subject belonged indisputably to the universal community of saints. . . . It is not so much a matter of plagiarism as of ensuring that the local saint is seen clearly to possess the attributes of, and to belong undoubtedly to, the universal community of saints."[19] The virtues, trials, and especially miracles are very often drawn directly from Scripture. This not only creates a continuity of sanctity but also reinforces that the Christian life in general and the monastic life in particular was understood as an ever-increasing progress in enacting the Scriptures—not only enacting its commandments and precepts but also receiving the same graces that biblical personages enjoyed. The citation and appropriation of Scripture in hagiography melded imitation of the saints with imitation of the Scriptures, all of it ultimately pointing to the imitation of Christ who is the source and pattern of both the saints and the Scriptures.

LITERARY CULTURES

Before discussing the literary habits of the early medieval monastics, the stark technical differences between their culture and the modern day must be addressed. Modern biblical scholars have massive advantages over their medieval counterparts. The printing press was a quantum leap forward; books could now be mass-produced so that individuals could have substantial libraries and even small institutions could own thousands of volumes. All the while, the text in each run of a given book was identical. Mass-produced Bibles of the same version all contain the same text.

---

[18] Lapidge, "The Saintly Life," 247. Ursula Lenker's magisterial study of Anglo-Saxon Gospel lectionaries records lectionary entries for 155 Sanctoral occasions, many of which commemorated multiple saints. See Ursula Lenker, *Die westsächsische Evangelienversion und die Perikopenordnungen im angelsächsiscen England* (Munich: Fink, 1997).

[19] Lapidge, "The Saintly Life," 254.

Furthermore, a common system of chapters and verses ensures identical references to any biblical passage. Such a system highlights and typically even footnotes minor variations where Hebrew or Vulgate verse numberings differ from the standard scheme. With the advent of computer-aided research tools, texts of all kinds can be parsed and searched with ease, placing at the fingertips of scholars amazing capabilities for locating cross-references and accessing primary and secondary sources. In addition to these textually-centered technologies, increases in productivity provided by innovations like electric lighting, central heat, word processing, and the internet further separate the two cultures.

By way of contrast, early medieval monastics had only the texts that could be copied by hand on expensive and laboriously prepared materials. Indeed, notes in the margins or at the end of manuscripts sometimes contain complaints written by the scribes concerning the poor ink, bad lighting, the poor quality of the vellum, and the physical pain caused by hours of writing under such conditions. Too often modern academics dismiss as plagiaristic scribal behaviors that functioned contextually as strategies for preserving and transmitting texts that would otherwise have been lost. Monasteries were supposed to have enough books such that each monk could have one book for edifying reading during Lent and for the daily practice of *lectio*, but this still does not imply a large number.

The primary advantage of monastic readers over their modern counterparts was the practice of *lectio*; due to this method of slow and meditative reading, monastics would have memorized far more of the biblical, patristic, and liturgical texts they read than most modern readers. The sheer volume of biblical references and allusions scattered through monastic writings of all types bear witness to the degree to which the biblical text was assimilated.

New Testament scholarship and early medieval monastic culture are both fundamentally literary ways of life, yet their purpose in reading the same texts is very different. Nowhere is this more plainly seen than in examining the very foundations of their interpretive projects: their hermeneutical frameworks and their basic approaches toward the New Testament compositions as found in introductions to the New Testament. Ælfric serves us in perfect stead as a voluminous author and teacher who has bequeathed both a clearly delineated hermeneutical framework and a text which may be regarded as the first introduction to the Bible ever written in an English language.

The Hermeneutical Framework of Early Monastic Medieval Culture

Reading through Ælfric's corpus, an attentive reader notices that he continually returns to certain themes grounded in an overarching narrative that holds together the Scriptures, world history, and the eschatological fulfillment. The numerous bits and pieces scattered throughout his writings point toward several texts that lay out a narrative of this kind. Virginia Day's 1974 article, "The Influence of the Catechetical *Narratio* on Old English and Some Other Medieval Literature" correctly identified the place of Ælfric's core narrative within its patristic and early medieval trajectory.

Day begins by defining the identifying characteristics of what she refers to as the "catechetical *narratio*":

> In medieval literature there are a number of examples of a type of writing which provides an outline of Christian cosmology and Christian history. These works deal, usually briefly, with the following: [1] God and his creative powers, [2] the creation, [3] the fall of the angels, [4] the creation and fall of man, [5] biblical history, [6] the redemption, [7] Christ's life, [8] the crucifixion, [9] the descent into hell, [10] the resurrection, [11] the ascension, [12] the second coming and last judgement. The subjects vary somewhat; the fall of man and his redemption are of central importance, and some outline versions are reduced to these essentials.[20]

Day identifies the originating source of this outline—particularly taking creation as a starting point and emphasizing redemption—as Augustine's *De Catechizandis Rudibus*. While correct in highlighting the importance of this patristic work, she misses a yet more basic source, indeed, Augustine's own: the Creeds. Of her twelve common elements only three—elements 3, 4, and 5—are not contained within the Apostles' and Nicene Creeds.

Day helpfully identifies a number of works that implement Augustine's catechetical pattern: Avitus of Vienne's *Libelli de Spiritalis Historiae Gestis*,

---

[20] Virginia Day, "The Influence of the Catechetical *Narratio* on Old English and Some Other Medieval Literature," ASE 3 (1974): 51–61, here 51. The numeration of the elements is my own for ease of reference.

Hrabanus Maurus's *De Fide Catholica*—a reorganization of the Hiberno-Latin *Altus Prosator*, Odo of Cluny's *Occupatio*, the Old Irish *Voyage of Snegdus and MacRiagla*, the poem *Saltair na Rann*, the prose version of the same in the Lebar Bec, Pseudo-Boethius's *De Fide Catholica*, and a handful of sermons—both freestanding and incorporated into martyrologies. The two most important early medieval adaptations of Augustine's work are Martin of Braga's *De Correctione Rusticorum* and Pirmin's *Scarapsus*.

Turning to the *Narratio*'s effect on Old English literature, Day mentions Cædmon's hymn, the Junius Manuscript's "Genesis," and "Christ and Satan," but focuses on three Old English sermons: the anonymous Vercelli XIX, Ælfric's *De Initio Creaturae*, and Wulfstan's Bethurum VI—a reworking of Ælfric's piece. All three bear the imprint of Martin of Braga's work; the first and last show clear signs of Pirmin's as well. Ælfric's, though, is more independent from its sources.[21] In short, Augustine's catechetical suggestions were widely influential in early medieval Europe and in Anglo-Saxon England; when compared with other catechetical works, Ælfric's contributions are largely typical rather than exceptional.

Ælfric presents his version of the *narratio* in a number of his writings:

> Ælfric produced other versions of the Christian cycle. There is one at the beginning of his *Letter to Sigeweard* and another at the beginning of his *Letter to Wulfgeat*. His *Hexameron* also contains similar material; although its structure is that of the six days' work [of creation], it closes with a reference to the redemption and eternal life and a passage of exhortation. . . . There is also evidence that the *Letter to Sigeweard*, the *Letter to Wulfgeat* and the *Hexameron* all lean on the *De Initio* [CH I.1] in diction and phraseology. The *De Initio* was Ælfric's most complete version; it is as if all the latter accounts presuppose the existence of this basic one.[22]

---

[21] Both Day and Godden—citing Day—emphasize the freedoms that Ælfric takes with his sources. While they both acknowledge his significant debt to Augustine and Martin of Braga, close verbal parallels are few and tentative. See Day, "Catechetical *Narratio*," 57; Malcolm Godden, *Aelfric's Catholic Homilies: Introduction, Commentary and Glossary*, Early English Text Society, supplementary series 18 (Oxford: Oxford University Press, 2000), 8.

[22] Day, "Catechetical *Narratio*," 57, 58.

Day also mention's Ælfric's works *De Creatore et Creatura* and *De Sex Etatibus huius Seculi*. Furthermore, verbal and thematic parallels may be found throughout Ælfric's sermons for the Annunciation of Mary, Christmas, and the "Memory of the Saints."[23] Truly grasping this narrative and its contours is essential to apprehending Ælfric's program.

Day touches on the crucial importance of this *narratio*. Since her intention is to place Ælfric's appropriation within a larger trajectory, she does not explore further but states:

> The catechetical background explains why he chose the *De Initio* to open his Catholic Homilies: the catechetical sermon is the traditional introduction to Christianity. In the *Letter to Sigeweard* the narratio serves as an introduction to a discussion of the bible and Ælfric's various translations from it. The Augustinian background makes clear how apt this is. Augustine considered that the catechetical narratio should provide the essential narrative and message of the scriptures interpreted for the ignorant: the narratio is to lay down the guidelines for the understanding of scripture. Accordingly, before allowing his reader to proceed to what he conceived of as the dangerous terrain of the bible itself, Ælfric took the opportunity to clarify the correct message to be derived from it. In the *Letter to Wulfgeat* also the context of the narratio is clearly "catechetical": Ælfric prefaces his advice on how to live the moral life with a brief outline of the Christian cycle, exactly as Augustine had recommended that the narratio be followed by exhortation. In general Ælfric's production of several versions of the narratio—as well as his use of some similar material in the *Hexameron*—has the aim of providing a framework for the unlettered, of placing each particular point of Christian doctrine in relation to the pattern of the whole.[24]

---

[23] These three sermons are, respectively, (1) Homily for the feast of the Annunciation, in *Ælfric's Catholic Homilies: The First Series, Text*, ed. Peter Clemoes, Early English Text Society, supplementary series 17 (Oxford: Oxford University Press, 1997), 281–89 (hereafter ÆCHom I, 13); (2) Homily for Christmas in *Ælfric's Catholic Homilies: The Second Series, Text*, ed. Malcolm Godden, Early English Text Society, supplementary series 5 (London: Oxford University Press, 1979), 3–11 (hereafter ÆCHom II, 1); and (3) ÆLS (Memory of Saints).

[24] Day, "Catechetical *Narratio*," 59.

Day rightly identifies the function of this *narratio*: to fix the framework of the Christian story in the minds of its hearers. Her point may be extended—especially given the verbal reminiscences and allusions in Ælfric's other writings—that it securely embeds itself within the worldview of the preacher and interpreter as well. Indeed, the *Letter to Wulfgeat* states that its summary of the *narratio* is in fact a remembrance of what Ælfric had expounded on his actual visit to Wulfgeat's hall, Ylmandune. This framework is the hermeneutical lens through which he views the biblical text and thus it deserves sustained attention.

The heart of the narrative is the story suggested by the Creeds. The lead characters are briefly introduced before the opening of the narrative proper: The Holy Trinity, one God in three persons, Father, Son, and Holy Spirit, is eternal and preexistent. The Trinity—primarily through the Father and the Son—created the world, all things seen and unseen. The Holy Spirit holds all things in life and forgives those who truly repent.

In the process of creation, God created ten angel hosts. The tenth host, led by Lucifer, rebelled against God on account of Lucifer's pride and were cast from heaven. This host exists now as the demonic order. In order to replace this host, God created humanity—first Adam, then Eve—and placed them in the garden, presenting the tree in the center of the garden as a test of obedience and loyalty, the loyalty that Satan and his host lacked. Through the devil's trickery Eve was deceived and humanity disobeyed God's command, receiving dismissal from the garden and death as a consequence.

From Adam came Noah who had three sons; after God led them through the flood, the eldest of the sons, Shem, was the ancestor of the Hebrews whom God rescued from Egypt and to whom the Law was given.

From the Hebrew people God chose the Blessed Virgin Mary from whom Jesus was born incarnate by the Holy Spirit. Jesus performed a great many miracles that the people might believe that he was the Son of God. He taught that humanity must believe rightly in God, be baptized, and demonstrate faith with good works. Fundamentally, though, he came for the redemption of humanity. The devil used Judas to incite the Jews to kill Jesus and he was crucified. After the crucifixion he was buried and descended into hell where he conquered the devil and freed Adam, Eve, and their descendants. He arose from the dead on the third day and rejoined his disciples, teaching them that they must go throughout the earth, teaching and baptizing. On the fortieth day he ascended bodily into heaven and was seated at the right hand of the Father. He will come at the end of time on the clouds with great power and will raise all souls that they may be judged. The wicked will be cast into eternal fire; the righteous he will bring into the heavenly kingdom.

Ælfric's fundamental hermeneutical outlook is that Scripture is the written record of a great eschatological epic that arcs seamlessly from creation to the great consummation. This view presents several exegetical implications. Scripture as a whole is understood with reference to itself—the Old Testament and New Testament are read together and mutually interpret one another. The dominant tools for interpreting Scripture are fundamentally literary and are the same as those used for interpreting other monuments of literate culture: grammar and poetics. To the early medieval mind, Scripture not only utilized grammatical and poetic techniques but also defined them. Scriptural phrases that would ordinarily be judged to be grammatically incorrect were passed over as not only acceptable but beyond critique. Furthermore, the identification of these tools means that the interpretation of Scripture is a learned art form that requires both skills and intelligence beyond the scope of the ordinary believer.[25]

Second, as a result of this literary character of Scripture, the Scriptures and their contents were subject to literary rules and devices rather than historical inquiry. As a result, literary strategies for meaning-making like prolepsis (foreshadowing), allegory, and typology are not only possible but also quite necessary. Furthermore, these were applied not only to the biblical text but also to the events narrated by the text. Strategies like typology discovered clues and hints in isolated passages and events that point to the larger drama of redemption being played out repeatedly on many levels within the pages of the divine text.

Ælfric deploys this kerygmatic framework within several different contexts. While the same core proclamation appears each time, Ælfric shifts its emphases and the surrounding, contextualizing material to suit his pedagogical, catechetical, or homiletical needs. As a result, the the-

---

[25] Ælfric's preface to Genesis displays his reluctance to translate Scripture into English lest the simple be misled by an overly literal understanding of the Law. Furthermore, his sermons abound with warnings that the depths of the Scriptures are beyond the ken of his listeners.

ology of the kerygma is not rigid or static but adapts itself to different situations.

Through these adaptations, worship, faith, and obedience form an interlocking set of concepts for Ælfric's subsequent reading of the Old Testament. Abraham, of course, exemplifies all three: "he worshipped God with his whole heart and the Heavenly God spoke to him often on account of his great faith. . . . God Himself promised him that through his kin all humanity should be blessed for his great faith and for the obedience that he had towards God."[26] Israel's temporal peace was dependent on praise and earnest worship of God. The summarized teachings of Jesus during his earthly ministry gather together ritual action, belief, and obedience as well: "[Jesus] said that no man may be healed unless he rightly believes in God, is baptized, and demonstrates his belief with good works."[27]

Ælfric's emphasis on obedience, particularly as filtered through exemplary characters of the Old and New Testaments and from the history of the church, locate his work squarely within the mimetic hermeneutic of traditional monasticism and, at the same time, enable it to speak to the Anglo-Saxon lay milieu. He follows in the footsteps of Cassian and Benedict, appealing to the same sainted examples, in his construction of a semi-Pelagian theology of salvation through imitation of Christ and his holy ones in belief and in deed.

Furthermore, this hermeneutic drives his fundamental approach to the biblical texts and to the gospels. The impulses present in this kerygma are made explicit in Ælfric's lengthy *Letter to Sigeweard*.[28] This letter melds Ælfric's kerygma with a treatise on the Bible and its interpretation that is the earliest surviving English-language introduction to the Bible. Ostensibly, the letter is a two-section work comprising an introduction to the Old Testament (lines 1–838) and an introduction to the New Testament (lines 839–1274). Its unifying vision, though, alternates between

[26] Ælfric's *Letter to Sigeweard*, in *The Old English Version of the Heptateuch*, ed. Samuel J. Crawford, Early English Text Society 160 (London: Oxford Univeristy Press, 1922 [repr. with additions by N. R. Ker, 1969]), lines 249–52, 257–64. Hereafter ÆLet 4 (SigeweardB); see also ÆLS (Memory of Saints) lines 25–27.

[27] Homily *De initio creaturae*, in *Ælfric's Catholic Homilies: The First Series, Text*, ed. Peter Clemoes, Early English Text Society, supplementary series 17 (Oxford: Oxford University Press, 1997), p. 188, lines 261–63. Hereafter ÆCHom I, 1.

[28] ÆLet 4 (SigeweardB).

the order of the canon and an explication of the eight ages of history that constitute the period from creation to the blissful existence of the righteous after the Last Judgment. Functionally, this letter accomplishes five tasks: (1) it communicates a sense of the whole canon through a listing of books and facts about them, (2) it serves as an index of Ælfric's English language treatments of Scripture up to the time of the writing, (3) it subsumes the canon within the apocalyptic battle between Christ and Satan, (4) it identifies the Scripture's import as prophesying and foretelling Christ's redemptive acts throughout history, and (5) it offers exemplars for imitation in the ongoing struggle.[29]

On one hand, the treatise looks like a modern introduction to the Scripture in that it works systematically through the biblical canon, concerning itself with matters of authorship, contents, and basic interpretation. The Old Testament portion covers the Pentateuch, the historical books to the Exile, the Psalms, the Solomonic Wisdom books, the apocryphal Wisdom books, the Prophets, and the later canonical and apocryphal historical books (including Job).[30] In the presentation of these books, Ælfric notes the author whenever possible, explains the Latin name of the book where necessary, and then gives a summary of the contents. These may be brief or lengthy.[31] Lastly, interpretive comments aid the reader in linking these books to Christ either through typological interpretation of narrative, typological etymology, or direct prophecy. In addition, Ælfric does not miss the opportunity to offer contemporary

---

[29] The latest work on the *Letter to Sigeweard* dates it toward the end of Ælfric's career, between 1003 and 1009. Larry Swain, "Ælfric of Eynsham's Letter to Sigeweard: An Edition, Commentary, and Translation" (PhD diss., University of Chicago, 2008), 46.

[30] Jerome's preface to Job—undoubtedly one of Ælfric's sources either directly or through Isidore's *Ety.* 5—gives no sense of the genre of the work. This rather irascible work prefers to speak of the meter, to excoriate Greek Old Testament translations other than the Septuagint, and to criticize those who would rather purchase or produce deluxe manuscripts than feed the poor. His famous (singular) reference to "*uncialibus*" appears in this preface. Of the books of the Old Testament, Lamentations alone is not mentioned directly though the passage "[Jeremiah] lamented greatly the sins of his people just as his book tells us" (ÆLet 4 [SigeweardB], lines 619–20 may be an oblique reference to it).

[31] The summary for the book of Ruth, for instance, occupies a mere three lines: lines 445–48. The longest summary and interpretation by far is for Genesis—175 lines long (lines 137–312). Exodus, by comparison, occupies almost 60: lines 313–70.

political commentary in his exposition by highlighting Old Testament exempla of kings, leaders, or women who took up arms against pagan armies,[32] apparently a jibe at the ineffectual English policies in regard to the Viking invaders.[33]

The New Testament introduction treats the evangelists, the apostolic authors and their epistles, the Pauline corpus including not only Hebrews but also the epistle to the Laodicians,[34] Acts, and Revelation. This section does not have the extensive exegetical remarks that the Old Testament section had. However, Ælfric does pause after his section on the Pauline epistles to summarize the interpretive center of the gospels, catholic, and Pauline epistles as love of God and obedience through good works.

Lastly, in his concluding matter, Ælfric takes up the topic of the canon as a whole. The two testaments, like the two seraphim in Isaiah 6, speak with a single voice "concerning Christ's humanity and concerning the

[32] See especially his comments on Judges (lines 427–45), Saul (lines 455–63), David (lines 464–71), the good and bad kings of Judah (lines 507–18), Judith (lines 772–80) which contains the very explicit admonition: "[This book] is also translated in English in our fashion to set an example for people that you should defend your own land with weapons against an attacking army," and a lengthy exposition on the Maccabees (lines 781–838).

[33] Compare the contemporary lament in the Anglo-Saxon chronicle on the martyrdom of Archbishop Ælfheah at the hands of Viking raiders: "All these disasters befell us through bad policy, in that [the Vikings] were never offered tribute in time nor fought against; but when they had done most to our injury, peace and truce were made with them; and for all this peace and tribute they journeyed nonetheless in bands everywhere and harried our wretched people and plundered and killed them" (Dorothy Whitelock, ed., *English Historical Documents: c. 500-1042*, 2nd ed. [London: Eyre & Spottiswoode, 1979], 244). Moreover, see the famous Sermon of Lupus to the English Nation by Ælfric's correspondent Archbishop Wulfstan of York, who particularly decries the practice of stripping churches to pay tribute to the Danes.

[34] Laodicians is transmitted in a handful of Latin early medieval biblical manuscripts. As Ælfric does not mention the work in any other extant context, it is impossible to say if the letter was included through knowledge of the apocryphal work or through the reference to such a letter in Col 4:16. (The Laodician textual variant in the title of Ephesians was not transmitted in the Latin tradition.) See Thomas N. Hall, "Ælfric and the Epistle to the Laodicians," in *Apocryphal Texts and Traditions in Anglo-Saxon England*, ed. Kathryn Powell and Donald Scragg (Cambridge: D. S. Brewer, 2003), 65–84.

Holy Trinity in true unity."[35] Like the seraphim, the unity of the testaments is further demonstrated in their endless praise of God in both words and works. Ælfric divides the canon into a total of seventy-two books that mirror both the number of nations who scattered from Babel and the number of apostles that Jesus sent out into the world as a further demonstration of the unity of the canon.

Thus, in one sense, the contents of Ælfric's *Letter to Sigeweard* anticipate the expectations that modern scholarship places on the genre of *einleitung* or critical introduction. The foremost questions treated include the identity of the biblical authors, the temporal context within the history of Israel (particularly for the Old Testament sections), the chief contents of the works, basic interpretive strategies, and even attention to the relationships between the parts of the canon and the whole canon. Certainly modern scholarship would disagree with many of Ælfric's findings in this regard, but the scope is familiar.

Despite these familiar aspects, Ælfric's framework is his kerygma in general, a periodization of history focused toward the end-times in particular, and a catechetical focus that continually draws him away from a tight focus on the biblical text. The organizing effects of Ælfric's kerygma on the *Letter to Sigeweard* are immediately apparent. He begins not with the Scripture but with the Trinity and immediately diverges from the biblical narrative to present a lengthy extracanonical account of the fall of Satan. As Ælfric continues, he moves in historical order—an order that agrees with the canonical order as far as 2 Chronicles. As he moves through the periods of history, he follows the standard apocalyptic device of dividing time into a set of ages.[36] As the ages run in their courses, they draw more inevitably to the time of the Last Judgment. Already we are in the sixth age, which will end with the Second Coming of Christ. The periodization comes, once again, from Augustine's *De Catechizandis Rudibus*.[37] As

---

[35] ÆLet 4 (SigeweardB), lines 1155–56.

[36] The first six ages are clearly temporal, the last two are somewhat extratemporal. Age 1: from Creation to Noah; Age 2: from Noah to Abraham; Age 3: from Abraham to David; Age 4: from David to Daniel; Age 5: from Daniel to Christ; Age 6: from Christ to the Last Judgment. Age 7 is, essentially, a stasis age wherein all who have died rest until the Last Day. Age 8 is the single eternal day of the Resurrection life.

[37] The idea also appears in Augustine's *Tract. in Ioh.* 9.6 and subsequently in Bede's *Hom* 1.14 where he expands on the theme.

a result, his scheme is fundamentally historical in as much as it follows the scope of the ages, rather than following the canon proper.

Despite the historical framework, Ælfric is not working with an understanding of history as an assembly of factual events; history is a subset of moral philosophy. As a result, Ælfric seems just as or more interested in authors than in books. The section on the four main prophets indeed focuses more on the authors than their books. He goes into detail on how each of the prophets died.[38] The inclusion of the Sibyls among the prophets is traditional; here Ælfric follows Isidore.[39] Again, as Ælfric presents the New Testament, he spends a substantial set of lines discussing the evangelists—but never discusses the gospels or the differences between them. The evangelists themselves absorb his attention. The apostles, like the prophets, are remembered not only for their writings but also for their martyrdom. Finally, in one of the most unusual features of the letter, Ælfric leaves the theme of the Scriptures altogether and recounts a legend concerning John taken from Rufinius's *Chronicon*. Apparently, establishing the character of the writer is just as important as recounting the contents of his work.

The focus on authors brings Ælfric's catechetical intention back into view. Throughout the work, Ælfric has repeatedly referenced the importance of good works. Indeed, obedience to God's commands—interpreted as faith revealed in good works and in the orthodox worship of the Triune God—is Ælfric's touchstone for interpreting Scripture. He makes this especially clear in this writing by inserting two interpretive summaries—one at the beginning serving the Old Testament and one in the midst of the New Testament section. After his initial greeting and before his usual description of the Trinity, Ælfric offers introductory remarks concerning God's will:

> God loves good works, and he wishes to have them from us for it is
> truly written concerning him that he is blessed by his own works. As
> the psalmist thus sang concerning him: *Sit gloria Domini in seculum
> seculi, letabitur Dominis in operibus suis*; that is in English: "Let there
> be glory to our Lord forever and ever; our Lord is blessed in his own

---

[38] Note that all of the prophets die for their faith but one who lives to an exceedingly ripe old age (Daniel). The same pattern holds true for the apostles where the sole peaceful death at an extended age is John.

[39] Isidore, *Ety.*8.8. PL 82.309C–10B.

works." Thus says the prophet. The Almighty Creator manifested himself through the great works which he worked at the beginning, and he willed that creation would see his joys and dwell with him in glory in eternity under his rule [*underþeodnisse*] ever obeying [*gehirsume*] him, because it is very perverse that worked creatures should not obey [*gehirsume*] him who shaped and worked them.[40]

Thus good works are placed in direct connection with the obedience due the overlord who is the creator of all things. The two concepts are inseparable.

The same connection appears in Ælfric's summary comments on the unity of the New Testament witness. Directly citing John 14:15, 23-24, Ælfric comments: "Here we may hear that the Savior loves the deed more than the smooth word. The word passes away; the deed stands."[41] Citations of James 1:22-23a; 1 John 3:18; and Titus 1:16 demonstrate for him the consonance of the various sections of the New Testament on this pivotal point. That is, loving Jesus and the God who sent him is demonstrated in obedience to his commands, good works; the apostolic witness agrees that true belief is obedience exemplified by action.

The biblical characters and authors that Ælfric introduces reinforce his point and provide examples of faithful action.[42] A key concern within this letter is the responsibility of the noble class—the warrior class—to the nation. In addition to consistently drawing attention to the defense of Israel from heathen armies, a concluding section at the end of the letter addresses the responsibilities of the three main classes of society, the working/tilling class, the praying class, and the ruling/fighting class. Without all three classes performing their specific function, society will collapse like a stool with a bad leg. Naturally, the work of the warriors is the protection of the other two classes. The thematic repetition leads a reader to conclude that Ælfric is encouraging Sigeweard not just to general good works but to a quite specific one—taking up arms to defend

---

[40] ÆLet 4 (SigeweardB), lines 18–28.

[41] ÆLet 4 (SigeweardB), lines 956–57.

[42] In this regard, a further examination of the parallels between the *Letter to Sigeweard* and ÆLS (Memory of Saints) would prove most profitable. ÆLS (Memory of Saints) is a general treatise on the saints but spends a great deal of time on biblical saints in particular.

his people from the Viking raiders. Here Ælfric demonstrates his ability not just as a generic catechist but as a savvy advisor as well, blending religious instruction with political suggestion.

Ælfric's treatment of Matthew within the *Letter to Sigeweard* is a treatment of the author more than the text. In doing so, he discusses Matthew twice but each time he is part of a larger group—the first time grouped with the other evangelists, the second time with the apostles. Ælfric's description of the apostles is commonplace and repeats the well-known material from Jerome's commentary on Matthew that served as a preface to the gospels in most early medieval gospel books:

> Four gospels were written concerning Christ's life. One was written by Matthew who was with the Savior, his own disciple following him in this life. He saw his wonders and wrote them in this book in the Hebrew tongue after Christ's passion in the land of Judea that they might believe in God. He is the first evangelist in the canon. [He then introduces the other evangelists.] These are the four rivers from a single well-spring which go widely from Paradise over God's people. These four evangelists were formerly signified as Ezekiel saw them: Matthew in a man's form, Mark in a lion's, Luke in a calf's, John in an eagle because they signified these significances. Matthew wrote concerning Christ's humanity.[43]

There is no discussion here of sources, of editorial work, or of the shaping of traditional material. Ælfric does address the target audience, language of composition, and a central theological theme—the humanity of Christ. He does not, however, produce any evidence for these claims. He presents the traditional wisdom which flowed from Eusebius to Jerome to Isidore. After this introduction, he summarizes the gospel story found in the works of the four evangelists, speaking of Christ's incarnation, the slaughter of the innocents, the selection of the apostles, the miracles, and finally the crucifixion and resurrection; no differentiation between sources is made.

The next discussion of Matthew comes in Ælfric's description of the Acts of the Apostles, but it serves to transmit the historically suspect material more commonly associated with the apocryphal Acts than the canonical Acts. Ælfric writes of Matthew, "Matthew preached in the land of

---

[43] ÆLet 4 (SigeweardB), lines 862–67, 880–85.

Ethiopia where there are Ethiopians and the king slew him, not converted but faithless."[44] Ælfric's sermon for the feast of St. Matthew (*CH* II.34) takes this as a jumping-off point and after an initial exegesis of the call of Matthew, includes a *passio* that tells of Matthew's martyrdom in Ethiopia.

Thus, Ælfric treats Matthew as an individual rather than a text. Ælfric's Matthew is almost entirely independent of the text that bears his name. No references are made to it or citations used. Ælfric's interest is not in Matthew as an editor but Matthew as a participant within the eschatological epic described by Scripture. He is a witness—a witness of the human life of Jesus as his disciple, and a witness in that he testified concerning the Christian faith up to and including martyrdom. Matthew transmits knowledge about the events of salvation history and also participates within it, ensuring the spread of the Gospel and therefore the kingship of Christ.

In summary, Ælfric understands the Scriptures to be the record of the great eschatological epic describing the enmity between God and Satan and laying forth the redemptive work of Jesus Christ. Within this framework, Matthew is important because he is a participant and a witness. His gospel records both the words and works of Jesus witnessed by Matthew, but Matthew himself is also an *exemplum* of a committed preacher and teacher who is willing to spread the message of Christ's redemption to distant nations even if it costs him his life.

The Critical Conversation: The Modern Situation

All four of the commentaries with which I am working participate in the critical conversation concerning the scientific study of the New Testament. Two of them—Luz and Davies and Allison—not only stand within it but also participate directly in the continuation of the conversation. The other two—Boring and Hare—stand within it just as surely as the other two but serve a different function. Their primary purpose is to mediate the insights of the critical conversation to those who stand outside of it: they offer insights to clergy and laity who have not been trained and inculturated into the scientific study of the New Testament. As a result, they offer an intermediary position, engaging two worlds: the scholarly and the (broadly construed) pastoral.

---

[44] ÆLet 4 (SigeweardB), lines 998–1000.

The Critical Commentaries

The work of Luz and that of Davies and Allison operate in a similar fashion. Surveying the scholarly tradition, they identify the major interpretive options for a given passage, discussing which scholars and schools took certain directions. Then, weighing these options, they choose one or another of these paths as the best reading of the text, supporting their choices with evidence that then adds to this critical conversation. An important part of this process, then, is identifying the contours of the conversation—noting who is included and who is not, and which interpretive philosophies are broadly accepted and which are not. The central virtues needed to satisfactorily participate within this endeavor are a broad knowledge of the voluminous secondary literature of the field, the ability to accurately synthesize the work of other scholars, grouping them into meaningful categories, then offering persuasive insights—preferably original insights—as to why one interpretive option or cluster of options are to be preferred over others. In regard to these tasks, both Luz and Davies and Allison are consummate professionals. Their abilities and credentials are validated by their invitation to contribute to two major critical commentary series, a certification of their scholarly worth and a statement of their authority to contribute to the continuing conversation.

One indication of the character of the tradition in which they stand is their use of language. The critical conversation is conducted in a formal and stylized dialect. English diction unfamiliar to outsiders is commonplace: words like "eschatological," "hermeneutic," and "chiastic" are used without explanation. Other words have a different meaning than their popular use: terms like "cult" and "miniscule" have different valences and meanings within the critical conversation. And, on occasion, the language itself is not English: the authors expect a basic knowledge of Greek and Hebrew—sometimes Latin and Aramaic too—and a sprinkling of German phrases is not unusual either.

Ulrich Luz begins the preface to the first edition of his commentary with a reference to the "flood of secondary literature that increasingly proves to be more than a hindrance to scholarly communication" and that may keep "one from dealing with the text itself."[45] An additional

---

[45] Ulrich Luz, *Matthew 1–7: A Continental Commentary*, trans. Wilhelm C. Linss, Hermeneia (Minneapolis, MN: Fortress Press, 1992), xv.

reference to the "immensely swollen secondary literature" also conveys the sheer volume of work that the critical conversation produces and that must be integrated to have a mastery of the tradition.[46]

Luz refrains from sketching the contours of the modern critical conversation, but a number of names surface in both the preface to the German edition and the preface to the English edition: Hermann Dörries, Joachim Gnilka, Eduard Schweizer, Hans Weder, Axel Knauf, and Helmut Koester.[47] For those in the conversation, these names on the whole identify a stream of German scholarship that is both historically grounded and interested in pastoral issues. He also helpfully adds a notice that defines the length of the tradition he will engage: "After the text [of Matthew] itself, I am probably most indebted to the church fathers and to the Protestant and Catholic exegesis of the sixteenth through the eighteenth centuries."[48] Thus, he consciously includes prescientific considerations of the text into the boundaries of his conversation. The ten-page double-column list of short titles of commentaries, studies, and frequently cited articles reflects the array of predominantly German, English, Latin, and French sources that he has drawn on and provides a comprehensive list of conversation partners;[49] a list of specific works engaged stands at the start of each passage that he addresses.

Furthermore, on a typical page of his commentary, a line dividing somewhere between a third and half the page denotes space reserved for footnotes, many of which either point to secondary sources or engage discussions held within the secondary literature. Other scholars are not visibly present in the text of his work above the line—but they certainly appear below it.

In terms of his purpose, Luz hopes that his work will not be solely academic:

> I have written this commentary primarily for priests, pastors and teachers of religion. One wonders whether it will help them engage in an intensive conversation with the texts in their study or whether its length

[46] Ibid.
[47] Ibid., xv, xvii.
[48] Ibid., xv.
[49] Ibid., xxviii–xxxvii.

will actually keep them from such a conversation. I would rather have a response to this question than to read all the critical reviews.[50]

He acknowledges with the nod to critical reviews that his work stands securely in the scholarly tradition, yet he hopes that that it will include those who have only been introduced and not immersed in it: the clergy. The laity are here not in view.

Davies and Allison begin their preface with arguments against the two main objections against new commentaries: the current state of flux in biblical studies and the presence of sufficient commentaries. In overcoming these, they present a sketch of their view of the conversation. In addressing the first they write:

> As it is important that each generation translate the Bible for itself, in its own idiom, so each generation should express its own interpretation of it. This will necessarily rest to a large degree on the work of previous generations. Any significant commentary will be an agent in the transmission of exegetical traditions: its wisdom accumulative. But each generation also brings its own peculiar insights to add to those of the past and helps to ensure that the Bible remains a living reality and not a static deposit.[51]

This is a succinct statement that holds two virtues in tension—the transmission of knowledge and its increasing growth. The work of a "significant" commentary is to do both.

A list of contemporary commentaries features in their answer to the second objection. In framing their answer, they identify these works as conversation partners—but partners that fall short or at least are in need of further supplementation:

> Willoughby C. Allen published his volume in this series in 1907, and A. H. McNeile's commentary in the Macmillan series appeared in 1915. These were on a large scale and based on a scrupulous scholarship. The recent work of Robert H. Gundry (1982) is

---

[50] Ibid.

[51] W. D. Davies and Dale C. Allison, *A Critical and Exegetical Commentary on the Gospel According to Saint Matthew*, 3 vols, International Critical Commentary 26 (London/New York: T & T Clark International, 2004), 1:ix.

massively learned and instructive but not a little idiosyncratic. There
have also appeared, among others on a smaller scale, the commentaries by W. F. Albright and C. S. Mann, F. W. Beare, Floyd Filson
and David Hill. The first of these was much criticized; and most of
the others—admirable as they are, especially that of Professor Hill—
were limited by the nature of the series in which they appeared, and
the same applies to the English translation of Eduard Schweizer's
influential commentary. On all these we have gratefully drawn as
upon the countless, often excellent, monographs dedicated to the
First Gospel. But in the conviction that the time is ripe for a fresh
attempt at a large scale commentary on Matthew we accepted the
invitation of the editors of this series.[52]

Here they have clearly identified the field of the English-language commentary tradition within which their work is located. David Hill is mentioned again as a reader of the manuscript.[53] A broader scope of their
conversation is given in their exhaustive bibliographical listing of "Commentaries and Other Literature." This list of bare bibliographical data
stretches twenty-seven pages and spans a wide range of writing on Matthew from Augustine and Pseudo-Anselm to Weiss and Wellhausen to
Weder and Wink.[54]

In contrast to Luz, Davies and Allison reserve relatively little space for
footnotes; only a fifth of the page at most is taken by them. Names of
other scholars and references, however, appear throughout the body of
the text. Rather than relegating interpretive differences and controversies
to the footnotes, they are present within the text proper.

Although they do not go as far as to state it, their implied audience is
certainly the scholarly community engaged in the critical conversation.
The closest they come to a clear statement of purpose is their concluding
remark: "Although we cannot be sufficient for this, our aim has been to
be loyal to the tradition of disinterested and objective study in biblical
criticism. We hope that this commentary will not prove unworthy of it."[55]

[52] Ibid., 1:ix–x.
[53] Ibid., 1:xi.
[54] Ibid., 1:xxi–xlvii.
[55] Ibid., 1:xi.

The catchphrase "disinterested and objective"[56] signals that the authors consider their work to be outside of dogmatic constraints imposed by any particular ecclesial body. It also situates them in a branch of the scholarly conversation not beholden to postmodernist philosophies that would call into question the possibility of achieving either objectivity or disinterest.

The Mediating Commentaries

The commentaries of Boring and Hare serve a different purpose. While the commentaries of Luz and Allison-Davies serve to synthesize, summarize, and move the critical conversation forward, the works of Boring and Hare serve to synthesize then mediate the conversation to outsiders not initiated into the conversation. Their commentaries are not primarily designed to speak to the community engaged in the scientific study of Matthew but to offer the fruits of scientific study to readers approaching the text from a position of faith who bring questions about the application of the text to the life of faith.

Both of these authors are scholars. They are trained in and stand within the critical tradition. While the tradition is present throughout their work, it appears more or less silently. That is, while insights from earlier scholars appear, they are not quoted and footnoted as they are—as they must be—in the critical commentary tradition. Furthermore, these authors move beyond the community invested in the critical conversation. Because they speak to believers in their lives of faith, they frequently address issues and interpretations that could be summarily dismissed by the critical conversation because they do not flow from responsible exegesis as defined by the conversation. Also, their language is that of the people. Far fewer foreign words or terms appear, and when they do, they are suitably explained. Thus, these commentaries must mediate between critical and popular conversations and use the former to shed light on the latter in a manner comprehensible to those who live in the latter.

Again, these authors are every bit as indebted to the critical conversation as those who write the critical commentaries—the difference is that the debt is far less apparent due to the audience for whom they are writing.

[56] Ibid.

Eugene Boring offers an introduction that sets up his approach and introduces readers to the Gospel of Matthew and its world. He makes a few brief comments that serve to situate his interpretation but, in a sense, does not make as broad of a statement as the previously surveyed texts because of the nature of his work; rather than being freestanding, it is incorporated within a multivolume work and is bound within one volume with several other essays and a commentary on Mark. He is subscribing to a common form. The remarks that he makes, though, are both helpful and instructive. The bulk of his introductory thoughts appear in one section. Boring writes:

> This commentary attempts to help the modern reader interpret the ancient text with a view to its translation into contemporary meaning.
> Historical study of the Gospel of Matthew is an ally in this task. Matthew was himself an interpreter, standing in the living streams of tradition, interpreting the meaning of the Old Testament into the new situation by looking back on the advent of the Christ, his ministry, crucifixion, and resurrection. In particular, Matthew stands in a Christian hermeneutical stream interpreting the sacred texts of Christian tradition revered in his church (namely, Q and Mark) and the M traditions unique to the Matthean community. Matthew's own interpretation represented in the Gospel of Matthew then entered into the living stream and has been the object of interpretation in the church for nineteen centuries. The contemporary interpreter stands with Matthew in this continuing stream, heir to Matthew's Bible and his Christian traditions (Q, Mark, M), the Gospel of Matthew itself, and the church's continuing interpretation of them all. Matthew is not the passive object of our interpretive work. He is a fellow interpreter who speaks not only to us, but also with us.[57]

Boring's work is intended for popular consumption—anyone from a scholar to a New Testament neophyte is able to pick up his text, understand it, and find insights there. As a result, he constructs his categories around the issue of interpretation with care.

Christian denominations hold varying views toward the role of critical scholarship; while some embrace it wholeheartedly, others do so with

---

[57] Eugene Boring, "Matthew," in *The Interpreter's Bible: Matthew–Mark*, ed. Leander E. Keck, vol. 8 (Nashville, TN: Abingdon, 1995), 57.

reserve—some with a wary eye—while others reject it entirely. Some go so far as to suggest that relying on any form of prior interpretation is itself a sin against the Spirit and should be avoided. Negotiating these topics with sensitivity, Boring avoids potentially inflammatory terms like "critical" or "scientific." While the term "historical" appears, its use is ambiguous; readers do not know whether he is referring to a type of interpretation or to the historical reality of Matthew's interpretation which he takes up immediately afterward.

Instead, Boring chooses to focus on the role of "interpreter." He notes that Matthew was himself an interpreter of both the Old Testament traditions and the Jesus traditions that came to him through Mark, Q, and M. Matthew's own interpretation then became part of the "living/continuing stream" which flows through nineteen centuries to the reader. The only two people specifically placed in this stream are Matthew and the reader; Boring is implicitly present—as are the voices of the nineteen Christian centuries, not to mention those of the Old Testament centuries as well.

Interpreters of the New Testament occasionally appear both in the text and in footnotes, playing larger roles in the introductions to materials and in the excurses that Boring presents on particular topics. Both past and present interpreters appear, and there seems to be no hard and fast dividing line between those engaging in the scientific study of the text and its unscientific study, but the former are mentioned and cited much more frequently.

Douglas Hare signals his intentions in a preface that mirrors his editors; both prefaces that begin this text emphasize that it is not intended as a replacement of scholarly commentaries but is a supplement to them. Hare carves a niche for himself by identifying a gap between the critical commentaries and ecclesial leaders:

> One of the deepest frustrations of ministers, seminary students, and lay Bible teachers is that scholarly commentaries so often provide answers for questions they are not asking and fail to address their basic questions concerning the theological meaning of the text. Scholarly commentaries are indispensable. The church has learned the hard lesson that there is no shortcut to meaning; if we are serious about discovering what the biblical authors are trying to say, there is no escape from the careful questioning undertaken by such studies. This commentary is by no means intended as a substitute for these. Its intention is to supplement their work by emphasizing what

each passage means to Matthew and, by extension, to the modern church.[58]

In a slightly different approach from Boring, Hare describes his work less as a direct mediation between the academic microculture and the ecclesial microcultures because he adds something that the scholarly commentaries do not contain—the theological meaning of the text.

In contrast to the other commentaries utilized, Hare uses neither footnotes nor endnotes. Interactions with modern scholars occur silently, with only a handful of exceptions. Even these exceptions (like an exegetical question suggested by a colleague on page 285) refer to other more popular treatments of the biblical text. The conversation is present but remains invisible to those not familiar with its contours.

Tucked in the back of the commentary is a bibliography divided into two sections: "For further study" and "Literature cited." The first is a half-page in length and refers to the main recent English-language treatments of Matthew (Davies and Allison appears here). The second is a page or so long and contains a smattering of articles, continental commentaries (Luz's work is listed here), monographs, and popular works. Again, the breadth and depth of the conversation is consciously limited.

The Early Medieval Situation

Ælfric's compositional technique and its relation to the tradition has been the focus of much study. The identification of his sources has continued over the course of a century. Förster's groundbreaking work laid a firm foundation for the study of the sources of the *Catholic Homilies*.[59] Smetana's recognition of the importance of the early medieval homiliary tradition and the place of Paul the Deacon's homiliary in reference to Ælfric added much-needed nuance to these studies.[60] Smetana's follow-up

---

[58] Douglas Hare, *Matthew*, Interpretation (Minneapolis, MN: Fortress Press, 1995), vii.

[59] Max Förster, "Über die Quellen von Ælfric's exegetischen Homiliae Catholicae," *Anglia* 16 (1894): 1–61.

[60] Cyril Smetana, "Ælfric and the Early Medieval Homiliary," *Traditio* 15 (1959): 163–204.

work on the homiliary of Haymo,[61] the works of Barré[62] and Grégoire[63] on Carolingian homiliaries, Gatch's first major synthesis of the homiletic environment,[64] Clayton's survey of the homiliary tradition with particular attention to the late Anglo-Saxon milieu,[65] and Joyce Hill's work on Smaragdus[66] have all led to a much better understanding of how Ælfric interacted with his source material and the means by which he accessed it. Godden's magisterial commentary painstakingly documents Ælfric's sources for the *Catholic Homilies*, often offering cogent suggestions from the homiliary tradition concerning how various pieces of patristic material came to Ælfric's attention. While, as Hill notes, more work remains to be done on the early medieval mediators of the tradition, it is now possible to speak intelligently concerning Ælfric's stated aims, implicit aims, and achievements in the *Catholic Homilies* with specific reference to the critical and popular conversations and the main lines of transmission.

Early medieval monastic homilies also come forth from and in continuity with a critical conversation, albeit one with different rules and purposes than the modern scientific study of Scripture. In order to fully appreciate their contents, we must understand that this conversation took place within a very different context and for a very different purpose than the modern one. The context is the liturgy and the purpose is the consistent handing down of an authoritative tradition of interpretation.

Homilies were transmitted primarily in homiliaries. These books were collections of sermons where the order and textual context were

[61] Cyril Smetana, "Ælfric and the Homiliary of Haymo of Halberstadt," *Traditio* 17 (1961): 457–69. Shortly after the publication of this article, Barré properly identified this homiliary as the work of Haymo of Auxerre.

[62] H. Barré, *Les homéliares carolingiens de l'école d'Auxerre*, Studi e Testi 225 (Rome: Biblioteca Apostolica Vaticana, 1962).

[63] Reginald Grégoire, *Les homéliaires du moyen âge*, Rerum Ecclesiasticarum Documenta, Series Maior, Fontes 6 (Rome, 1966); and Reginald Grégoire, *Homéliaires liturgiques médiévaux: analyse des manuscrits*, Bibl degli studi medievali 12 (Spoleto, 1980).

[64] Milton McC. Gatch, *Preaching and Theology in Anglo-Saxon England: Ælfric and Wulfstan* (Toronto: University of Toronto Press, 1977), 27–59.

[65] Mary Clayton, "Homiliaries and Preaching in Anglo-Saxon England," *Peritia* 4 (1985): 207–42.

[66] Joyce Hill, "Ælfric and Smaragdus," *Anglo-Saxon England* 21 (1992): 203–37.

determined by the rhythms of the liturgical year. Preeminently, they were books for use in liturgy. They could be used at Masses, in the Night Office, in Chapter, or in other liturgical functions outside of these three. Only after these purposes did they serve other functions, particularly as sources for holy reading in the monastic practice of *lectio divina* or as resources for study of the Scriptures, theology, and the church fathers. Clayton, in dialogue with McKitterick and Gatch, identifies three types of homiliaries based on function: those for use in the Night Office, those for private devotional reading, and those for preaching to the laity.[67] She notes that these categories were quite flexible, however, and certainly Ælfric himself shows little discrimination between them when looking for source material, drawing from all three without regard.

Where the goal of the modern critical conversation is to move the conversation forward, the purpose of this critical conversation was not motion but stasis—handing on the authoritative teachings of the officially sanctioned tradition with as little deviation as possible. The complication of the situation, though, is that the teachings of the tradition do not apply to something static but to life itself. As a result, change was inevitable; the tradition and those who handed it on had the responsibility of making sure the fundamentals of the tradition were handed on in ways that engaged the emerging circumstances that impacted the often tumultuous lives of early medieval Christians.

Because of the nature of this conversation, an ongoing problem was identifying the proper participants. One important arbitrating mechanism was the council, gatherings of clerics that ranged anywhere from local synods attended by clergy of a certain region to the grand ecumenical councils attended by metropolitans, patriarchs, archbishops, and bishops from across the known world. Often the business of these councils included consensus declarations on whether an author or the opinions of an author were in continuity with the apostolic faith as understood and interpreted by the gathered assembly.[68] Lists of teachers and authors both

---

[67] Clayton, "Homiliaries and Preaching," 216.

[68] Note the untextual nature of the criteria and the acclamations of Pope Leo's *Tome* as recorded in the Acts of the Council of Chalcedon: "This is the faith of the fathers, this is the faith of the Apostles. So we all believe, thus the orthodox believe. Anathema to him who does not thus believe. Peter has spoken thus through Leo. So

approved and condemned were drawn up and circulated. Inevitably these lists were compared with one another and a general consensus formed in areas defining who was and was not part of the conversation.

In addition, certain writers certified as trustworthy produced their own lists of trusted authors based on who they read and cited with approval in their works. Often these lists were implicit, but sometimes they became explicit lists, detailing the lineages of students and teachers, their various writings, and the fate of them and their various writings. The *Ecclesiastical Histories* of Eusebius, Sozomen, Orosius, and others performed this function. The polemical works against heretics by Eusebius, Pantaneus, and others identified positions to be specifically rejected, while Jerome's work, *On Illustrious Men*, continued by Gennadius upon Jerome's death, focused on authors and the texts they produced, approving and rejecting as needed.

While the church attempted to maintain control over the boundaries of the conversation by regulating the content of texts, one factor made true control impossible: the technology of textual transmission. Texts were transmitted by handmade copies. However much the organizational levels of the church attempted to centralize and control the conversation, it was unable to control the scribes.

This lack of control manifested itself in a variety of ways. One had to do with the problem of authenticity. A key document that now serves as a main primary source for our knowledge of received and condemned works, the Gelasian Decretal, is itself considered a forgery. While probably an authentic list produced by some synod or council, it is currently dated in the sixth century and therefore half a century after Pope Gelasius I, its purported author. Furthermore, identifications of authors sometimes depended on whatever heading a scribe wrote down. In one of the great ironies of the tradition, the extant texts believed to be by Pelagius survived destruction because of their ascriptions to his adversary Jerome.

---

taught the Apostles. Piously and truly did Leo teach, so taught Cyril. Everlasting be the memory of Cyril. Leo and Cyril taught the same thing, anathema to him who does not so believe. This is the true faith. Those of us who are orthodox thus believe. This is the faith of the fathers" (NPNF, 2.14). The criteria were not whether the consensus was most biblical but whether the teaching matched the faith of the apostles, of which biblical fidelity was one component.

Pseudonymous works, whether falsely or simply incorrectly attributed, are common throughout the medieval period, the intent sometimes benign and accidental—but sometimes quite deliberate and deceptive. Codex construction played its part as well; packets of pages, individual leaves, and even whole sections called quires could also be inserted into codices, further complicating issues of authorship and authenticity.

Thus, despite efforts to the contrary, the borders of the critical conversation were sometimes more porous than the church preferred, requiring constant vigilance against the introduction of distortions or heresies. Some times and places, of course, were more vigilant than others; for the most part, throughout the early medieval north, vigilance seems to have been the exception rather than the rule.

Gregory the Great (†604)

The main stream of the homiliary tradition can be said to begin with the chief patron of Benedictine life in the West, Pope Gregory the Great. A member of his congregation—most likely a member of his staff—recorded a number of homilies he preached in the years 591–592.[69] These were edited into a collection of forty gospel homilies that received wide circulation in the medieval period. Based on contextual clues, these all seem to have been preached at public Masses.

Although he may stand at the head of the Western homiliary tradition, Gregory would resist any suggestion that his writings are original. Rather, they draw broadly on patristic sources and are sometimes completely or partly adaptations of the writings of predecessors, particularly Augustine, Leo the Great, John Cassian, and others; his homily for the First Sunday in Lent stands as a suitable example: his teaching on the temptation of Jesus contains traditional material found in Irenaeus, Origen, and others. Gregory's treatment, in fact, is most likely an adaptation of John Cassian's *Conferences* 5.6. Similarly, the trope that the one who turned water to wine could surely make bread of rocks had he chosen is likely indebted to Leo the Great's *Homily* 40.3. His numerological discussion of the timing of Lent corresponds with widespread ancient tradition. Thus, even here at the start of the chain, Gregory is passing along a self-consciously traditional reading of the text.

---

[69] The standard English edition is Gregory I, *Forty Gospel Homilies*, trans. David Hurst, CS 123 (Kalamazoo, MI: Cistercian Publications, 1990). Note that Hurst renumbers Gregory's homilies from the usual scheme found in Migne and elsewhere.

The Venerable Bede (†735)

The homiliary of Bede represents a second step in the movement of the homiliary tradition. Bede composed fifty sermons on the gospels arranged according to the liturgical year. He does not always appoint his homilies for particular occasions but leaves some for general use in certain liturgical seasons. Comparing the series carefully with Gregory's, a distinctive trend emerges; although Gregory was one of Bede's favorite authors, there is no overlap between the biblical texts treated by Bede and Gregory. Martin suggests plausibly that Bede produced his homilies intentionally to supplement and flesh out Gregory's cycle.[70] Indeed, such a service would be in keeping with the rest of Bede's corpus: with regard to the gospels he wrote commentaries only on Luke and Mark—the two that lacked earlier authoritative patristic treatment.

Bede's style was fully patristic, and he seamlessly interwove patristic material and his own interpretations derived by patristic exegetical techniques. An admirer of Augustine, Bede similarly produces thickly textured homilies that pull in a multitude of biblical references from across the canon and focus on details of grammar and vocabulary. Unlike Augustine, whose style is rambling and often hard to follow, Bede's writing is tight and concise. While he was constantly in dialogue with and drew freely from Augustine, Gregory, and the other fathers, Bede does not cite them directly in his homilies. (His commentaries are a different story; with a set of marginal references, Bede seems to have invented and pioneered the use of the source footnote.)

Bede's homilies were clearly intended for the monastic Night Office and also as material for holy reading. Unlike Gregory, Bede includes no stories to provide local color, preferring to save those for his historical writings. Bede's audience, without a doubt, consisted of other monastics and the clergy. His homilies both participated in the critical conversation and were intended to remain within it. His choice of languages, his use of language, and his choice of styles ensured that they would remain accessible to and for the benefit of those within the conversation.[71]

---

[70] Bede the Venerable, *Homilies on the Gospels: Book One: Advent to Lent*, trans. Lawrence T. Martin and David Hurst, CS 110 (Kalamazoo, MI: Cistercian Publications, 1991), xvi.

[71] The style of the *Ecclesiastical History* is quite different from that of his homilies, inviting wider circulation. It is no surprise, then, that King Alfred the Great selected

Paul the Deacon (†799)

The next point in the tradition is the great homiliary of Paul the Deacon. Appointed by Charlemagne to pluck flowers from amongst the Catholic fathers, Paul collected 244 items representing 125 liturgical occasions for the Night Office. Following the needs of the Night Office, Paul supplied most Sunday and festal occasions with two texts: a "*sermo*" for the second nocturn and an "*omelia*" for the third.[72] For his texts, Paul used homilies of the fathers whenever possible, preferring works from Bede, Gregory the Great, Chrysostom, Jerome, and Augustine and using passages from commentaries or other works when an appropriate homily was not available. For instance, of the fifty-six works attributed to Bede in the original collection, thirty-six are homilies and twenty are sections drawn from Bede's commentaries on the two less popular gospels, Luke and Mark.

In each case, the source was identified so that those hearing would know from whom the teaching came and that it stood within the tradition. Inevitably, though, some of these attributions were incorrect. In fact, of the fifty texts attributed to Maximus, modern scholarship believes that only fourteen of them are actually his; of the nineteen attributed to John Chrysostom, only one is certifiably the work of Chrysostom. In addition, other material was added as the centuries passed—and included more dubious material: many of the so-called Augustinian sermons added later were not written by Augustine. (Migne's edition in PL 95 is representative of the expansion of the collection—it contains 298 texts, up fifty-four from the original scope.)

In one sense, Paul only transmits materials previously written by others and introduces no changes to their texts. In another, he exercises important editorial power by shaping the transmission of the tradition. Paul provided all of these texts with a new and uniform context—the Night

---

Bede's *Ecclesiastical History* for translation in his project to make key Latin texts available to those literate in English.

[72] Smetana notes that there are 151 texts identified with the title *sermo*, ninety-three identified as *omelia*, and that the distinction in the texts closest to Paul's original work seems to have accurately reflected the difference between the two. See Cyril Smetana, "Paul the Deacon's Patristic Anthology," in *The Old English Homily & Its Backgrounds*, ed. Paul E. Szarmach and Bernard F. Huppé (Albany: State University of New York Press, 1978), 75–97, at 78. See the discussion of the difference between the two terms in the discussion of the Night Office in chap. 2.

Office. Each homily or commentary pericope selected by Paul was newly contextualized by the sermon paired with it and the responsories that would interrupt it two or three times in the course of its reading. Furthermore, he was, for all practical purposes, drawing the bounds of the critical conversation by what he included and excluded. For many monasteries with limited libraries, Paul's homiliary served as the primary repository of patristic wisdom. While more texts were added as the centuries passed, Paul the Deacon's homiliary passed into the heart of the tradition and became the source for the readings in the Roman Breviary. Like Bede, Paul the Deacon's work was intended to remain within the critical conversation as well as establishing its foundation. It is directed specifically to the clergy and monastics participating in the Night Office.

Neither the works of Gregory nor Bede were in any way "official." They were widely read and eagerly sought out but had no official standing.[73] Paul the Deacon's work was different. The prefatory letter originally accompanying it documents Charlemagne's commission to Paul and authorizes the homiliary as the official text for the Frankish kingdom. Charlemagne demanded the establishment of a purified core tradition, and Paul's homiliary was an important aspect of that program of reform. The texts were to be strictly orthodox, coming from the recognized fathers, and compiled by one whose orthodoxy and commitment to the tradition was known to the authorizing powers.

Smaragdus (†840)

The next logical step in the homiliary tradition is the "homiliary" of Smaragdus. While often described as a homiliary in the literature, it is something less than a homiliary: it is an exegetical help for the construction of homilies. Smaragdus treats 109 occasions of the liturgical year, providing each with three kinds of material: a catena of patristic material on the appointed epistle, a patristic catena on the gospel, and a brief statement on the harmony between the two. Like Paul the Deacon, Smaragdus draws entirely from patristic material. He offers original material only in the third section that describes the relationship between the

---

[73] The letters of the English missionary bishop Boniface working in the territory that would become Germany and the Low Countries constantly request copies of Bede's works from his English patrons and relatives.

readings. He also cites his sources, enabling those using the work to know from whom the interpretations were coming. Unlike Paul, he makes selections from patristic works and places them in silent conversation with one another, placing them side by side without further comment. He moves through the biblical texts in a line by line fashion, deploying patristic material as he goes—usually providing between one and three patristic excerpts per line or phrase. Also unlike Paul, Smaragdus's incorporation of the epistle shows that he intended his work to assist with the biblical readings for Mass, since the epistle is particular to the Mass and does not appear within the Night Office.

Applying the term "homiliary" to this work is not completely accurate, because it utilizes the literary form of the catena rather than the homily. Nevertheless, its shape raises questions about how it was used and what it may teach us about preaching in early medieval contexts. How much did the written text determine the content of the act of proclamation? Did a preacher simply read off what was on the page before him, or does the text of Smaragdus represent starting points and options for the exposition of each verse, allowing the preacher with Smaragdus's text before him to pick and choose as he went, perhaps even translating or paraphrasing on the fly for non-Latinate congregations? Furthermore, what does this format suggest about how early medieval preachers understood the literary form of "homily" itself? The approach taken by Smaragdus dovetails with the notion of a homily as a set of verbal glosses that clarify the meaning of the biblical text rather than a methodical treatment of each line of the text or the exposition of a general theme extracted from the whole of the biblical passage.

Clearly, this work is intended to remain within the critical conversation. Like Paul's homiliary, it provides a foundation for the conversation by identifying the authors to be read and, moving beyond Paul, focuses patristic material on each line of the liturgically selected biblical texts.

Haymo of Auxerre (†855)

The homiliaries produced by the school of Auxerre, and especially Haymo of Auxerre, represent the next logical step beyond Smaragdus. In a telling footnote, Smetana refers to the work of Smaragdus as "brief excerpts from the Fathers," then to the homiliary of Haymo as "little more than judicious excerpts of the Fathers welded together into a continuous discourse."[74] Like Smaragdus, Haymo uses multiple selections from the fathers, but he chooses between various options, adds connecting material rather than presenting bare citations, and presents a new homily composed of patristic interpretations and insights cast into a new form. In short, Haymo's homilies may well be examples of what contemporary preachers did when they had a work like Smaragdus before them in the pulpit.

Ælfric of Eynsham (†c. 1010)

The only complete manuscript of both cycles of the *Catholic Homilies* is Cambridge Gg.3.28.[75] It contains more than just the homilies. It begins with a dedicatory letter to Sigeric, archbishop of Canterbury, in Latin and English, contains the first cycle of the *Catholic Homilies*, another letter prefacing the second cycle, and the second cycle itself, as well as some additional brief catechetical materials. Ælfric's prefaces to his cycles of *Catholic Homilies* are important for understanding what Ælfric wanted to achieve and how he saw himself as a participant within the critical conversation of his day and a mediator of it. Both cycles have, in fact, two prefaces (for a grand total of four); each cycle received a Latin preface and an English preface. Broadly speaking, the content of Ælfric's prefaces was fairly uniform: "Each preface generally includes Ælfric's self-identification, his explanation for the creation of the work (often relating it to a request from an ecclesiastical or secular superior), an account of the work's sources and style, and remarks about its transmission."[76]

Wilcox's studies of Ælfric's prefaces confirm that Ælfric utilized his prefaces to establish his authority by identifying his place within the conversation and its transmission and his reliability to mediate the tradition to those who only understand English. Wilcox states:

> Ælfric's self-identification in the prefaces is a reflection of his attitude towards authority and his concern with maintaining a rigorous standard of orthodoxy. The opening of Preface 1b [the Old English Preface to *CH I*] is characteristic in the way that Ælfric uses his identity

[74] Smetana, "Ælfric and the Early Medieval Homiliary," 181n6.
[75] Designated by Clemoes as "K." Godden and Pope both retain Clemoes's manuscript sigla.
[76] Jonathan Wilcox, *Ælfric's Prefaces*, Durham Medieval Texts 9 (Durham: University of Durham, 1995), 67.

to validate the following work. He begins by identifying himself in terms of his ecclesiastical credentials and position: he is a monk and mass-priest (1b.1) and his current position is validated with respect to both ecclesiastical and civil authority through reference to Bishop Ælfheah and Æthelmær the thane (1b.2-5). The ecclesiastically-reliable persona defined in this first sentence is the identity which is opposed to error in the second sentence. Here further theological validation is provided (the decision to translate was "I trust through God's gift" 1b.5-6) and the reason for translating is emphasized: "because I saw and heard much error in many English books, which unlearned men through their ignorance reckoned as great wisdom" (1b.7-9). Ælfric has economically created a persona which can be relied upon to provide orthodoxy in opposition to the "much error" usual "in many English books."

Ælfric sometimes establishes his authority in other ways. In Preface 1a [the Latin Preface to *CH I*] the epistolary opening formula equates "I, Ælfric" with "a student of . . . Æthelwold" (1a.1), a commonly recurring validation through association with the important Benedictine reformer. Further validation is provided in Preface 1a by the naming of a range of sources, patristic and Carolingian (1a.4 and 12-15). A final guarantee of authority is provided by the appeal to Archbishop Sigeric to correct "any blemishes of malign heresy or dark fallacy" (1a.36-40): the work which survives such correction must be reliably orthodox.[77]

Thus the English preface warns against heresies in other English books, suggesting—accurately[78]—that many theologically suspect writings exist among English materials and stand outside of the proper lines of tradition and transmission. As a monk, mass-priest, and client of both Bishop Ælfheah and Æthelmære, Ælfric is a reliable source of orthodox material in English. The Latin preface provides more detail and is intended for those familiar with the critical conversation. Only those who understand the language will understand the proofs that Ælfric offers there—he is the student of Æthelwold and cites the proper patristic sources.

---

[77] Wilcox, *Ælfric's Prefaces*, 68–69.

[78] The Blicking and Vercelli books, the only two major surviving collections of homilies before Ælfric, contain Old English translations of condemned works including the *Visio Pauli* and the Apocalypse of Thomas, about which more will be said in chap. 4.

Citing the patristic sources explicitly places Ælfric within the critical conversation. He writes to Sigeric that he has translated materials from "Gregory, Augustine, Jerome, Smaragdus and also Haymo." Thus Ælfric identifies both the major patristic sources he used and the early medieval homiliaries in which he found them. Hill has argued convincingly that the absence of Paul the Deacon from this list is due to Paul's homiliary circulating without the prefatory documents that identify its editor, not an uncommon state of affairs among English manuscripts of Paul's work.

This list matches what Ælfric puts forth in the homilies themselves. Typically right after the translation of the scriptural text, he identifies a patristic author who has guided his interpretation. Within the *Catholic Homilies*, Augustine, Gregory, Bede, and Haymo are most often identified as his sources.

Ælfric also invokes patristic authors whenever he needs to bolster a decision made in favor of orthodoxy. For instance, in his second homily for the Assumption of the BVM, he specifically warns against untoward speculation with a patristic appeal:

> If we tell more concerning this feast-day than we read in holy books which were set down by God's direction then we will be like those *dwolmen* [foolish men, heretics] who write many false narratives according to their own direction or through dreams; but the faithful teachers, Augustine, Jerome, Gregory, and whatever others, cast them down through their wisdom. There are, nevertheless, *dwollic* [foolish, erroneous, heretical] books both in Latin and in English, and ignorant people read them. . . . Let everyone cast away the *dwollic* falsehoods which lead the incautious to destruction, and may everyone read or listen to the holy teachers who will guide us to the kingdom of heaven, if we are prepared to hear it.[79]

The three fathers from the preface return here as well as the central arbiters of orthodox teaching.

Ælfric's prefaces speak of his work as translations from Latin sources. These statements are intended as further guarantees that the material is

---

[79] ÆCH 2.29, lines 119–33. Translation from Wilcox, *Ælfric's Prefaces*, 28.

reliable. However, Ælfric's use of the term "translate" (*interpretatio/awen-dan*) turns out to be different from its normal contemporary meaning:

> The modern term "translation," however, is inadequate for conveying the range of medieval practice, since it suggests rendering content as closely as possible from one language to another. Ælfric's practice is often closer to the modern sense of "adaptation" or "interpretation" entailing the transmission of Latin learning into English. . . . "I know it is possible to translate words in many ways," Ælfric observes at Preface 3a.10. He explicitly points out that his practice is not confined to the narrowest sense of transferal from one language to the other; rather he repeatedly describes his translations as not word for word but sense for sense (Prefaces 1a.9-10, 29-30, 5a.21-22, 8e.5-8). Such a formulation has a long tradition: he is probably drawing on Jerome's statement about biblical translation, which was, in turn, derived from classical tradition.
>
> Other aspects of Ælfric's description of his translation technique make clear that the process is far from literal. He describes his translations as both abbreviating and rearranging his sources (Prefaces 1a.28-33, 5a.21-26), and he attaches comments on the plainness of his style and the orthodoxy of his content to his process of translation (Prefaces 2a.8-12, 3a.10-11, 5a.21-26, 1a.33-35, 36-38, 2a.22-24). He makes it clear that a literal transfer from one language to another would be counter-productive: "He who translates (*awent*) or he who teaches from Latin into English must always arrange it so that English may have its own way, otherwise it is very misleading to read for those who do not know the way of Latin." (Preface 4.96-99)[80]

Thus his own statements about his work demonstrate a consciousness of the importance of the translating process and a concern to present material in such a way that the orthodox meaning is clear. In practice, this includes not only translation but also a significant amount of editorial work.

Thanks to Godden's magisterial commentary that meticulously identifies the patristic material that Ælfric wove together into his homilies, we now have a much better idea of Ælfric's range as an interpreter, editor, and author. While he derives much of his authority from his self-presentation as a patristic translator, Godden reveals that the degree to which Ælfric is

---

[80] Wilcox, *Ælfric's Prefaces*, 63–64.

a faithful interpreter of his patristic sources depends entirely on the homily under consideration. Ælfric most often departs from the patristic text when he moves to engage the popular conversation. He does this both to explain something either in the text or source that would not be clear to an Anglo-Saxon audience and to engage mistaken readings or opinions in his environment. Even when he departs from his sources, he remains within a patristic and orthodox framework. That is, he tends to be just as orthodox when he goes off-book as when he remains close to his sources.

Thus Ælfric participates fully within the critical conversation of the early medieval world in that he works with the Latin texts of the orthodox fathers of the Western church and the early medieval editors who collected and arranged their exegetical insights in accordance with the liturgical year. However, his intention was to serve as a mediator between the monastic microculture and the larger English-speaking macroculture. Distressed at the heresies found in the materials offered to those outside of the monastic microcultural conversation, Ælfric's lifework—of which the *Catholic Homilies* represent a central pillar—is to transmit the Christian orthodox of the Latin books into a language and style accessible to all.

SUMMARY

Conventional wisdom suggests that early medieval exegesis is derivative at best and plagiaristic at worst. I suggest that this criticism is overly harsh for two reasons: first, it judges early medieval exegesis on a set of criteria alien to the culture. If the purpose of the early medieval conversation had been the generation of new insights on the biblical text, then it would indeed be guilty as charged. But the conversation itself existed for a different purpose. It sought not to create new data but to preserve insights from being lost through neglect, heresy, losing touch with Christian experience, or destruction—a danger made all the more real by the technological limits of manuscript production. No doubt early medieval monastics, like some current Christian microcultures, would accuse the modern academic microculture of an insatiable lust for exegetical novelties and a disconnect between exegetical possibilities and their application to the Christian moral and spiritual life.

Second, the judgment seems blind to the fundamental character of critical conversations. That is, a modern critical commentary like that of

Luz or Davies and Allison could stray close to the line of being called "derivative" quite easily. We recognize, however, that the charge of being derivative is directly related to the degree to which a work is rooted in the critical conversation and indebted to its predecessors; "derivative" is the shadow side of being "informed" and "engaged" in the ongoing conversation.

In summary, the modern American academic microculture of biblical studies and the early medieval English monastic microculture have more in common than might at first be immediately obvious. They are both communities that take engagement with the New Testament text seriously; both use mimesis as central formative practices; and both participate in critical conversations. The purposes and goals of the two cultures are, however, quite different. Indeed, the difference between the goals has required modern distinction from and, ultimately, modern misunderstandings of the medieval monastic project. My study now moves from similarities and takes up the practice that most clearly defines the early medieval monastic project and sets it apart in its intention and rigor from the modern academic project and from most other communities that shape themselves around the New Testament text: the early medieval monastic liturgy.

Chapter 2

How Monastic Praying Shaped Reading

INTRODUCTION

The primary difference between modern academic culture and early medieval monastic culture is liturgy. If we understand liturgy in its broadest sense as a cycle of repeatable public rituals, then we can see that modern academic culture is not without its liturgical moments. The convocations and graduations that mark the turning points of the academic year have their origins in the Christian liturgies of the first universities and cathedral schools. In addition, there is no denying a ritual quality to certain rites of passage connected with oral defenses of exams, proposals, and dissertations. Academic conferences and attendant meetings have their own rites as well, but these do not have the pervasive and determinative character that marked the place of the liturgy in early medieval monastic life.

Jean Leclercq leaves a discussion of the liturgy to the final chapter of his study of monastic culture. It does not come last as an afterthought but as the climax to which the rest of monastic culture builds. The last paragraph of the last full chapter of Leclercq's work pulls together the importance and place of the liturgy in monastic culture:

> The liturgy is at once the mirror of a culture and its culmination. Just as the office of Corpus Christi, in the composition of which St. Thomas [Aquinas] surely participated, crowns his doctrinal work, so the

hymns, sequences, and innumerable poems written by the monks
are the culmination of their theology. The liturgy had been the motive
for the renewal of monastic culture in the Carolingian period, and
was also its fruit. During the following centuries, it is in the atmo-
sphere of the liturgy and amid the poems composed for it, *in hymnis
et canticis*, that the synthesis of all the *artes* was effected, of the literary
techniques, religious reflection, and all sources of information
whether biblical, patristic, or classical. In the liturgy, all these resources fully attained their final potentiality; they were restored to
God in a homage which recognized that they had come from Him.
Thanksgiving, eucharist, theology, *confessio fidei*—all these expressions, in monastic tradition, expressed only slightly differing aspects
of a single reality. In the liturgy, grammar was elevated to the rank
of an eschatological fact. It participated in the eternal praise that the
monks, in unison with the angels, began offering to God in the abbey
choir, and which will be perpetuated in heaven. In the liturgy, love
of learning and desire for God find perfect reconciliation.[1]

The liturgy is the great engine of monastic culture that gives it its indelible
character and is its greatest product. It is pervasive and deeply formative.

As a result, when Leclercq speaks of the speculative character of monastic theology, he identifies it as: "the outgrowth of the practice of monastic life, the living of the spiritual life which is the meditation on Holy
Scripture. It is a biblical experience inseparable from liturgical experience."[2]
Indeed, the liturgy provided both the normative locus for the encounter
with Scripture and also its interpretation: "it was the liturgy itself which
formed the usual and ordinary commentary on Holy Scripture and the
Fathers."[3] Any attempt to separate what is "biblical" or "exegetical" in the
monastic experience away from what is "liturgical" is a project doomed
at the outset. Scripture—whether in blocks or sentences or phrases—
formed the heart and texts of the monastic liturgy.

In discussing the liturgy and the early medieval experience of it, I shall
begin with an overview of the liturgies themselves. From there, I will return

---

[1] Jean Leclercq, *The Love of Learning and the Desire for God: A Study of Monastic
Culture*, trans. Catharine Misrahi (New York: Fordham University Press, 1982),
250–51.

[2] Ibid., 213.

[3] Ibid., 237.

to the monastic formation and will demonstrate how monastic education ties together the strands from the previous chapter—mimesis, a literary culture, and the critical conversation—into formation for the liturgy focused on the goal of a holy life. Then I will look at how biblical interpretation occurs with the liturgy and demonstrate this by looking at the season of Christmas as celebrated within Benedictine Revival liturgies.

THE THREE KINDS OF LITURGICAL SERVICES

In order to understand the mechanics of liturgical formation, it is necessary to sketch the outline of the monastic services, the daily *ordo*. I begin with an overview of the three fundamental kinds of liturgical services, where the greatest interpretive possibilities lay, then will examine how these liturgies interrelated within the specific context of England's Benedictine Revival.

Within the monastic *ordo*, there are three basic kinds of services that serve slightly different functions. The primary purpose of all liturgy, in the medieval mind, is the praise of God. In connection to this primary purpose are three secondary purposes specific to certain services: the Daily Office or *synaxes* had a catechetical role, the Masses had a sacramental role, and the Chapter had an administrative role.

Two primary sources lay out the bare bones of the services: the Rule of Benedict and the *Ordines Romani*. While Benedict's Rule gives a snapshot of early sixth-century Italian customs that gained traction and use in Europe as the centuries wore on, the *Ordines Romani* is the name given to a broad collection of materials that traveled in general groupings compiled anonymously from the seventh through the eleventh centuries that told how the various services were to be performed.[4] Beyond these base texts, documents called "customaries" explained them, elaborated on them, and gave practical instructions on local practice. Thankfully, two customaries survive from Anglo-Saxon England, enabling us to know

---

[4] The modern edition of the fifty *ordines* is Michel Andrieu, ed., *Les Ordines romani du haut moyen âge*, 5 vols., *Spicilegium Sacrum Lovaniense* 11, 23, 24, 28, 29 (Louvain, 1931–1961). The single best brief treatment of the *ordines*—and a helpful summary of the contents of each—is Cyrille Vogel, *Medieval Liturgy: An Introduction to the Sources*, trans. and rev. William Storey and Niels Rasmussen (Portland, OR: Pastoral, 1986), 135–224.

quite a lot about how these services were actually performed at the time of the Benedictine Revival. The first is the *Regularis Concordia* (hereafter *RC*), written by Bishop Æthelwold, Ælfric's teacher; the second is Ælfric's own customary, the *Letter to the Monks of Eynsham* (hereafter *LME*). [5] These will be used in combination with the other documents to sketch a sense of the main structure of the liturgies that shaped monastic days.

The Daily Office

The Daily Office is a set of fixed services of prayer whose central characteristic is the weekly recitation of the Psalter. From the earliest days in the Egyptian deserts, the psalms were considered the truest guides of life, the most fertile source for reflection, and the most certain path to holiness. The *Apothegmata Patrum* records Epiphanius as saying: "The true monk should have prayer and psalmody continually in his heart."[6] Similarly, the first two chapters of Smaragdus of Saint-Mihiel's early medieval collection of monastic wisdom, the *Diadema Monachorum*, are on prayer and the discipline of the psalms, respectively.[7]

The monastic practice of the Daily Office as first described by Cassian has been understood as the embodiment of Psalm 118:164 (Vulgate): "Seven times a day I praise you."[8] By the time of Benedict, a rather literalistic reading required the introduction of another service; since one of the monastic services began in the middle of the night, it could not be counted among the seven "day" services, thus Benedict legislates seven day offices and a night office (with an obligatory reference to VgPs 118:62: "At midnight I arose to give you praise"). Confusions of counting and terminology be-

---

[5] The *Regularis Concordia* is found in Thomas Symons, *Regularis Concordia Anglicae Nationis Monachorum Sanctimonialiumque: The Monastic Agreement of the Monks and Nuns of the English Nation* (London: Nelson, 1953). Ælfric's letter is edited and translated in Christopher A. Jones, *Ælfric's Letter to the Monks at Eynsham* (Cambridge: Cambridge University Press, 1998).

[6] *The Sayings of the Desert Fathers: The Alphabetical Collection*, trans. Benedicta Ward, Cistercian Studies 59, rev. ed. (Kalamazoo, MI: Cistercian Publications, 1984), 57.

[7] PL 102: Col. 0594C-0596A.

[8] English Scripture translations are taken from the Douay-Rheims version of the Bible, a translation of the Vulgate. See citations of this passage in John Cassian, *The Institutes* 3.4.3, trans. Boniface Ramsey, Ancient Christian Writers 58 (New York: Newman Press, 2000), 63; and RB 16.1-3.

tween the older scheme recorded by Cassian and the newer scheme legislated by Benedict has plagued monastic customaries ever since.

Ælfric's overview on clerical duties contained in his first Latin Letter to Archbishop Wulfstan speaks of seven offices:

> I will speak plainly to you now about the clergy. Concerning them, the holy fathers established that they should sing the seven synaxes, thus every day you ought to sing every [canonical] hour each day. Of these, the first synaxsis is *nocturnes*, the second is the "Prime" [first] hour of the day, the third is the same hour itself which we call "Terce," the fourth is truly the Sext [sixth] hour, the fifth is the None [ninth] hour, the sixth however is the hour of Vespers, the seventh *synaxis* we call Compline.[9]

Here Ælfric—quoting directly from *Excerpts of Pseudo-Ecgbert* 28.2—follows a convention that can still be found today. The term "Night Office" can be ambiguous; since there is only a formal break between the Night Office and Lauds, the term can be extended to both. As the practice of aggregation (saying several liturgical hours at one sitting) expanded among secular clergy, Prime could also be included within the "Night Office." To avoid ambiguity, within this work the term "Night Office" refers only to the first and longest liturgical office of the night.

As there is no universally accepted terminology used by the medieval sources, modern scholars prefer to enumerate the seven-plus-one services of the Daily Office as the Night Office, Lauds, Prime, Terce, Sext, None, Vespers, and Compline. Within these eight services, three groups emerge based on structure: the Night Office, the Greater Offices (Lauds and Vespers), and the Lesser Offices (Prime, Terce, Sext, None, and Compline).

The Night Office

The Night Office is by far the longest and most complicated of the services or "hours" of the Daily Office. It is also where long readings happen. Within this service, both Scripture and patristic sermons are read. Charting the Night Office is complicated because it has several forms based on the time of year, whether the day is festal or ferial, and local traditions. Since

[9] Bernhard Fehr, *Die Hirtenbriefe. In altenglischer und lateinischer Fassung*, Reprint ed. (Darmstadt: Wissenschaftliche Buchgesellschaft, 1966 [1914]), 43.

all of the homilies we shall be examining are appointed for feast days, I shall, for the sake of convenience, display a festal monastic scheme only:

	6 Psalms with Antiphons
Opening Versicles[10]	Versicle and Response
Psalm 3	Lord's Prayer
Antiphon and Psalm 94	Absolution
Seasonal Hymn	Blessing
1st Nocturn: Scripture	Lesson, part 1
2nd Nocturn: Sermon	Respond 1
3rd Nocturn: Homily	Blessing
Te Deum	Lesson, part 2
Gospel of the Day	Respond 2
Te decet laus	Blessing
Kyrie	Lesson, part 3
Lord's Prayer	Respond 3
Preces	Blessing
Collect of the Day	Lesson, part 4
	Respond 4

Table 1: Monastic Festal Night Office

The content of the lessons vary according to the nocturn. The first is always from Scripture. The second and third nocturns only appear on a day when a liturgical occasion of import—either a feast day or a Sunday—is being celebrated. The lesson for the second nocturn is a *sermo* that relates information about the occasion itself. It could be a life or passion if a saint is being commemorated or simply a sermon about the season in the case of Sundays. The lesson for the third nocturn is an *omelia*, a homily or a section of a commentary that treats the gospel ap-

---

[10] Charts adapted from John Harper, *The Forms and Orders of Western Liturgy from the Tenth to the Eighteenth Century: A Historical Introduction and Guide for Students and Musicians* (Oxford: Clarendon, 1991), 93–95.

pointed for the day. By the time of Ælfric, these readings were generally taken from a homiliary like that of Paul the Deacon.

The Greater Offices

Occurring around the times of sunrise and sunset, Lauds and Vespers ground the hinges of the day and share the same basic structure:

Opening Versicles
Psalms with Antiphons
Sentence from Scripture
Respond
Seasonal Hymn
Versicle and Response
Gospel Canticle with Antiphon
Collect of the Day
Concluding Blessing

Table 2: Monastic Festal Lauds and Vespers

Four psalms are sung at Vespers and, liturgically speaking, six are sung at Lauds, but this includes an uncounted Old Testament canticle inserted after the fifth psalm, and what is reckoned as the "sixth psalm" is actually three psalms taken together (Pss. 148–150).[11] The gospel canticle was invariably the *Benedictus* (Luke 1:68-79) at Lauds and the *Magnificat* (Luke 1:46-55) at Vespers.[12]

The Lesser Offices

Among the Lesser Offices, the three midday hours (Terce, Sext, and None) have an identical structure; the early and late offices of Prime and Compline are similar both to each other and to the middle hours but display differences based on their function and contain seasonal variations. As none of these differences impact the liturgy's interpretation of

---

[11] These three begin in Latin with *laudate* and thereby give the Office its name.
[12] The third great Lukan canticle, the *Nunc Dimittis* (Luke 2:29-32), does not appear in the Monastic Office but is used at Compline within the Secular Office.

Scripture, I display here the pattern of the middle offices as an indication of the contents of these offices:

Opening Versicles
Invariable Hymn
Psalms with Antiphons
Sentence from Scripture
Versicle and Response
Collect of the Day
Concluding Blessing

Table 3: Monastic Little Offices

The offices of Prime and Compline include rites of confession and absolution as well that promote their functions as offices that prepare the community for the day's work or for the night's rest.

The Mass

While Benedict's Rule makes passing reference to Mass as a once-weekly affair—and speaks of admitting priests to the monastery only with reluctance—by the time of the Benedictine Revival ordained monks were quite common and Masses were celebrated twice daily. The first Mass, which occurred on Sundays and feast days after Prime, was the matitudinal Mass or the "Morrow Mass," which was used for votive masses that celebrated various events or salvific persons, or addressed a need facing the community or nation.[13] The second Mass that occurred after Terce[14] was the Mass of the Day where the Propers appointed for the day's liturgical observance were used.

---

[13] Ælfric directs that on Sundays the Morrow Mass is of the Holy Trinity unless another feast is in occurrence with the Mass of the Day in *LME* 10 (see Christopher A. Jones, *Ælfric's Letter to the Monks at Eynsham* [Cambridge: Cambridge University Press, 1998], 114–15). This is in agreement with the *Regularis Concordia* (see *RC* 1.23). The Missal of Robert of Jumièges—as a typical early medieval missal—includes some fifty-three votive Masses for a host of occasions and honorees, such as two for the Blessed Virgin Mary, one in time of war, one against the pagans, one against carnal temptations, one for the royal family, and so on.

[14] On ferial days the Mass of the Day followed the Litany after Sext (*RC* 1.25).

A typical sung Mass outside of a penitential season would have the following elements (elements in small capitals are sung by the choir):

Ordinary (Unchanging)	**Proper** (Variable based on the day & season)
	Introit[15]
Kyrie Eleison[16]	
Gloria in Excelsis	
	Collect(s)
	Epistle/Reading[17]
	Gradual
	Alleluia/Tract
	Sequence
	Gospel
Creed	
	Offertory
	Secret
Beginning of Canon of the Mass	

[15] Note that these names are not always what is found in contemporary sources. For instance, when looking at the Leofric Missal—the only surviving Anglo-Saxon Sacramentary to include the incipits of the choir texts—the following abbreviations are used to identify the corresponding liturgical elements: Introit—A. (antiphon for the following verse) and PS. (as introit texts were typically psalm verses); Gradual/Alleluia—R. (first half of the gradual), V. (second half of the gradual), AL. (the alleluia verse); Offertory—OF.; Communio—COM.; Reading—EP. (as it was frequently taken from an epistle); Gospel—EV.

[16] Evidence from surviving manuscripts indicates that tropes and proses—proper additions into the sung ordinaries (i.e., the Kyrie, Gloria, Sanctus, and Agnus Dei) and further additions to the sung Propers—were introduced into England with the Benedictine Revival. These were, however, highly variable and probably used at cathedral and larger monastic establishments.

[17] Epistle is the usual term for this biblical reading but is technically incorrect; readings on fasting and penitential days came from the Old Testament.

Ordinary *(cont.)*	Proper *(cont.)*
	Proper Preface
SANCTUS WITH BENEDICTUS	
Conclusion of the Canon of the Mass	
Lord's Prayer	
Peace	
AGNUS DEI	
	COMMUNIO
	Benediction[18]
	Postcommunion Prayer
Dismissal	

Table 4: Static and Variable Elements of the Mass

Note that a "Sermon" does not appear in this list of elements. Evidence concerning the place of sermons with Masses is complicated. On the one hand, it seems certain based on contemporary legislation and internal evidence within the *Catholic Homilies* that sermons were delivered within the Mass of the Day. Both the *Excerpts of Pseudo-Ecgbert* and the *Rule of Chrodegang* mandate preaching by the clergy to the people: the first requires it weekly, the second fortnightly—but expresses a clear preference for preaching on all Sundays and feast days.[19] Also, Ælfric's sermons often incorporate material from the epistle, suggesting that he had specifically reworked the sermons for that series for the Mass.[20] On the other hand, none of the liturgical documents from the period mention a sermon in

---

[18] The benediction was the prerogative of the bishop. Generally there were separate books for bishops called benedictionals where these prayers were located, but occasionally they were integrated into the text of sacramentaries as in the Leofric Missal. Furthermore, the early medieval Benediction was offered at a different place in the service from modern rites; the bishop gave this blessing when the sacrament would have been distributed.

[19] Chrodegang, *Rule of Chrodegang*, chap. 44 (PL 89:1079C-D).

[20] A greater discussion of this tendency appears below in chap. 3.

the Mass; none of the *ordines* specify when it would have fallen. Certainly a sermon would not have appeared within the Morrow Mass; the evidence in support of preaching implies that it would have occurred in Masses of the Day on Sundays and major feast days, most likely after the gospel.

The Chapter

Chapter was the daily monastic business meeting. Discussions of community business, admission of faults, and preparations for upcoming events—liturgical and otherwise—were all part of this meeting. Symptomatic of the pervasive quality of liturgy in the monasteries, this business meeting also had a fundamentally liturgical structure. The *RC* contains a thorough description of how Chapter was to occur within Benedictine Revival monastic houses:[21]

Salute of the Cross
Martyrology
Versicles and Response
Collect
Reading and Explanation of the Gospel of the Day[22]
Confession of Faults
5 Psalms for the Departed Brethren

Table 5: The Monastic Chapter

The martyrology was the reading of the life or passion of the saint or saints who would be celebrated on the following liturgical day. The *RC* does not go into detail concerning the required "exposition of the Gospel," but given the monastic preference for maintaining traditional expositions, it would seem likely that this would be another opportunity for the use of a prepared homily rather than a truly extemporaneous discussion from the abbot. Indeed, Symons notes that other monastic customaries from the period explicitly direct the reading of an "omelia" at this point.[23]

---

[21] *RC* 1.21 (Symons, *RC*, 17).
[22] On ferial days a section of RB was read.
[23] Symons, *RC*, 17 note b.

THE MONASTIC DAY CYCLE

By the time of the Benedictine Revival, these liturgies had been supplemented with additional offices that both preceded and followed the regular hours and occasions to the degree that monks spent over half of their waking hours in liturgies of one sort or another. A monastic feast day was longer than other days in the calendar. Rather than being reckoned from midnight to midnight, a feast began at Vespers on the evening before the feast and ran through Compline on the feast itself. In later medieval parlance, these were referred to as "doubles" in part because the day had two Vespers Offices that were therefore distinguished as the First and Second Vespers. Thus, monastic Sundays and feast days in the summer according to the *RC* would look something like this:

6:00 PM	**First Vespers** Psalms, etc., for the royal house Anthems of Cross, BVM, patron saints Vespers & Matins of All Saints Vespers, Vigils, Lauds for the Dead
7:30 PM	Change into night shoes *Collatio* (drink and reading from *Conferences* or *Vita Patrum*)
8:00 PM	**Compline** *Trina Oratio* (Set of psalms and collects for the royal house)
8:15 PM	Retire
3:30 AM	**Night Office** **Lauds** Miserere Psalms, etc., for the royal house Anthems of Cross, BVM, patron saints Matins of All Saints Change shoes/wash
5:00 AM	*Trina Oratio* Reading
6:00 AM	**Prime** Psalms and Prayers **Morrow Mass** **Chapter** Five psalms for the dead

7:30 AM	Work
8:00 AM	**Terce** **Mass of the Day**
9:30 AM	Reading
11:30 AM	**Sext** Psalms, etc., for royal house
12:00 PM	Dinner
1:00 PM	Siesta
2:30 PM	**None** Psalms, etc., for royal house Drink
3:00 PM	Work
5:30 PM	Supper
6:00 PM	**Second Vespers** Psalms, etc., for the royal house Anthems of Cross, BVM, patron saints Vespers & Matins of All Saints Vespers, Vigils, Lauds for the Dead
7:30 PM	Change into night shoes *Collatio* (drink and reading from *Conferences* or *Vita Patrum*)
8:00 PM	**Compline** *Trina Oratio* (Set of psalms and collects for the royal house)
8:15 PM	Retire

Table 6: The Monastic Day according to the *Regularis Concordia*[24]

Just as the three types of liturgical services interwove between one another, so the scriptural materials and cycles that defined each one were shared to form a whole that created the theological and liturgical shape of life within the monastic enclosure.

[24] Adapted from the chart in David Knowles, *The Monastic Order in England* (Oxford: Clarendon, 1968), 714–15.

MONASTIC EDUCATION AS FORMATION FOR LITURGY

The Psalms

It is impossible to overstate the intimate connection between early medieval monastic education and the early medieval monastic liturgy. Learning was about acquiring the skills to participate within the liturgy, to comprehend the depths of the liturgy, to incorporate it into monastic practice, and—in turn—to enrich it.

At the heart of this educational program was mastery of the psalms.

You have to imagine what it would be like entering a monastery in tenth-century England. A child, somewhere between the ages of seven and eleven would be taken from their family, mother tongue, and the world of fields and woods and home handcrafts and would be placed within an utterly alien environment. The central experience would be that of trooping into the oratory many times a day to sing unknown songs in an unknown tongue. Liturgist Mary Berry has reckoned that, in summer time, the monks would be awake for nineteen hours of the day; about eleven of these would be spent in song!

At first, no doubt, new boys and girls would be overwhelmed by the sheer volume of unfamiliar material. They would mumble along, trying to follow the pitch and to throw in a word or two when they could. At least they would have the benefit of singing alongside a number of other people—strong voices from whom they could take their lead. As daunting as this sounds, children are adaptable, and the presence of music itself would be a help

Furthermore, once the initial tsunami of unfamiliar experiences had passed, the children would discern (perhaps with the help of their peers or teachers) that certain songs show up far more frequently than others. In a Benedictine Reform monastery, the seven penitential psalms were sung several times every day as part of the prayers for the king, queen, and benefactors (the *trina oratio*). Indeed, it would be a slow monk who didn't quickly learn Psalm 51, chief of the penitential psalms; during Lent, it would have been sung at least eight times a day. Also, the Night Office invariably began with a recitation of the fifteen gradual psalms (Pss 120–134). Charting out the liturgical provisions of the *RC*, there were thirty-five psalms that would be sung every single day. Surely the young novices would have learned these quickly, at least to the point where they could confidently sing them in the midst of a group who knew them well. Naturally, they would have the additional impetus of knowing that those who made faults in the singing of the songs were subject to punishment during daily Chapter.

Thus the constant liturgical cycle was a means for passive education. The children would sing along as they were able and absorb a massive amount of Latin. It would, however, only be meaningless sounds to them without further help. The Old English edition of Ælfric's *Colloquy* opens with this exchange between teacher and student:

> Teacher: What is your work?
> Student: I am presently a monk and I sing seven times each day with my brothers, but meanwhile, between them, I want to learn how to speak in the Latin tongue.[25]

Both monastic rules and surviving educational books help give us a sense of how this mass of memorized sounds was converted into useful language. First, memorization of the psalms outside of the choir was an essential activity. Despite the passive learning of the choir, the monks worked with teachers, other students, and by themselves to memorize the psalms. The Rule specifically identifies the time after the Night Office in winter and after None throughout the year as a period to learn the psalms and readings. (A bit later in the text, Ælfric's *Colloquy* clarifies that the learning experience described in the text is taking place after None.)

Benedict's source, the Rule of the Master, describes the process in detail and demonstrates that the active memorization of the psalms occurs in parallel with the learning of literacy. The passively memorized sounds are transformed into written words as the process of active memorization unfolds:

> During these three hours [between Prime and Terce] the boys, in their deanery [groups of ten], are to learn letters on their tablets from someone who is literate. Moreover, we exhort illiterate adults up to the age of fifty to learn letters. Again, we wish it kept in mind

[25] G. N. Garmonsway, *Ælfric's Colloquy*, Methuen's Old English Library (London: Methuen, 1938).

that during these same periods the psalms are to be studied by those who do not know them, directed by the deans in their respective deanery. So during these three hours, they are to read [aloud] and listen to one another, and take turns teaching letters and psalms to those who do not know them. (RM 50.12-15)[26]

And throughout [the] summer season, whether the meal is at the sixth hour or at the ninth, for whatever time remains between None until time for Vespers to begin, the various deaneries having been separated from one another in different places, some as directed by their deans are to read, others listen, others learn and teach letters, others study psalms which they have transcribed. When they have mastered and memorized them perfectly, let their deans take them to the abbot to recite by heart the psalm or canticle or lesson of any kind. And as soon as he has recited it in its entirety, let him ask prayers for himself. Then when those present have prayed for him, the abbot concludes and the one who has done the reciting kisses the abbot's knees. Either the abbot or the deans immediately order something new to be transcribed [for memorization], and after anything has been transcribed, before he studies it, let him again ask those present to pray for him; and in this way the learning of it is to be undertaken. (RM 50.62-69)

There is one other factor we have to account for. The Rule of the Master was written in the early sixth century somewhere in the region of Rome or Campania. The Latin of the psalms would still be largely comprehensible to these monastics. To the tenth-century English novices, it would have been a completely foreign tongue.

This initial stage of education—the passive acquisition of the psalms and their active memorization—provided a foundation that the monks and nuns would use the rest of their lives both in and outside of the liturgy. This childhood memorization would be reinforced daily as the psalms were sung in the Daily Office. Also, psalm verses and portions were sprinkled throughout Office and Mass in the form of prayers, responsories, and minor Propers. Indeed, the vast majority of the minor Propers are pieced together from the psalms. Furthermore, the monks were to continue running through these memorized psalms outside the oratory as well. The

---

[26] All citations from the Rule of the Master come from *The Rule of the Master*, trans. Luke Eberle (Kalamazoo, MI: Cistercian Publications, 1977).

RC, in harmony with longstanding monastic tradition, recommends that the psalms be silently recited and meditated on during the periods when the monks were at work in the fields or in the workshops.

This initial stage of education would be complete once the entire psalter and canticles were committed to memory. Exactly how long that would take depended entirely on the student, but contemporary sources do give us a sense of the range. In speaking of an early medieval saint, Gregory of Tours expresses his wonder that the saint was able to memorize the entire psalter in only six months instead of two or three years. It is hard to say if two to three years was normal or if Gregory was exaggerating slightly for the sake of promoting the saint. Either way, this does give us something to go on—exceptional students might be able to get through this process in six months to a year, while more ordinary students could take as long as three years.

Elementary Education

As the words of the psalter, the canticles, and the hymns were embedding themselves in the young monastics' memories, the drilling would begin on the analysis and effective use of Latin as a living language. Three kinds of texts would work in conjunction with one another—grammars, glossaries, and colloquies. As part of his commitment to education, Ælfric wrote a set of the three with an emphasis on moving monastics who had grown up speaking Old English into literacy and fluency in Latin as quickly as possible.

Basic grammar was taught through the study of Donatus, the pagan grammarian who instructed the young St. Jerome. While Donatus might be studied directly, many of the authors of the English church produced grammars of their own, mostly working off Donatus. We have grammars written by Tatwine composed around 700, Alcuin, the missionary Boniface writing around 716, and other anonymous English authors. Ælfric's English-language grammar for learning Latin was based on Donatus and an excerpted edition of Priscian that covers topics like the cases and endings of Latin nouns and verbs and the various parts of speech. As with other Christian authors, he frequently provides examples of Latin usage directly from the psalms and liturgy. For instance, his discussion of adverbs is reinforced by the phrase "But thou, O Lord, have mercy on me and raise me up," which is simultaneously a quotation from the psalms (VgPs 40:11) and the response to the readings in the Night Office.

Glossaries were much like modern dictionaries; there would be a Latin headword—the word to be understood—accompanied by its gloss. Depending on the kind of glossary, the explanatory gloss might be in Old English or might explain the Latin headword using simpler Latin terms. There were two main kinds of glossary that circulated in the early medieval period—an alphabetic type and an encyclopedic type. The alphabetic was structured in dictionary fashion with the headwords arranged in alphabetical order. The encyclopedic grouped words into particular useful categories. Ælfric's own glossary was of this type and was frequently copied and bound with his grammar:

> Its first grouping could be titled "elements of the universe": it begins with Deus omnipotens: þæt is god ælmihtig, followed by heaven, angels, the earth and the sea, human beings, and their division into sexes. From there it moves to parts of the body, occupations and classes of people, common adjectives including physical and mental characteristics, birds, fish, animals, plants, trees, dwellings, food and drink, and so on. The structure is encyclopaedic, and the connection with original glossing contexts is distant and hard to recover.[27]

Other glossaries can be tied more tightly to their source texts. That is, we can get a sense of what texts were being read by the students by the type and order of difficult words that appear within them.

Colloquies were set dialogues between one or more speakers. The monastics would memorize the texts, then recite them—each student taking a different part—before the master in class. Most foreign language classes today still use this dialogic method for gaining basic conversational fluency; once the dialogue has been memorized, the stock phrases used for greetings and other basic social functions could be adapted as needed to begin real conversation in the new language. Ælfric's *Colloquy* is a fascinating walk through early medieval society. He sets his as a conversation between a master and an array of pupils, all of whom have different jobs across the early medieval landscape. One is a monk, but others are hunters, fisherman, peasants, and other figures who populated everyday life outside of the monastery. By describing the world and so-

---

[27] Robert Stanton, *The Culture of Translation in Anglo-Saxon England* (Woodbridge, Suffolk: D. S. Brewer, 2002), 16.

ciety about them, the young monks were gaining a facility in describing events and activities for which the psalms offered no vocabulary. While the psalms speak wonderfully about the soul's various emotions toward God or about the travails of the Israelites, the vocabulary for negotiating an average medieval day in the monastery was lacking and required this additional supplement.

Memorization of the psalter, work on grammar, and the acquisition of skill in Latin leads naturally into the study of the psalter's meaning. As the students gained literacy, they would not only grasp the meaning of the Latin words but also begin to pick up insights about what the text meant to them and for them. The central text that brought together grammar, the fundamentals of rhetoric, an introduction to the interpretation of Scripture as a whole, and the meaning of the psalms in particular was the commentary of Cassiodorus.

Cassiodorus was a fifth-century monastic teacher who achieved a synthesis of classical and Christian edification at his southern Italian monastery, the Vivarium. This synthesis is reflected in his commentary, the *Explanation of the Psalms*.[28] On the one hand, it draws from traditional Christian readings of the psalms, predominately from St. Augustine's sermons. On the other, he takes care to point out the figures of speech and thought as he sees them, demonstrating that—as he saw it—David prefigured the schoolmasters' flowers of rhetoric and that sound rhetorical knowledge was an advantage in mining the deeper meanings of Scripture. While Augustine's *On Christian Teaching* recommends a knowledge of these techniques, the African saint does not offer it there; what Augustine failed to convey, Cassiodorus provides. Thus, the schemes and tropes of classical wisdom are important for true monastic literacy because of their primary function in making the meaning of Scripture—and particularly the psalms—more available.

The commentary examines each of the 150 psalms and uses a structured four-part approach to analyze them:

> [Cassiodorus] invariably begins with an explication of the psalms-heading, and then passes to a discussion of the division of the psalm,

---

[28] *Cassiodorus: Explanations of the Psalms*, 3 vols., trans. P. G. Walsh, Ancient Christian Writers 51–53 (New York: Paulist Press, 1990).

in which he seeks to identify the speaker (David, or Idithun, or Asaph, or Christ, or the Church, or the synagogue) or the speakers, for some psalms are visualised as dramatic dialogues. He next offers a verse-by-verse explanation of the meaning of the psalm; and finally he appends a conclusion, in which he seeks to demonstrate the lessons which the psalm offers to contemporary Christians. The originality of this fourfold treatment lies in the second and fourth sections. Earlier psalm commentators in the west, notably Jerome and Augustine, regularly offer only brief comment on the psalm heading and proceed directly to detailed analysis of the verses. Cassiodorus's second section, the division of the psalm, offers a more general appreciation of the structure and the literary art of each poem. Some psalms are visualised as dramatic dialogues with different sections allotted to different [speakers]. . . . In his analysis of other psalms, Cassiodorus is content to signal the appearance of diapsalms, where these divisions denote changes of topic within the economy of the whole poem. The fourth section . . . enables our commentator to take a retrospective view of the main significance of the psalm. As we shall later observe, he is especially eager to exploit the psalms in refutation of the major heresies, and the *Conclusio* is a convenient section in which to underline the need for theological orthodoxy.[29]

Thus, in addition to providing orthodox explanations for the meanings, Cassiodorus teaches key skills in the interpretation of the biblical text. First, he teaches readers to ask about the identity of the speaker of each psalm section. This step encourages his readers to carefully parse the text for clues and hidden meanings as the identity of the speaker has the potential to change the meaning of what is said quite radically. Second, he provides 150 examples of structural analysis of biblical texts. Here he teaches readers that texts cannot be approached flatly, but that they need to be attentive to shifts in topic, meaning, or speaker. Although most patristic exegesis operates on a phrase-by-phrase or sentence-by-sentence level, Cassiodorus is awakening his readers to larger shapes and structures within the text. Third, his phrase-by-phrase exposition includes an encyclopedic analysis of the application of secular learning to the art of biblical interpretation.

---

[29] *Cassiodorus*, 1:6.

In his concluding comment on Psalm 150, Cassiodorus states: "We have shown that the series of psalms is crammed with points of grammar, etymologies, figures, rhetoric, topics, dialectic, definitions, music, geometry, astronomy, and expressions peculiar to divine Scripture."[30] This statement is neither a boast nor an exaggeration. The appendices of the latest English translation of Cassiodorus identify twenty-six different kinds of arguments that he identifies in a host of psalms, 143 different etymologies, and 106 different figures of speech and thought. Cassiodorus is a self-contained study of advanced grammar, biblical interpretation, and rhetoric as well as an introduction to a wide variety of other topics.

The manuscript British Library, Royal 2 B V gives us a fascinating perspective into how this elementary level of education that combines the psalms, grammar, and Cassiodorus all come together. The manuscript is a psalter that includes all 150 psalms plus the monastic canticles. It does not seem to have been used in choir as it lacks the necessary psalm divisions but was a classroom book. The psalms are written in Latin in clear, large letters. Above these, between the lines, a running gloss in Old English explains the meaning of the Latin words. In the margin are excerpts from Cassiodorus's commentary on the psalms. Working through this book, a student would be learning to read Latin, to read Old English, to acquire an understanding of the Latin text, and to learn how the psalms were interpreted by an important monastic author. A companion book written by the same scribe and presumably used alongside it (or at least in the same classroom) contains Jerome's fifty-nine homilies on the psalms.

Music Education

For people who spent most of their waking hours engaged in liturgical song, music was an essential part of the basic curriculum. Most of the music theory and writing about music from the period uses terms from the study of grammar to discuss music and its uses. As the young oblates learned the grammar of the texts they were singing in choir, they were instructed in the music they were singing as well. The Cluniac customaries from the time of Ælfric and in the century after lay out the heavy liturgical demands on the oblates:

---

[30] Ibid., 15.

> [They] pronounce the versicles of each psalm at all the canonical
> hours, intone the antiphons on ferial days, and intone whatever is
> sung at the morning mass, unless it is a major feast day; at Lauds
> and Vespers, they sing a responsory and say the versicles; in the
> summer at Matins they say the single short lesson; they always read
> in chapter, never in the refectory.[31]

In a time when music notation was still in the process of development, the chief mode of learning was still oral. Monastic customaries from Cluny during the period describe the oblates sitting in the chapter house, learning the chant from a teacher singing it to them. These records also describe the cantor coming by and checking up on the learning process. Each day he would listen to the oblates to be sure they had learned the music correctly from their instructor before they sang in the services, and he was the one responsible for disciplining the boys if they made any errors in the singing as well. If learning the psalms was a long and complicated affair, learning all of the music was even more so; Guido of Arezzo († ca. 1033) mentions that it took roughly ten years to master the entire musical corpus of the Mass and Office.

The connection between liturgical music and grammar, however, goes far deeper than the reuse of terminology. Emma Hornby's groundbreaking work *Medieval Liturgical Chant and Patristic Exegesis: Words and Music in the Second-Mode Tracts* patiently works through a small part of the chant corpus to demonstrate exactly how grammar, music, and the interpretations of Cassiodorus come together in early medieval liturgical music. The tract, it will be remembered, falls between the epistle and the gospel during penitential seasons. There are a few second mode tracts that are old—likely compositions of the papal *schola cantorum* sometime before the mid-eighth century. Another was a Frankish composition, probably written between 790 and 820. Four others were composed around 900.

Hornby's analysis of the oldest second-mode tracts demonstrates conclusively that the music of the chants is tightly tied to the grammar of the texts: there are four main phrases that are used within the tracts, and their use is governed by the grammatical structure of the psalm texts being set

---

[31] Susan Boynton, "Training for the Liturgy as a Form of Monastic Education," in *Medieval Monastic Education*, ed. George Ferzoco and Carolyn Muessig (London: Leicester University Press, 2000), 7–20, here 8.

to music. By analyzing the grammar, the music becomes apparent—there is a clear formula being used. However, there are points where the tracts vary from the formula. In each case, a break from the usual formula serves to heighten something found in the text to draw out a theme and underscore its connection to the liturgical occasion being celebrated:

> In each second-mode tract, the musical reading of the text connects to the liturgical themes of the day in question, as evidenced by the readings and by the other Proper chants which surround it. On Passion Sunday, the emphasis in *Deus deus meus* is on Psalm 21 [22] as prefiguration of the Passion of Christ. In *Domine exaudi* on Holy Wednesday, the dual interpretation of Psalm 101 [102] as referring both to Sion (the Church) weighed down by sin and also to Christ's blameless suffering and resurrection is reflected in the music. *Qui habitat*, sung on Quadragesima Sunday, speaks of the battle between Christ and the devil in the Temptation, which Lent symbolically re-enacts. The chant is also sung on Good Friday, together with *Domine audiui*, and both touch on the triumph of the risen Christ Crucified; *Domine audiui* refers to the life of Christ from Nativity through Passion to Resurrection. At the same time, and particularly notable in the exegetical emphases of *Deus deus meus* and *Domine exaudi*, the attentive listener is invited to share in the psalm narrative on a personal level. Medieval exegesis, particularly as experienced in a liturgical context, collapses to some degree the hermeneutical distance between the reader and the world of the biblical text; the world of past salvific events becomes, not just a moral ideal to be striven for but a preset reality to be embraced.[32]

Thus, the music is responding to both the grammar of the psalm selections and the interpretive tradition, relying in particular on the work of Cassiodorus.

Now—it is a fair question as to whether this mid-eighth-century chant formula was understood beyond the composers in the papal *schola*. The Frankish tract *Eripe me* becomes important here for what it tells us about how later ages comprehended the musical scheme. Hornsby's analysis shows that, by and large, the formula is present but was not expertly executed.

---

[32] Emma Hornby, *Medieval Liturgical Chant and Patristic Exegesis: Words and Music in the Second-Mode Tracts* (London: Boydell Press, 2009), 112.

The conventions were understood well enough to be used and properly transmitted but not well enough to be fully replicated. By the beginning of the tenth century, the four new second-mode tracts are entirely different—the formulas are used in a fairly haphazard manner, and the particular phrases used to highlight are not applied in the same way at all.

Based on this evidence, we can conclude the following. First, the composition of the second-mode tracts combined the basic fundamental arts—grammar, rhetoric, biblical interpretation, patristic learning, and music—for the beauty and elaboration of the liturgy. Second, the patterns embedded within these compositions could be discerned by later musicians as the Frankish *Eripe me* demonstrates. The four later tracts show, however, that not all composers either understood or attempted to replicate this form of compositional technique. Nevertheless, the patterns were there, waiting to be uncovered by those who pondered them deeply.

Advanced Education

Once the Psalter and the liturgical music was well in hand, other works would be added. The students were now ready for the five core texts of the Anglo-Saxon monastic curriculum: the pseudepigraphal *Distiches of Cato*, Prosper of Aquitaine's *Epigrams*, Juvencus's *Books of the Four Evangelists*, Caelius Sedulius's *Paschal Song*, and Arator's *On the Acts of the Apostles*.[33]

The proverbs ascribed to Cato are not explicitly Christian but contain brief wise sayings reminiscent of the biblical book of Proverbs. Prosper's work was similar but explicitly Christian. Prosper of Aquitaine was a dedicated student of Augustine, and his epigrams are brief distillations of Augustinian thought in a neatly packaged, easily memorized format. The glosses written into the surviving editions of these works from the Anglo-Saxon period are largely grammatical—helping to identify what part of speech various words are or clarifying what a clause refers to—showing that these books were still used relatively early in the learning process.

The other three books are poetic paraphrases of New Testament Scripture. Juvencus was a Spanish Christian poet of the fourth century who

---

[33] For a much deeper discussion of these five works and their use in Anglo-Saxon England, see Michael Lapdige, "The Study of Latin Texts in Late Anglo-Saxon England," in *Latin and the Vernacular Languages in Early Medieval Britain*, ed. Nicholas Brooks (Leicester: Leicester University Press, 1982), 99–140.

wrote the earliest surviving paraphrase of the gospels in Latin epic verse. His treatment is a fairly straightforward harmonization of the four gospels in metered hexameter verse. Caelius Sedulius likewise composed a Latin epic in hexameters based on the gospels and the life of Christ, but where Juvencus stays fairly close to his source material, Caelius Sedulius goes farther afield. Sedulius uses miracles and the miraculous power of God as the orienting theme of his work. Of the five books of the *Paschal Song*, the first describes miracles from the Old Testament that either point to or show the power of Christ before launching into the story of Christ with a particular focus on his miracles in the other four books.

The readings from the gospels in the Mass and the Night Office are disjointed; they appear in the form of brief excerpts that are arranged to follow the liturgical year and its cycles, not the narrative stream. As a result, Juvencus was probably a monastic student's first presentation of the whole story of the incarnation, life, crucifixion, resurrection, and ascension of Jesus. Sedulius, then, would be a student's first introduction to the interpretation of the gospels.

Just as Sedulius issued an improved and interpreted edition of what Juvencus wrote, Arator's epic treatment of Acts is itself an imitation and elaboration of Sedulius. Arator's central focus is the mystical interpretation of the events of Acts; he weaves allegorical interpretation and moral exhortation into the fabric of his paraphrase. Again, this text would have been an early example for monastic students on the art of the spiritual reading of the Bible.

Ælfric's perspective on the Bible, understanding it chiefly as an eschatological epic, is clearly indebted to these three epics at the core of the monastic curriculum. There were, however, other direct influences from them as well. Pieces of Caelius Sedulius's *Paschal Song* were incorporated directly into the liturgy; the text for the *introit* for a votive feast of the Virgin Mary beginning "Salve sancta parens" comes directly from a line in praise of the Virgin in book two.

A look into further learning comes through a more advanced set of colloquies. Ælfric's own *Colloquy* is clearly intended for introductory students gaining basic fluency in Latin. We also possess intermediate and advanced colloquies from one of Ælfric's students named Ælfric Bata. While the master's colloquy presents us with a scene of several village boys sitting at the feet of their master learning, Ælfric Bata provides a colorful set of colloquies that walk through the monastic day with a rambunctious set of boys who alternately cheat on their homework, get threatened with beatings by their angry teacher for failing their lessons, and break monastic rules in a variety of ways. Indeed, one dialogue consists almost entirely of Latin words for the different kinds of agricultural manure used as insults traded between master and teacher! Needless to say, references to the liturgy, participation within the liturgy, and preparing for it are found throughout these colloquies, confirming that what was seen in the Cluniac customaries about the role of the oblates in worship was equally true for Benedictine Revival England.

At this point, it becomes more difficult to trace the direction of monastic instruction. We can say for certain that works like Aldhelm's *On Virginity* in both its prose and poetic form were studied at centers of learning like Winchester, but whether monks at smaller houses would have encountered it is another story altogether. The question has to shift from what was read to what was available. When we picture a medieval monastic library in our mind's eye, we probably think of a building or tower filled with books—like the great library depicted cinematically in *The Name of the Rose*. The reality, though, was far more basic. The library of the average monastery of the time contained no more than fifty books. Instead of a building, or even a set of large rooms, we should picture a modestly sized cupboard. The great libraries of Benedictine Reform England—like Winchester and Ramsey—probably had twice that number. As a result, the state and shape of intermediate to advanced education depended entirely on situation and placement of the monastery.

Working from surviving booklists and manuscripts, there seems to have been a core of roughly twenty titles from the church fathers that served as the heart of the monastics' theological education. These titles were grouped around four central figures: Gregory the Great's *Dialogues, Forty Gospel Homilies, Morals from Job*, and the *Pastoral Care*; Isidore of Seville's *On the Church Offices, On the Nature of Things, Etymologies*, and *Synonyms*; Jerome's *Letters* and *Commentary on Matthew*; and Augustine's *City of God, On the Trinity, Narrations on the Psalms, Enchiridion*, and selected *Letters* and *Sermons*. Additionally John Cassian's *Institutes* and *Conferences*, Benedict's *Rule*, and Rufinius's translation of Eusebius's *Church History* rounded out the list.[34]

---

[34] Michael Lapidge, *The Anglo-Saxon Library* (Oxford: Oxford University Press, 2008), 127.

Only after considering the realities of what the monastics did and didn't have can the true importance of the homiliaries be appreciated. By excerpting sermons and homilies from a wide range of orthodox teachers, homiliaries played an essential role as a patristic anthology and exposed the monastics to a breadth of Christian thought and teaching that would have been otherwise inaccessible to them.

A concluding note that serves to firmly fix the deep relationship between monastic education and the liturgy regards the study of Horace at Winchester. Horace was the great poetic master of the Augustan age who did for the ode what Virgil did for the epic. However, his Latin and his meter—in particular, his adaptation of Greek meters for Latin poetry—was very complicated. We know without a doubt that Horace was studied in Winchester around the time that Ælfric studied there under Bishop Æthelwold. The evidence rests in the hymns composed by Ælfric's contemporary Wulfstan Cantor, written in praise of Bishop Æthelwold. The complex meters that Wulfstan uses—correctly—could only have been accomplished through a thorough and exacting study of Horace and his compositional techniques. The study of Latin meter was the pinnacle of the literary arts, and our foremost evidence regarding its presence is through works produced for the glory of God and a sainted bishop for the embellishment of the liturgy.

LITURGICAL INTERPRETATION

Liturgy interpreted Scripture in a variety of ways. The simplest and most obvious way is by discursive means. That is, a composed, nonscriptural text would make an exegetical observation or connection that would interpret an image, unpack an allegory, or praise an action as worthy of imitation. These connections are often found in hymns, collects, and Proper prefaces, but sermons and homilies as fundamentally liturgical genre also appear in this category.

A second, selection, is a broad category that ranges from highlighting individual verses—as for use as Little Chapters at Vespers or Lauds—to identifying large portions of text as particularly suitable for certain occasions such as selecting gospel or epistle texts for Mass. The appointed gospel, which grounds both the final reading of the Night Office and also the Mass of the Day, provides a defining theme for the entirety of the occasion. Furthermore, the selection of the gospel and epistle for a Sunday or other major feast had broader liturgical implications. Significant verses from these texts would be further selected for use throughout the week. Isolating a single verse out of a text highlights it and gives it particular importance for establishing the meaning of the larger text when it is encountered again.

Repetition, a third means, takes a selection of whatever length and reuses it for a specific purpose. For instance, certain versicle and response pairs are repeated daily throughout certain liturgical seasons. The effect is that these two verse snippets become an integral part of the monastic experience of the season. Certain selected texts are used and reused on a weekly or even daily basis. Over a period of decades, even centuries, their repeated use has given them a privileged place within the tradition. The Lord's Prayer, the Song of Mary (Luke 1:46-55), the Song of Zechariah (Luke 1:68-79), these and texts like them have earned a special place in the heart of the church and serve as central passages against which other texts and their interpretations are tested.

The fourth builds on the others and is far more common, pervasive, and complicated than the first: pregnant juxtapositions. Many liturgical forms like the antiphons used with the invitatory, the psalms, and the gospel canticles, the *preces* (prayers), responsories, little chapters and others consist of taking the material selected from Scripture and placing it in relation to other scriptural materials. That is, the liturgy may take two passages from two entirely different parts of the canon but by placing them next to each other has created, in essence, a new scriptural concept or narrative. No interpretation is given or even suggested, yet the liturgy presents an interpretive puzzle; there is no explicit interpretation, yet the arrangement implies that they belong together. The connection between texts is loaded with potential meaning, but the liturgy leaves it in a potential state—a state pregnant with yet-undelivered meaning. The underdetermined character requires the reader and the whole reading community to actively participate in the process of meaning making by creating comprehensible connections. These texts and the relationship between them have a spiritual meaning; it is up to the participants to uncover what it may be. The connections showcased in the writings of medieval liturgists like Amalarius of Metz and the whole *expositio missae* (exposition of the Mass) genre sometimes strike modern exegetes as quite fanciful. Nonetheless, these authors were operating from the firm conviction that no texts that appear together in the liturgy do so by mere chance; rather, the Spirit is speaking a spiritual truth that the participant must uncover.

Indeed, to a large degree the success and longevity of the liturgy is due to a fundamentally underdetermined approach to meaning. By using scriptural selections and creating pregnant juxtapositions, the liturgy creates many different opportunities for reading that are open ended. The range of possible or potential meanings suggested can never be completely exhausted and, as a result, the same texts in the same configurations can continue to speak to new readers in new ways over generations.

Because of the underdetermined character of this arrangement, though, tracing direct influence of the liturgy on a given text is difficult. The best sign that liturgical suggestions lay behind interpretations is when the same texts suggested by the liturgy appear in conversation with the primary text in a homily or sermon.

SCRIPTURE AND THE CHURCH YEAR

Keeping time in the early medieval church was a complicated affair. John Harper, in his standard introductory handbook on the medieval liturgy, notes that:
The daily liturgy is regulated by four overlapping and interacting cycles:

the daily cycle of Office and Mass;

the weekly cycle;

the annual cycle of liturgical seasons (Temporale);

the annual cycle of feast days (Sanctorale).[35]

Within these cycles of keeping time, there were several operative lectionaries. Each of these four different cycles required their own sets of readings, totaling no less than eight distinct lectionaries. These were:

1. A psalms lectionary that ordered all 150 psalms within the eight daily liturgical offices, repeating every week;
2. A program of continual reading (*lectio continua*) that read through the Old and New Testaments (excluding the gospels) once every year at the Night Office, sometimes spilling over into mealtimes;

[35] Harper, *Forms and Orders*, 45.

3. A Gospel Mass/Night Office/Chapter lectionary for the Temporale;
4. The Mass Propers for the Temporale taken primarily but not exclusively from the psalms;
5. A Readings (*Lectiones*) Mass lectionary for the Temporale;
6. A Gospel Mass/Night Office/Chapter lectionary for the Sanctorale;
7. The Mass Propers for the Sanctoral taken primarily but not exclusively from the psalms;
8. A Readings (*Lectiones*) Mass lectionary for the Sanctorale.

Lectionaries 3–5 and 6–8 were roughly correlated with one another, although they were typically kept within separate liturgical books.[36] The gospel readings that fell on Sundays and feast days were repeated three times; first at Chapter, then at the principal Mass of the Day along with the other readings, but also at the end of the Night Office. With the standardization of the Mass liturgy and its lectionaries in the Carolingian period, yet another cycle of nonscriptural readings evolved as homiliaries (like that of Paul the Deacon) that identified pertinent passages from patristic sources to be read as sermons on the occasion and homilies on the appointed gospel to be read in the second and third nocturns of the Night Office respectively.[37]

The early medieval church year was composed of two yearly cycles of seasons and daily observances—both feasts and fasts—superimposed on

---

[36] Our physical evidence for gospel and reading lectionaries from Anglo-Saxon England is scant: only six gospel lectionaries survive (see Helmut Gneuss, "Liturgical Books in Anglo-Saxon England and Their Old English Terminology," in *Learning and Literature in Anglo-Saxon England: Studies Presented to Peter Clemoes on the Occasion of His Sixty-Fifth Birthday*, ed. Michael Lapidge and Helmut Gneuss [Cambridge/New York: Cambridge University Press, 1985], 91–141, here 109) and no epistolaries (Gneuss, "Liturgical Books," in Lapidge and Gneuss, 110). Both Gneuss and Lenker concur that there were also mixed lectionaries containing both gospels and readings, but none survive beyond possible fragments (Gneuss, "Liturgical Books," in Lapidge and Gneuss, 105–6, 110; Ursula Lenker, "The West Saxon Gospels and the Gospel-Lectionary in Anglo-Saxon England: Manuscript Evidence and Liturgical Practice," *Anglo-Saxon England 28* [1999]: 141–78).

[37] For more on homiliaries, see the discussion of the critical conversation in chap. 1.

one another.[38] The first, the Temporal cycle or Temporale, was a yearly remembrance of the birth, life, death, acts, and teachings of Christ. The second, the Sanctoral cycle or Sanctorale, was theologically a continuation of the Temporale that celebrated the people whose lives, deaths, and intercession after their earthly lives demonstrated the power of Christ working through them, maintaining Christ's presence in the world through the church by the power of the Spirit. Structurally and theologically, the Temporale was the more important of the two; functionally, though, the second increased at a rapid rate as saints worthy of veneration continued to be produced by the church through the ages.[39]

Within the life of the early medieval monastic establishment, a change of liturgical seasons signaled a change in life—liturgical and otherwise. The beginning of a season marked a change in the biblical texts that a community read, a change in the musical settings and the textual contents of the life of prayer, possibly changes in the colors of vestments in the oratory, even changes in what the monastics ate and wore. The changes of seasons affected life throughout the monastery; as a result, they affected thinking within the monastery. The seasons were comprehensive periods of formation, a mimetic modeling of an aspect of Israel, her Christ, or his church that engaged the mind with doctrines, the heart with religious affections, and the body with acts of penance, *ascesis*, or holy joy. Reading the gospels within these contexts foregrounded either primary or latent meanings in the text that accorded with these doctrines, affections, and acts. Thus, reading sermons as monastic exegesis must consider the season as a primary interpretive influence.

The seasons, however, are also not as straightforward as they appear. In discussing the various periods of liturgical time, monastic authors tended to focus on celebrations as days and fasts as seasons. Thus, authors

[38] The early medieval church year was very similar but not identical to the church year celebrated in modern liturgical Western churches (like the Roman Catholic, Anglican, and some Lutheran churches).

[39] The two main liturgical reforms of the Roman Catholic Church, the Council of Trent and Vatican II, both pruned back a Sanctorale that had, by the sheer number of observances, threatened to eclipse the Temporale. Indeed, many of the Protestant Reformers in the sixteenth century asserted the primacy of the Temporale through their resistance to the cult of saints although—certainly—other factors were at work there as well.

like Ælfric, Isidore, Rabanus Maurus, Amalarius, and even the anonymous author of the *Old English Menologium* and *Seasons for Fasting* gave catalogs of feasts but discrete periods of time for fasts. These complicate a facile or even an early twenty-first-century ecclesiastical notion of the relationship between seasons and shorter periods of time like octaves and days. The paucity of customaries and comprehensive ordinals prevents sweeping generalizations about a host of issues like the definitive beginnings and endings of all seasons or aspects of seasonal celebrations within any given monastic community. Particular problematic issues include the status of the season after Epiphany, the use of liturgical color in the early medieval period, or the beginning of the Advent season—which differing traditions located around either the feast of St. Andrew (November 30) or St. Martin (November 11). As a result, it is more useful to utilize the word "season" in its most ambiguous sense as a general period of time rather than its most strict sense of a rigidly proscribed unit of time.[40]

The hermeneutics of any given season were constructed dialogically in relation to the biblical passages read during the season. That is, any given gospel pericope read within a season was acted on and interpreted by all of the other Scripture which gave the season its character. Furthermore, that pericope itself was both interpreted through the seasonal hermeneutic and contributed to it, adding its distinctive elements and images to the seasonal *gestalt*. Understanding and reconstructing a seasonal hermeneutic, then, means exploring at least four elements:

1. How do the primary feasts of the season establish the mimetic and doctrinal emphases around which everything else is oriented?

2. How do the lectionaries of both Mass and Office orient themselves around these emphases and add scriptural images, affections, and notions to the character of the season?

3. How do the liturgical changes of text, tune, and liturgical action of the season and its secondary feasts concentrate the religious affections established by the first two?

---

[40] Our ambiguity need not be theirs, though. Just because we do not know when a given season stopped and started at a given time and place does not mean that they did not know.

4. Finally, how do the seasonal life changes in diet and activity cement the mimetic and affectional character of the season into a holistic process of spiritual and moral formation?

Consideration of these factors in creative tension with seasonally shaped exegesis and proclamation will lead to a much better understanding of the interpretive forces acting on any particular text read within a season. I will demonstrate how this works practically by looking at the season of Christmas and its hermeneutic using the fourfold schema above.

LITURGY AND THEOLOGY IN THE CHRISTMAS SEASON

The Primary Occasions of the Christmas Season

The season of Christmas spans a spare thirteen days,[41] the period of time from the Vigil of Christmas (December 24) through Epiphany (January 6). Within this time span, thirteen different liturgical occasions have their own Proper texts and readings.[42] The primary feast days of the Christmas season are two: Christmas and Epiphany. These two serve as hinge festivals, defining the formal beginning and ending of the season as well as its primary emphases.

The feast of Christmas celebrates the birth of Christ and the subsequent rejoicing of celestial beings, Israel, and the church. Doctrinally, the feast establishes and celebrates the incarnation of Christ, noting both Jesus' assumption of humanity through his birth from the Virgin Mary and his preexistent divinity that rested—coeternal—in the bosom of the Father.

Epiphany celebrates the manifestation of Christ to Israel and beyond through a conflation of scriptural events, most notably the gifts of the magi, the baptism of Christ by John, and the first miracle of Jesus in the

---

[41] This thirteen includes the traditional twelve days from Christmas to Epiphany plus the Vigil of Christmas.

[42] They are: (1) the Vigil of Christmas, (2–4) three Masses for Christmas Day, (5) the feast of St. Stephen, (6) the feast of St. John the Evangelist, (7) the feast of the Holy Innocents, (8) the feast of St. Silvester, (9) the Octave of Christmas/Holy Name, (10) the First Sunday after Christmas, (11) the Second Sunday after Christmas, (12) the Vigil of Epiphany, and (13) Epiphany.

wedding at Cana. The main doctrine and image of the feast combine in a single scriptural phrase, Christ as "the light for revelation to the Gentiles" (Luke 2:32), that lent its force to the characterization of the entire Christmas season. The season places both Israel and the church before the eyes of the community as patterns for imitation. The emphasis in Christmas and Epiphany sermons is on witnessing the miracle of the incarnation with the shepherds and the angels and on recognizing Christ in his manifestations with the magi, John the Baptist, and the first disciples.

The gospel lectionaries for the season of Christmas draw their texts from the beginning of the gospels of Matthew, Luke, and John; the exceptions are the feasts of St. Stephen, St. Silvester and St. John which draw their readings from the ends of Matthew and John respectively. In all, readings for the season encompass Matthew 1:18-21;[43] 2:1-23;[44] Luke 2:1-40;[45] and John 1:1-14.[46] The readings of the Night Offices are dominated by Isaiah, particularly the familiar messianic texts and passages of celebration. Thus both the *RC* and the *LME* appoint Isaiah 9:1ff.; Isaiah 40:1ff.; and Isaiah 52:1ff. for the Christmas readings.

Liturgically speaking, the Christmas season blossoms. The Gloria, which had been removed from Mass for the Advent fast, is restored. Across both Mass and Office, the ordinary texts are musically ornamented with more complex and beautiful arrangements including the addition of tropes. The proper texts utilize both the theology and the images of the biblical texts.

One example, a representative liturgical book, serves as a suitable demonstration of how these seasonal principles are applied to the liturgy of the Mass. The Leofric Missal[47] is a well-preserved missal in use during the Benedictine Revival. Containing three layers of texts, the most recent editors[48] have hypothesized that the manuscript at the core of the book was

[43] Vigil of Christmas.

[44] Epiphany: Matt 2:1-12; Holy Innocents: Matt 2:13-23; Vigil of Epiphany/Second Sunday after Christmas: Matt 2:19-23.

[45] Christmas I: Luke 2:1-14; Christmas II: Luke 2:15-20; Octave of Christmas: Luke 2:21-32; First Sunday after Christmas: Luke 2:33-40.

[46] Christmas III.

[47] Oxford, Bodleian Library MS. Bodl. 579. The Leofric Missal is online in its entirety at: http://image.ox.ac.uk/show?collection=bodleian&manuscript=msbodl579.

[48] Nicholas Orchard, ed., *The Leofric Missal*, 2 vols., Henry Bradshaw Society 113 and 114 (Rochester, NY: Boydell, 2002).

used by St. Dunstan of Canterbury (†988), one of the three great monastic bishops of the Revival. Its texts represent a standard liturgical book of the "Eighth-Century Mixed Gelasian" type appropriate to the period.

The Leofric Missal's kalendar[49] is well preserved and is laid out in orderly columns, dates on the left side with golden numbers and letters and names of liturgical and astronomical occurrences in the right column. The pages identify five levels of feasts by script hierarchies. Proceeding from least to most important they are: (1) solemnities with no prefix, written in a black Anglo-Saxon miniscule; (2) solemnities prefixed by a red "S," but with the name of the occasion written in black Anglo-Saxon miniscule; (3) solemnities prefixed with a red F with the name written in black rustic capitals; (4) solemnities written in red rustic capitals; and (5) solemnities prefixed by an F and written in multicolored rustic capitals. Of the Christmas observances, the feast of Christmas itself and the next three days—St. Stephen, St. John, and Holy Innocents, are grade 5, the Vigil of Christmas is grade 4, the Circumcision and Epiphany are grade 3, and the Octave of Epiphany and St. Silvester are grade 2. The Sunday occasions are not present as they are moveable rather than static feasts.[50]

Of the eighty-one liturgical texts for the Christmas season in this book, several themes reappear. Certain doctrinal and conceptual terms occur frequently. The doctrine of the incarnation is mentioned through references to commingling of humanity and divinity or the incarnation itself twenty-one times. Terms for birth are also central and appear seventeen times. Terms for light appear seventeen times as well. In addition to doctrinal language, affectional language also adds to the character of the season. Various forms of the word "rejoice" appearing as a noun, verb, or adjective occur twelve times.

Out of these prayers, a few deserve special attention for the way they illustrate the interplay between liturgical texts, seasons, and the exegetical

---

[49] Fols. 39r-44v. Manuscript pages are usually not numbered like printed pages. Each page or folio (fol. or fols.) receives one number and the two sides are identified by letters; "r" for the *recto* or front side, and "v" for *verso* or back side.

[50] By way of comparison the highest graded feast in December or January not part of the Christmas season is the feast of St. Thomas (December 21) which is grade 3. Even other occasions celebrating biblical feasts do not rank as high; the Conversion of St. Paul (January 25) is only a grade 2.

project. Some, like the preface for the Octave of Christmas, are broadly synthetic, drawing together a number of images, doctrines, and themes to illuminate the season:

> Through Christ our Lord to whom, celebrating today the day of his circumcision and the octave of his birth, we venerate your wonders, Lord: she who gave birth is both mother and virgin, he who was born is both baby and God. Deservedly, the heavens spoke, the angels gave thanks, the shepherds rejoiced, the magi changed, kings were disturbed, the little ones through their passion were crowned with glory. And therefore with angels . . .[51]

This preface begins by identifying the specific observance it celebrates, both the liturgical octave and a biblical event, the circumcision of Jesus (Luke 2:21). Then, it succinctly summarizes the twin paradoxes of Christmas: the incarnation and the perpetual virginity of the Virgin Mary. It places in service of these two events a host of biblical events by way of allusion, touching not only the gospel accounts but also typological cross-references. Thus, "angels gave thanks" alludes to Luke 2:13ff.; "shepherds rejoiced" alludes to Luke 2:18, 20; "the magi changed" refers to Matthew 2:12 but possibly also to apocryphal accounts of the conversion of the magi; "the little ones through their passion were crowned with glory" alludes to the slaughter of the innocents in Matthew 2:16-18.

The phrase "the heavens spoke" can be understood as a figure of speech referring to the angels; a direct citation of angels as the next item of the list, however, would render it repetitive. More likely this phrase is a reference to Psalm 18:1 (Vulgate), especially given the incarnational interpretation of Psalm 18:1-6 (Vulgate) in the early and medieval church (see the Christmas hymn *Veni redemptor gentium*). Similarly, "kings were disturbed" appears to refer directly to Matthew 2:3—and it does: "And king Herod hearing this, was troubled, and all Jerusalem with him." The use of the plural "kings" where Matthew uses the singular "king" accomplishes two purposes. First, it preserves the parallelism and the use of the distributive plural helping verb "are" which, in the Latin, is shared with

[51] Item 389; Orchard, *Leofric Missal*, 111. The "VD" beginning this and all other Proper prefaces is an abbreviation for the first two words and thus the whole of the transitional phrase leading into the Proper preface: "Vere dignum . . ."

all of the other nouns in this string. Second, it links the passage with Psalm 2:1 (Vulgate; "The kings of the earth stood up, and the princes met together, against the Lord, and against his Christ"), a psalm whose messianic implications were patently clear to the church. In particular, the use of the plural in the psalm was read as a figure of speech following Acts 4:25ff.

Through this piling up of reference and metaphor within the preface, the liturgical occasion, theological doctrine, and the biblical text are joined through the liturgical prayer.

Other prayers directly present a variety of exegetical interpretations of the appointed texts. For instance, the collect for the feast of St. Stephen highlights one particular aspect of the Acts account:

> Grant us, Lord, we beseech you, to imitate him whom we honor, that we might also learn to love our enemies, for we celebrate the [heavenly] nativity of him who yet knew to intercede on behalf of his enemies to our Lord Jesus Christ, who lives and reigns with you and the Holy Spirit.

Stephen is presented as an example for moral imitation and emulation. Out of the Stephen narrative, the collect identifies Acts 7:60—Stephen's prayer of forgiveness for his killers—as the central point of the reading. Correctly following Luke's intention back to Luke 23:34, the collect identifies Stephen as a type of Christ, emulating his death. This, in turn, is connected to Christ's command in Matthew 5:44 to love enemies and to pray for those who persecute.

Two of the Propers for the feast of the Holy Innocents utilize a shared figure to establish a meaning for the feast. The collect reads:

> God, whose praise today the innocent martyrs, not in speaking but in dying, confessed; mortify all evils of vices in us, that as our tongues might speak of your faith, our lives also might declare [it] with habits; through Jesus Christ our Lord.

The second prayer of the benediction is:

> And he who granted to them, who confessed his only Son our Lord not in speaking but in dying, grant to you [pl] that as your tongue

might declare the true faith, also upright habits, that a blameless life
might declare it. Amen.

Utilizing rhetorical paradoxes, the prayers exhort the congregation to
emulate tropologically the infant martyrs by an appeal to honor. Just as
those who cannot speak witnessed to Christ, so we too should bear witness to Christ without speech through the silent witness of virtuous
living.

Furthermore, the triple benediction for the Octave of Christmas packs
a substantial amount of exegesis into a few lines:

> May Almighty God, whose only begotten Son on today's day did not
> undermine the Law but come to satisfy it in the flesh received cir-
> cumcision, purify your minds with the spiritual circumcision from
> all incentives to vices, and pour his benediction upon us. Amen.
>
> And he who gave the Law through Moses, that he might give the
> blessing of our mediators, may he draw from us the mortification
> of vices and make us persevere in new virtue. Amen.
>
> That thus in the number six you might live in perfection in this
> age, and in seven you might rest among the host of blessed spirits,
> in order that in the number eight, renewed by the resurrection,
> enriched with the remission of the jubilee, you may attain to the joys
> that will remain without end.

The first blessing utilizes the spiritualization of circumcision found in the
prophets and in the New Testament to make a tropological point about
vice and virtue in the contemporary congregation. Both the first and the
second draw attention to the value of the Law, although they do not suggest that the Law be followed literally; again, a tropological interpretation
dominates. The third blessing utilizes numerological interpretation to
interpret the eighth day, connecting the circumcision with resurrection
according to the standard interpretation of numbers popularized by
Augustine and others.

The Secondary Occasions of the Season

The secondary feasts of the Christmas season that add texture and
nuance are the feast of the Holy Name/Circumcision (January 1) and
three irregular feasts. The term "irregular" fits these occasions because

Christmas is one of the few seasons where Sanctorale occasions are co-opted into the Temporale.[52] The three days immediately following Christmas Day are celebrated as the feasts of St. Stephen (December 26), St. John (December 27), and the Holy Innocents (December 28). While the feast of the Holy Name continues to emphasize the particularity of the incarnation—that Jesus was born to a specifically Jewish household where he was circumcised on the eighth day as a matter of course—the other three add a different cast to an otherwise joyful season.

The first and third feasts provide a dark undertone because they focus on two occasions of death. St. Stephen is the Protomartyr, the first Christian to die for his faith. The liturgical emphasis of the feast is on St. Stephen's exemplary love for his enemies, following in Christ's own footsteps, as manifested in the collect for the day.

The feast of the Holy Innocents, the remembrance of those children slaughtered in the search for Jesus recorded in Matthew 2:16-18, both maintains the canonical contents of the birth narrative but also juxtaposes images of infants—a key Christmas image—with death. The gospel reading, Matthew 2:13-23, is treated both tropologically and typologically in the Propers. In addition to the collect and benediction addressed above, the preface emphasizes the tropological significance of these children-saints and further identifies them as types of Christ:

> Eternal God, even the precious deaths of little ones, who the cruel rage of the bestial Herod killed on account of the infant of our salvation, proclaim your immense mercy in which only more grace shines as volition and confession is manifest prior to speech. Before the passion, as worthy members of the passion, they were witnesses to the Christ whom they did not yet know. O infinite goodness, O ineffable mercy to those slaughtered on account of your name, the merit of glory will not be allowed to die. But, to their own blood poured out was also added the salvation of regeneration and on them was the crown of martyrdom bestowed. And behold with angels . . .

---

[52] While the feast of St. Silvester is celebrated on December 29, the celebration of this prelate has not been integrated into the Christmas season in the same fashion as the biblical saints. The prayers of the Mass set are those of a confessor pope.

The death of the infants foreshadows the death of God's Son—the Christmas infant. Just as the shedding of their blood produced regeneration and the crown of glory, so too will his. These Sanctoral occasions, then, add to the sense of the season by reminding the community that the incarnation is completed in the cross; Bethlehem is preparation for Calvary. Although the occasion of a joyful birth, Christmas is the birth of the perfect sacrificial victim.

The second feast, St. John, returns to the main theme of the season and reinforces the divinity of Christ. The Propers for the festival emphasize both the hidden (*archana*) language of John and his emphasis on the divinity of Christ.[53] The preface for the feast makes the explicit connection between the feast of St. John and Christmas by ending the prayer with a direct citation of John 1:1, the gospel for the principal Mass of Christmas:

> Eternal God, we venerate the birthday of your blessed apostle and evangelist John who was called to his vocation by our Lord Jesus Christ, your Son, making a disciple from a fisherman. Exceeding the human way of understanding, he contemplated with his mind and revealed with his voice prior to others the divinity of your very Word who was without beginning, for in the beginning was the Word and the Word was with God and the Word was God.

The preface neatly gathers the two factors that link John and his gospel so closely to the Western church's conception of Christmas: John's special emphasis on the divinity in the midst of Jesus' humanity and on the paradox of the preexistent Word taking on corruptible flesh.

Despite the shadow of the cross cast by two of these feasts, the ways of life in the Christmas season reinforce its predominately joyful character. The food restrictions of Advent (which was known in the Irish Rules as "the winter Lent") are relaxed, and the twelve days of the season are times of feasting. Sensual aspects of the liturgy enrich and enliven the celebration; Ælfric ordered that in his community all of the bells are to be rung during Mass, Vespers, and the Night Office. Furthermore, a thurible provides incense at the Mass and gospel canticles at Lauds and Vespers.[54]

---

[53] The use of *archana* ties into other prayers for the season that use *archana* and *mysterium* to speak of the incarnation.

[54] *LME* 22.

The prayers of the Leofric Missal's Mass sets, then, present Christmas as a season focused on the joy and mystery of the incarnation. Morally, it calls for a rededication to a life of virtue and holds up the first martyrs both as exempla and as types of Christ's own death—the ultimate purpose of the incarnation. As John perceived the divinity within the human Jesus, the congregation is invited to likewise understand the Christmas child to be true God as well as true man.

When we turn to the office hymns of the Christmas season, we find the same themes. Because of their length, however, the hymns were able to interweave theology with biblical narrative in a more comprehensive fashion. Not departing from the intentions that we find in the Mass sets, here the thoughts are expanded, expounded, and further connected to other theological themes and to even more scriptural texts.

In the Anglo-Saxon hymnals,[55] the Christmas season appears in a block typically containing eleven hymns—four (sometimes three) for Christmas itself, three for the feast of St. Stephen, four for Epiphany. While the same hymns usually appear, going back to a common Continental source brought to England with the Benedictine Revival, there is often not agreement as to which of the offices a given hymn was to be sung—First Vespers, the Night Office, Lauds, or Second Vespers. Of particular importance for the season are the Christmas Day hymns—these would be sung throughout the Octave (if not the season) if no other feast superseded them.

As noted above, certain words and concepts inevitably appear over and over again, maintaining the focus on the doctrinal, theological, and scriptural themes highlighted by the Christmas season. The notion of incarnation appears some seventeen times, birth appears fifteen times, and light ten times. The affectional cues of "rejoice" and "praise" appear three and nine times, respectively. While the counts on affectional words are rather few, the primary affectional vehicles for these selections—their music—are mostly lost to us; only a few of the tunes were transmitted in the Anglo-Saxon hymnals.

---

[55] Helmut Gneuss identifies eight hymnals that survive from the Anglo-Saxon period (Gneuss, "Liturgical Books," in Lapidge and Gneuss, 118–19). The definitive modern treatment of the genre is found in Millful's edition of the Durham Hymnal with collation of the other works in Inge B. Millful, *Hymns of the Anglo-Saxon Church* (Cambridge: Cambridge University Press, 1997).

The hymn *Christe, Redemptor Omnium* contains a classic example of the kind of exegetical play that links different liturgies through common scriptural threads. The third verse addresses the universal praise of the cosmos at the birth of Christ: "Heaven praises this day, the earth and the sea praise it, everything that is in them praises it joyfully with its song as the occasion of your coming."[56] The language here is largely shared with the Offertory of the Midnight Mass drawn from Psalm 95:11, 13 (Vulgate): "Let the heavens rejoice and the earth be glad before the face of the Lord because he comes." Given this connection, the appearance of "sing a new song" (*ymnum novum concinimus*) later in verse V would inevitably remind a monastic audience of the opening of Psalm 95 (Vulgate): "Sing to the Lord a new song [*cantante Domino canticum novum*], sing to the Lord, all the earth."

Just as the prayers for the feast of St. Stephen explored the parallels between Christ and Stephen, the hymn for the Night Office *Ymnum Cantemus Domino* is constructed of seven antitheses that explore the theological relationship between the incarnate Christ and the first Christian martyr:

> [Let us sing] . . . to Christ because he was born to the world,
> to Stephen because he died [to the world]
> to Christ because he conferred life,
> to Stephen because he endured death,
> to Christ because he descended,
> to Stephen, because he ascended
> to Christ, because he came to earth,
> to Stephen because he went to heaven.[57]

Another hymn opens with the same exegetical observation as found in the collect for the day:

> You who are holy and of great worth, first of God's martyrs, Stephen,
> you who were supported at every point by the miraculous strength

---

[56] Millful, *Hymns*, Hymn 36.5, 192.
[57] Ibid., Hymn 40.3-4, 204–5.

of charity and thus prayed to the Lord for the people who were your enemies.[58]

Thus the dominant themes drawn from the readings run across the liturgies of the monastic day.

The hymns of Epiphany focus on the concept of "manifestation" pre-eminently by connecting scriptural events. The hymn *Hostis Herodes Impie* (actually a section of a longer hymn whose initial verses were also used as the hymn *A Solis Ortu Cardine*) was composed in the fifth century by Sedulius Scotus and connects several events: the star guiding the magi,[59] the slaughter of the innocents by Herod,[60] the baptism of Jesus by John in the Jordan,[61] a summary of healing and raising miracles,[62] and the changing of water to wine at Cana.[63] The three central themes taken up by the hymn *Iesus Refulgit Omnium* are the magi and their star, the baptism of Jesus, and the changing of water to wine; these were also crystallized into the gospel antiphon used with the Magnificat at the Second Vespers of Epiphany:

> We keep this day holy in honor of three miracles: on this day the star led the magi to the manger; today wine was made from water at the wedding; today in the Jordan Christ willed to be baptized by John that he might save us, alleluia.

Thus, the hymns participate in the same interpretive themes as seen in the prayers and readings of the Christmastide Masses. They contribute to the seasonal focus on certain doctrines and texts, keeping them before the eyes of the worshipping community. Also, the length and scope of the hymns enable them to connect more items together than can be reliably assembled into a brief collect, extending the interpretive possibilities of the liturgy.

---

[58] Ibid., Hymn 41.1, 206. This hymn is attributed to Eusebius Bruno (†1081) of the generation after Ælfric.

[59] Ibid., Hymn 45.2, 206.

[60] Ibid., Hymn 45.3, 206.

[61] Ibid., Hymn 45.4, 206.

[62] Ibid., Hymn 45.5, 206.

[63] Ibid., Hymn 45.6, 206.

Summary

The liturgy was a pervasive aspect of monastic life. The seasons directed the cycles of scriptural reading that grounded the Mass and the Night Office. The selection of antiphons and *preces* and the composition of prayers and hymns of the Mass and Office offered underdetermined interpretive possibilities. These meanings that appeared implicitly within the monastic rhythms and centrally in the Mass and Office appear explicitly within the homilies of the Mass and Office.

Chapter 3

The Temptation and the Beatitudes

In the next two chapters we are going to put the four modern New Testament scholars into conversation with Ælfric of Eynsham, looking at four specific passages from Matthew's gospel. I begin each section with a brief introduction to the text in question. In exploring the character of the text and its gospel parallels, I make reference to the Eusebian Canons. This was a system of dividing the gospels that goes back to the beginning of the third century. Following the work of his predecessor Ammonius of Alexandria (†ca. 220), Eusebius of Caesarea (†340) split the gospels into a set of sentence or paragraph level divisions that accomplished two functions: first, it created a standardized way of referring to passages used in lectionary; second, it enabled him to display—by means of ten elaborate tables—which gospels shared common material between them. Remember, the gospel books that Ælfric and his companions were using did not use the chapter and verse divisions that we are accustomed to today. Rather, there were quite a variety of different competing schemes for dividing the gospels into chapters; there were at least fifteen different ways that Matthew was broken up resulting in anywhere from twenty-eight to eighty-eight chapters! Our current set of chapters was established by Stephen Langton (c. 1155–1228), English biblical scholar and later archbishop of Canterbury; verse divisions didn't appear until the first printed editions of the gospels by Robert Estienne in 1551.

I use these Eusebian Canon references for several reasons. First, to remind modern readers that precritical readers were not necessarily uncritical—or unaware of shared material between the gospels. Second, because the Eusebian Canons and accompanying Canon tables were standard features of early medieval gospel books; in the era before standardized chapters and verses, lectionaries and other references used the Eusebian divisions to identify text portions. Third, Old English sermons often bring in parallels from other gospels to shed light on the texts in focus, and recent scholarship has demonstrated that the surviving Old English gospels marked certain parallel passages to aid the exegetical process.[1] Fourth and finally, the Eusebian divisions present a method of connecting parallel passages without reference to modern interpretive arguments. Thus, the Canons are a critical tool common to both early medieval and modern readers of Matthew.

I then address in turn each of the four modern authors. My purpose is not to give a point by point summary of how they interpret every jot and tittle of the text but to sketch their approach and areas of interest in broad terms. In part, this approach is recommended by the diversity of the sources. For instance, Hare sometimes covers in a page what Davies and Allison require a dozen to accomplish due to the differences in purpose between them.

Once the modern authors have been surveyed, I turn my attention to Ælfric's interpretation. In each case, I begin with a reading of the sermon. Again, I am primarily looking for the main themes and angles of approach on the text but, because of the unfamiliarity of the medieval methods, I give more space to understanding and presenting this foreign voice than to the more familiar modern ones. Once I work through Ælfric's sermon on the passage, I examine the liturgical context from which the sermon comes. This illuminates interpretive choices found in the sermons, identifies interpretive themes suggested by the liturgy, and locates the sermon as one aspect within the liturgy's treatment of the Matthean text.

After the interpreters have been given separate hearings, I attempt to synthesize the conversation. My goal is not to judge between readings in order to select which reading is the best—or worst. After all, the point of chapter 1 was that, while similar in some respects, the modern scholarly and early medieval monastic cultures are doing different things for different purposes. Instead, my central question comes from the modern perspective: what insights can modern readers of the New Testament

---

[1] Ursula Lenker, *Die westsächsische Evangelienversion und die Perikopenordnungen im angelsächsiscen England* (Munich: Fink, 1997).

gain from the text of Matthew by engaging early medieval monastic readers on their own terms?

MATTHEW 4:1-11

Introduction

Matthew 4:1-11 relates the temptation of Jesus in the wilderness by Satan. A self-contained narrative incident, a disjunctive "Then . . ." starting at 4:1 separates this account from the preceding baptismal narrative (Matt 3:13-17), while a change of scene in 4:12 separates it from a summary statement on the inauguration of Jesus' public ministry (Matt 4:12-17). The text clearly comes from Q, the sayings source that lays behind both Matthew and Luke. Eusebius attributes the first verse to canon II, the Triple Tradition of material common to Matthew, Mark, and Luke, recognizing Mark 1:12ff. as a parallel, but the next ten are canon V, Double Tradition (Matthew and Luke) only. The final verse he assigns to canon VI, Matthew and Mark. Precisely the same parallels appear in Kurt Aland's *Synopsis Quattor Evangeliorum* with the addition of John 1:51 as a rather questionable parallel with verse 11. Matthew has retained the Q text to a large degree, making only a few minor additions.

The thoroughly mythological character of the narrative has posed interpretive difficulties for modern scholarship. The appearance of Satan as a literal character in particular has been problematic. In an attempt to distance both Jesus and the evangelist from the passage, many scholars—led by Bultmann—have explained it as a late addition to the gospel.[2] Kloppenborg in his *Formation of Q* refers to it as "something of an embarrassment" for modern Q scholars. He notes several scholars who have sought to exclude this passage from Q altogether.[3] Nevertheless, he concludes by stating: "The anomalous character of the story must however, be balanced against the strong Matthew-Luke agreements, especially in the speech portions, which in fact make the account one of the strongest of candidates for membership in Q."[4] Following this defense, he too assigns it a late date in the formation of Q.

---

[2] Rudolph Bultmann, *The History of the Synoptic Tradition*, trans. John Marsh (New York: Harper & Row, 1976), 328.

[3] John S. Kloppenborg, *The Formation of Q: Trajectories in Ancient Wisdom Collections* (Harrisburg, PA: Trinity, 1999 [1987]), 246.

[4] Ibid., 247.

Modern Interpreters

Ulrich Luz

Ulrich Luz reads the pericope as a mythical narrative created by the early church to interpret the baptismal narrative's identification of Jesus as Son of God. Ultimately, Luz states that "Jesus authenticates his divine sonship" by "obedience to the word of God in the Old Testament and in this way defeats Satan."[5] Luz is careful to state that this christological focus does not exhaust the meaning of the text; he notes that it is "indirectly open to a paranetic interpretation"[6] but prefers to leave its teaching simply at the level of demanding obedience to God's word from Christians.

After noting that Matthew makes very few changes to Q, Luz lays out a "brief sketch of the overall meaning" of the passage that focuses on possible meanings of the temptations; the chief categories that he sets up require a decision whether the temptations are "to be understood as universally human or as specifically messianic."[7] He presents four possibilities:

1) the classical paranetic interpretation that sees Jesus overcoming common human temptations with the psychological interpretation as a variant of this theme;

2) the christological interpretation that exists in two variants:

   a) Jesus rejects the *theios aner* ("divine man") approach and ostentatious miracles (working from the first two temptations) and

   b) Jesus rejects the political, Zealot understanding of the messiah (working from the third temptation);

3) Jesus typologically represents the true people of God living out the wilderness experience but this time in obedience—which leads back to either the paranetic or the christological; and

4) Jesus portrays the three dimensions of his messiahship—the prophetic, priestly, and royal.[8]

---

[5] Ulrich Luz, *Matthew 1–7: A Continental Commentary*, trans. Wilhelm C. Linss, Hermeneia (Minneapolis, MN: Fortress Press, 1992), 150.

[6] Ibid., 151.

[7] Ibid., 149.

[8] Ibid., 149–50.

Luz locates himself primarily, but not exclusively, in option 2a. The temptations are christological in nature and focus on unpacking the events of the baptism by demonstrating a central aspect of what it means to be Son—Jesus is obedient to the will of God as revealed in the Scriptures.

The key passage for Luz's interpretation is the third temptation, which he calls "the core and highpoint of the three scenes";[9] rather than taking the anti-Zealot approach (option 2b of his schema), he notes that Jesus does not reject the notion of political power nor even power over the world (after all, Jesus claims all authority at the gospel's conclusion)— rather, Jesus rejects worshipping Satan. Obedience is the point of the episode: Satan is rejected, not power or authority.

An important theme appears throughout Luz's interpretation: intertextuality. Luz notes that, in an open-ended and suggestive way, this passage has underdetermined and thought-provoking ties to other parts of the gospel—particularly in the material unique to Matthew. These connections work on a verbal level, tying episodes one to another through the use of repeated words. Thus the "high mountain" of the third temptation reminds the readers not only of the Moses narrative but also of the transfiguration— where Jesus' identity as the Beloved Son is proclaimed once again—and the end of the book where on a mountain Jesus does claim all authority.

The intertextuality also functions at the thematic level. Within this text, Luz points to a number of connections between the second temptation and conflict in Jesus' life including the passion. Interpreting the temptation as the temptation to ostentatious miracles, Luz believes that when readers encounter "Matthew's two demands for a 'sign from heaven' (16:1; cf. 12:38-39) [they] will again be reminded of this text."[10] The temple location sets up the importance of the temple in the events of Jesus' last days. The temptation of angelic assistance and protection appears again in Gethsemane. Last but not least, the words with which the scribes taunt the crucified Jesus repeat the devil's tempting words: "If you are the son of God, come down from the cross" (Matt 27:40b). Thus, the temptation episode informs the latter action in the Matthean narrative. Luz does not claim a particular purpose for this set of connections except that they underscore the obedience of Jesus in relation to temptations to act differently.

[9] Ibid., 153.
[10] Ibid., 152.

Davies and Allison

W. D. Davies and D. C. Allison present a thickly textured account that focuses closely on the formation of the Greek text of Matthew. Much of the space in their interpretation is devoted to identifying the language of Q and redactional elements added by Matthew or, conversely, changes to Q in Luke's parallel account. Additional space is devoted to presenting an impressive array of parallels with ancient literature, focusing particularly on apocryphal and rabbinic works. Because of this attention to technical features, a relatively small amount of the twenty-five pages is occupied with their own exegesis.

Nevertheless, the interpretation that appears is clearly identified and consistently presented throughout the analysis: The appearance of three quotations from Deuteronomy 6–8

> is the key to the narrative: we have before us a haggadic tale which has issued forth from reflection on Deut 6–8. Jesus, the Son of God, is repeating the experience of Israel in the desert (cf. Tertullian, *De Bapt.* 20).[11] Having passed through the waters of a new exodus at his baptism (cf. 1 Cor 10.1–5), he enters the desert to suffer a time of testing, his forty days of fasting being analogous to Israel's forty years of wandering. Like Israel, Jesus is tempted by hunger. And, like Israel, Jesus is tempted to idolatry. All important for a right understanding of our pericope is Deut 8.2–3: "And you shall remember all the ways in which the Lord your God has led you these *forty* years *in the wilderness*, that he might humble you, *testing you* to know what was in your heart, whether you would keep his commandments, or not. And he humbled you and let you *hunger*."[12]

Thus, the first temptation is connected to the hunger of Israel in the wilderness where they grumbled and demanded food. The second temptation is

[11] In this passage Tertullian addresses whether the newly baptized should fast following the pattern of Jesus. Tertullian rejects this notion, saying that by fasting Jesus was casting a reproach on Israel for its gluttony after coming through the Red Sea waters by showing the power of abstinence over gluttony. The other two temptations are not mentioned.

[12] W. D. Davies and Dale C. Allison, *A Critical and Exegetical Commentary on the Gospel According to Saint Matthew*, 3 vols. International Critical Commentary 26 (London/New York: T & T Clark International, 2004), 1:353.

linked by way of Jesus' response to the incident at Massah. The third temptation is to idolatry—a common temptation to which Israel succumbed several times—the most central to the narrative being the golden calf.

Because of the focus on Jesus as a type of Israel in the wilderness, passing the trials that Israel failed, the dualism between Jesus and Satan is softened a bit. While Davies and Allison note the change in the character of Satan between the Old Testament and the New Testament from an agent of the divine court to "a demonic, wholly evil figure"[13] (adducing many texts to prove their point), they almost see Satan in this passage as reverting back to an accuser figure or, at the very least, acting as an unwitting agent of God:

> As for Mt 4.1 and 3, the activity of the Spirit and the presence of Satan give the verb [*peirazō* (*to test or tempt*)] a double connotation: Jesus is at the same time being "tested" by God and "tempted" by the devil (cf. Gundry, *Commentary*, p. 55). That is, the hostile devil, "that slinking prompter who whispers in the heart of men" (*Koran* 114), is here the instrument of God.[14]

The devil is the mechanism by which Jesus can experience in a compressed form the temptations that Israel faced. In doing so, he serves God's purpose and sets the stage for Jesus' demonstration of his obedience to God in all things.

Last, unlike several of the other commentaries, Davies and Allison make no attempt to connect the text to the Christian life, ancient or modern. There is a brief reference that identifies this pericope as the source of the "Easter fast" mentioned in the fifth Canon of Nicaea, well within the realms of history-of-religion. Rather, their exposition exemplifies a solidly scientific approach that seeks to understand the text and its backgrounds entirely within its literary contexts.

Douglas Hare

Douglas Hare offers a position very similar to Davies and Allison but presents it in a framework explicitly pointed toward modern preaching and teaching. He opens with a clear thesis:

---

[13] Ibid., 1:356.
[14] Ibid., 1:360.

> This passage is not to be reckoned a historical narrative in the strict
> sense. . . . It constitutes a piece of haggadic midrash. . . . In its
> present form . . . the story is less involved with the vanquishing of
> Satan than with the meaning of Jesus' divine Sonship. It is, in effect,
> a theological meditation on the baptismal narrative addressing the
> question: What is implied in the heavenly declaration, "This is my
> Son, the Beloved, in whom I am well pleased"?[15]

The personal characteristics inherent in the baptismal title are demonstrated in the temptation narrative.

Hare compares the narrative to the testing of Abraham through the common word "beloved," but he, like Davies and Allison, prefers to see Jesus as a type of the wandering Israel:

> The three temptations in Matthew's order reflect the chronological
> order of three tests faced by Israel. Whereas Israel, called "son" by
> God (Hos. 11:1; see Deut. 8:5), failed each of the tests, Jesus demonstrates his worthiness to be the Son of God by responding to the
> tests with resolute faithfulness.[16]

Hare thus expands on the claim made by Davies and Allison to include chronological order. The first temptation is connected to Exodus 16:1-4, the second—again, by virtue of Jesus' response—to Exodus 17:1-7, and the third rather loosely to Exodus 32:1-6. More than Davies and Allison, Hare works with the underlying logic of the second temptation arguing that the events at Massah were about the presence of God ("Is the LORD in our midst or not?" Exod 17:7) and about improperly challenging God. Jesus, in their place, neither questions God's promises nor takes advantage of them.

The turn to modern application comes in a brief section after the exegetical work itself. Hare notes the typical lectionary placement on the first Sunday of Lent but denies that it "is of direct relevance for Christians as they enter a period of penitence."[17] Since modern Christians are not confronted by a physical devil or "whisked from place to place,"[18] the story

---

[15] Douglas Hare, *Matthew*, Interpretation (Minneapolis, MN: Fortress Press, 1995), 23.

[16] Ibid., 24.

[17] Ibid., 26.

[18] Ibid.

has little that it can tell us. Furthermore, the specific temptations are not modern ones: "the temptations that Jesus faces are peculiar to him; they seem very remote from those we face day by day."[19] Hare's answer is to move to abstraction and to note that all of the temptations share a common underlying problem—choosing to treat God as less than God.

Eugene Boring

Eugene Boring presents a brief but forceful reading of this pericope that focuses less on obedience than on laying out the central conflict that continues throughout the gospel: "Conflict with Satan is not limited to this pericope, but is the underlying aspect of the conflict between the kingdom of God and the kingdom of this world, which is the plot of the *whole* Gospel of Matthew."[20] Such an apocalyptic reading sees the particular conflict with Satan as the root conflict driving the action forward; this same conflict is repeated in all of Jesus' encounters with the Jewish authorities. The readers know from this text that the leaders act as they do because they are agents of Satan playing a role in a clash of kingdoms.

While this emphasis on the clash of kingdoms proceeds throughout the exegesis, Boring notes that the literary form of the passage closely matches that of haggadic tales of arguing rabbis, giving it the character of a controversy story. He unites this observation with the parallel between Jesus and Israel wandering in the desert and states in his analysis of 4:2 that: "The whole story can be seen as a typological haggadic story reflecting on Deut 8:2-3 (Jesus quotes exclusively from Deuteronomy). In contrast to Israel in the wilderness, whose faith wavered until it was restored by the miraculous manna, Jesus is hungry but remains faithful without a miracle."[21] Boring never again addresses the typological character of the story; it has served its function at this verse.

After the exegetical portion, Boring presents *Reflections* that link the exegesis with modern issues of interpretation for teaching and preaching. Here he addresses the key issue of how the story should be interpreted; he presents three ways: (1) a psychological/biological interpretation where Jesus wrestles with his calling; (2) an ethical interpretation; and (3) a

---

[19] Ibid.

[20] Eugene Boring, "Matthew," in *The New Interpreter's Bible: Matthew-Mark*, ed. Leander E. Keck, vol. 8 (Nashville, TN: Abingdon, 1995), 162. Emphasis in the original.

[21] Ibid., 163.

christological interpretation looking not at how Jesus saw himself but how Matthew, his community, and we see Jesus. He rejects the first quickly as contrary to the gospel genre, and dismisses the second just as quickly, noting that the things Satan tempts Jesus to do were good, not evil. He clearly lands on the third, presenting this episode as an example of a kenotic or self-emptying Christology in Matthew. As a result, the meaning of the text for moderns is limited:

> Thus we do not have in this pericope an example of a Jesus who "could have" worked miracles but chose not to do so as an ethical example for the rest of us. So understood, the text is of little help to us mortals who do not have the miraculous option. The same is true when the tempter reappears at the cross (27:40-44). To the extent that Jesus' temptation serves as a model for Christians, it might teach us that to be a "child of God" (a Matthean designation for Christians; see 5:9; cf. 28:10) means to have a trusting relationship to God that does not ask for miraculous exceptions to the limitations of an authentic Christian life.[22]

At the end of the day, then, Boring sees the text presenting a kenotic Christianity that underscores an apocalyptic drama that will run throughout the rest of the book. The Jewish leaders functioning as demonic agents will again test Jesus as their leader did but will be repulsed. The narrative of the testing as such offers no practical guidance beyond a general trust in God that does not seek the miraculous.

Ælfric's Interpretation

The Homily Proper

Ælfric offers a three-part interpretation of Matthew 4:1-11. He begins with an initial translation (lines 8–26) that leads into a verse-by-verse exposition (lines 27–137). Then he moves to a two-part section that approaches temptation more thematically, first looking at the spiritual and psychological dimensions, then locating the role of temptation within salvation history. Finally, he offers an introduction to the theology and practices of the liturgical season of Lent. The overarching theme of this

----

[22] Ibid., 166.

interpretation is that Christ is the exemplary contemplative who over-comes the devil through the practice of virtue and the correct deployment of Scripture; following in his footsteps, Christians also have the tools to overcome temptation and emulate the virtues of Christ.

The verse-by-verse exposition begins with an initial theological question: "Now every one wonders how the devil dares to approach the Savior that he might tempt him," providing the opportunity for a theological answer: "The Savior came to mankind so that he would overcome all of our temptations with his temptation and overcome our eternal death with his temporary death."[23] Redemption is the answer, and setting this question and answer at the head of the exposition puts everything that follows in the light of redemption.

Ælfric further unpacks the nature of the redemption, how our temptations were overcome, by summary statements that bracket the whole of this interpretive section. He begins this section by stating: "Now [the Savior] was so humble that he tolerated the devil to test him, and he permitted vile men to slay him."[24] The concluding statement of the exegetical section is longer and clarifies that the redemptive nature of the temptation was not just Christ's victory but also his example in the face of temptation:

> Great was our Savior's humility and his endurance in this deed. He could, with one word, have sunk the devil into the deep abyss but he did not display his might. Rather, he answered the devil with the Holy Scriptures and gave us an example with his endurance that, as often as we suffer anything from depraved men, we should turn our mind to God's teaching rather than to any revenge.[25]

Again, humility (*eaðmodnysse*) is the key virtue emphasized. Using the term "humility" in these bracketing summary statements is no accident. It places Ælfric's moral vision squarely within the monastic tradition;

---

[23] The Old English text and line-numbering is from *Ælfric's Catholic Homilies: The First Series, Text*, ed. Peter Clemoes, Early English Text Society, supplementary series 17 (Oxford: Oxford University Press, 1997), lines 28–32, pp. 266–74. Hereafter ÆCHom I, 11.

[24] ÆCHom I, 11, lines 32–34.

[25] ÆCHom I, 11, lines 132–38.

Benedict devotes the longest chapter of the Rule (RB 7) to a discussion of the twelve steps of humility that include all other virtues ending ultimately at the perfect love of God. Ælfric is constructing Christ as the perfect moral being as defined by his monastic tradition.

An explanatory frame further clarifies Ælfric's intention. The devil is presented as being confused as to who and what Jesus is precisely because of his virtue:

> The devil was in great doubt as to what Christ was; his life was not arranged as the lives of other men. Christ did not eat with gluttony, nor did he drink to excess, nor did his eyes go wandering aimlessly for lusts, so that the devil pondered what he was—whether he was God's son who was promised to mankind. Then he said in his thoughts that he would test what he was.[26]

Jesus' moral nature is established by identifying a set of vices in which he did not participate—vices that will be revisited later in the homily: gluttony, drunkenness, and lust. We are to understand these specific vices as functioning as a shorthand reference for all the vices. His outward purity is specifically what attracts the devil to him.

The first temptation for Ælfric has nothing to do with either power or a messianic sign. He interprets the reaction of Jesus as being purely contrarian: "Easily could the God who turned water to wine and who worked all creation from nothing—easily could he have turned the stones to bread, but he would not do anything at the devil's direction."[27] Jesus' scriptural rebuke is glossed as describing parallel sources of sustenance: just as bread feeds the body, so "God's teaching which he set down through wise men in books"[28] feeds the soul, making it "strong and ardent for God's will."[29] For Ælfric, then, the indeterminate "everything that proceeds out of the mouth of the Lord" of Deuteronomy 8:3 refers specifically to the words of Scripture. The invigorating power attributed to Scripture here further interprets Jesus' citation of Scripture in the following verses.

---

[26] ÆCHom I, 11, lines 37–42.
[27] ÆCHom I, 11, lines 49–50.
[28] ÆCHom I, 11, lines 53–54.
[29] ÆCHom I, 11, line 57.

The second temptation concerns ostentatious miracles. Again, Ælfric takes pains—as with the previous temptation—to stress that Christ could have performed the wonder. Rather, he consciously chose not to give the devil the satisfaction of doing so. Specifically, Ælfric connects this temptation with pride in a form particularly significant within Anglo-Saxon culture—the boast (*gilp*):

> That would be an exceedingly boastful [*gilplic*] deed if Christ would shoot down (though he easily could without harm—the limbs that bent the arch of the high heavens would not break) but he would not do anything for a boast [*gylpe*] for boasting [*gilp*] is a mortal sin. Therefore he would not shoot down because he rejected boasting [*gilp*]. But he said, "Man shall not test his Lord." The man tests his Lord when he trusts with foolishness and with boasts [*gilpe*] that a certain wonderful thing will be done in God's name or when he would command a certain wonder from God foolishly and without need.[30]

Ælfric counters the machismo of Germanic warrior culture with another appeal to humility.[31] At the same time, however, he issues a subtle rebuke to a danger more common within the monastery than the feasting hall; in a time when hagiography was replete with saints asking and receiving miracles of all sorts, Ælfric warns against commanding miracles from God—the kind of spiritual pride more tempting to monks than beer-hall boasting.

Ælfric spends more time on the verse the devil delivers than on Christ's countercitation. Regarding Satan's citation of Psalm 90 (Vulgate), Ælfric argues that it willfully misinterprets the verse: "Here the devil began to quote

---

[30] ÆCHom I, 11, lines 76–84.

[31] The poem *Vainglory* from the Exeter book provides a fascinating parallel to this section. The poem is a paranetic work based on the introduction to the *Rule of Chrodegang* where the poet describes a drunken boasting warrior, shows him growing in vice through his boasts, draws a comparison with Satan and the demonic horde who foolishly assaulted heaven due to their pride, and the boaster is referred to as "the devil's son" (*feond bearn*). This figure is contrasted by the man who loves humility (*eaðmod leofað*) and who receives the title of "God's own son" (*godes agen bearn*). For more on boasting as it appears throughout Norse and Germanic literature, see Carol J. Clover, "The Germanic Context of the Unferþ Episode," *Speculum* 55 (1980): 444–68; reprinted in *The Beowulf Reader* (New York: Garland, 2000).

Holy Scripture, but he lied in their exposition because he is a liar and no truthfulness is in him for he is the father of all lying. This [passage] was not written concerning Christ—as he had said—but is written concerning holy men."[32] Ælfric simultaneously identifies the devil's exegetical error and uses the correct interpretation to link this passage with the common Christian experience of temptation. Taking "strike your foot against a stone" morally, he parallels the testing of Christians with that of Jesus; God permits their testing as he did Jesus' but, recognizing their weakness, God sends angels to assist mortals—Jesus has no need of them.

> [Holy men] need the help of angels in this life so that the devil might not tempt them as severely as he could. So faithful is God to mankind that he has set his angels as guardians over us that they should not permit the cruel devils to destroy us. They may test us, but they may not compel us to do any evil except what we do of our own will through the evil incitement of these devils. We will not be perfected unless we are tested; through the testing we may grow if we continually renounce the devil and all his teaching, if we approach our Lord with faith and love and good works, and—if anywhere we should slip—immediately we rise again and eagerly amend what was broken.[33]

Thus at the center of the temptation narrative, Ælfric uses the very text that the devil cites as an opportunity to connect the temptations of Jesus to universal temptation and to assure those reading or hearing that God assists them with angelic help. Temptation is for the sake of progress in the spiritual life. Demonic forces can only tempt—not compel. This perspective is thoroughly monastic; several passages in the Rule and in Cassian's *Conferences* allude to the importance of testing and humility with it. Even if the saints are overcome by temptation, repentance is the road back.

The third temptation falls into two parts: an explanation of the devil's claim, and an exposition on worshipping God alone. The first begins by characterizing Satan. Just as Jesus has been identified with a primary characteristic, humility, and therefore with its attendant virtues, the devil's primary characteristic is identified as presumptuousness with its attendant vices. This was what got him kicked out of heaven and would spell

---

[32] ÆCHom I, 11, lines 62–65.
[33] ÆCHom I, 11, lines 65–75.

his ultimate demise through Christ's passion. Ælfric explains that "he thought that he owned all earth because no man could stand against him before Christ came who conquered him."[34] He notes that Scripture records God's possession of all creation in Psalm 23:1 (Vulgate) and that all creation clearly worships him except for evil men—those who exhibit lives of vice rather than virtue—and who thereby reject their creator.

Ælfric appeals to the Old Testament with its repeated prohibitions of idolatry but once again ties God's worthiness for worship to his status as Creator: "It is written in the old law that no man shall pray to any devil-idol nor to anything except God alone because no created thing is worthy of this dignity, but rather the One alone who created all things."[35] He goes on to explain that saints are not worshiped; rather, "We ask intercessions from holy men that they should intercede for us to their Lord and to our Lord. We do not pray, however, to them just as we do to God. They will not permit it."[36] This is grounded by the angel's rejection of John's worship in Revelation 22:8-9.

After his commentary, Ælfric turns to a two-part section that examines the mechanisms of demonic temptation. The first part examines the mental and psychological means by which it occurs and examines how it failed in this particular scenario; the second part reveals the meaning of this episode in the scope of salvation history. The two parts are related to one another primarily by topic and schematization, but the language of the first appears in the second, showing how these mechanisms were operative in practice.

The first examines the psychology of temptation. Following the idea that devils cannot compel evil deeds, Ælfric presents a three-step process (basically paraphrasing Jas 1:12-15) that explains how compulsion occurs. The devil entices his victim; the victim then desires the evil. Sin occurs when the victim then consents to what his mind desires. Thus, what is external (the enticement) is met by an internal movement (desire, which is original sin);[37] then consent may occur. Ælfric explains that in the case

---

[34] ÆCHom I, 11, lines 94–95.

[35] ÆCHom I, 11, lines 116–19.

[36] ÆCHom I, 11, lines 120–23.

[37] See ÆCHom I, 11, lines 143–45. "Often man's mind will be inclined to this desire—and sometimes it will fall into consent because we are born of sinful flesh."

of Christ, the temptations failed because "The Savior was not tempted in this way because he was born without sin from a maiden and had nothing perverse within him."[38] Because of the fact of the incarnation, Christ had no desire to sin that could be awakened by diabolic enticement and therefore did not consent nor fall into sin.

The second section presents a reading that could be dismissed as typological but, in fact, reveals not simply typology but narrative reversal. Returning to Genesis, Ælfric states that the devil tempted Adam with three temptations:

> Through gluttony, [Adam] was overcome when he ate the forbidden apple through the devil's teaching. Through vainglory, he was overcome when he believed the devil's words that "You will be as excellent as the angels if you eat of this tree" and they believed his lies and, with idle boasts, wished to be better than how they were created—but became worse. With greediness, he was overcome when the devil said to him: "You will have knowledge of both good and evil"—for greediness is not only for wealth but is also in the desire for greater dignity.[39]

The garden narrative is reordered for the sake of putting these three temptations in the order in which the devil deployed them in the encounter with Jesus in the wilderness. The temptation of Jesus presents him overturning the original Fall by resisting these three primal temptations: the bread temptation is gluttony; the temple, vainglory; the temptation of the riches of the nations is greed. Thus, Ælfric once again returns to the notion of redemption by exposing the scope of the victory. This story is not simply about Jesus besting the devil; it is a story about the new Adam resisting and overcoming both the temptations and the tempter who felled the first Adam.

The final portion of the homily connects this text to the liturgical observance of Lent. The ostensible point of connection is with the time span; Ælfric begins by noting that Christ fasted for forty days and nights—a superhuman achievement only possible through "the great might of his divinity through which he might have lived his whole life

---

[38] ÆCHom I, 11, lines 145–47.
[39] ÆCHom I, 11, lines 157–65.

without earthly food had he wished it."[40] This is contrasted with Moses and Elijah who accomplished the same feat only through the miraculous intervention of God.

Then Ælfric moves to contemporary practice of his hearers: the forty-day fast of Lent in imitation of Christ. He is not content with explaining the period by appealing to the length of the temptation, rather, he connects it back to the Levitical law of tithing:

> Why is this fast calculated as forty days? A whole year has three hundred and sixty-five days. Then, if we take a tenth of the year's days, then there are thirty-six tithe days and from this day until Holy Easter there are forty-two days. Taking then the six Sundays away from the total,[41] there are thirty-six of the year's tithe days for us to observe with restraint. Just as God's Law commands that we should pay a tenth of all things from our year's toil to God, so we should also in these tithing-days tithe our bodies with restraint to the praise of God.[42]

This interpretation seems to move his discussion away from the gospel pericope; the return is implicit in the following discussion of the nature of a true fast:

> Put away all strife and all quarreling and keep this time with peace and with true love for no fast is acceptable to God unless you reconcile and do just as God teaches. Break your loaf and give the other portion to hungry men. Lead into your house the destitute and poor and foreigners, and cheer them with your goods. When you see the naked, clothe them and do not overlook your own flesh. The man who fasts without almsgiving—he is sparing in his meat but afterwards eats what he previously set aside with restraint—this fast mocks God. If you wish your fast to be acceptable to God then help

---

[40] ÆCHom I, 11, lines 178–80.

[41] Sundays are subtracted from the length of the fast because according to Christian practice from the earliest days, no Sunday could be a fast day. See in reference to this Canon 20 of the First Council of Nicaea. (Cassian mentions this indirectly in *Conferences* 21.11.)

[42] ÆCHom I, 11, lines 189–99.

poor men with the portion which you withhold from yourself—and with more also if it is possible.[43]

This explanation, thick with biblical quotations and allusions, is strongly reminiscent of Benedict's description of the Tools of Good Works, listed exhaustively in RB 4. Ælfric makes clear—following monastic tradition— that fasting is not fundamentally about self-denial but rather is a pathway for cultivating the virtues in direct action on behalf of the poor and needy.

Ælfric concludes both this section and his homily with a warning for those who fast for the sake of spiritual pride:

> And so that we may do well, let us do this without boasts and idle praise. The man who does good in order to boast praises himself, he does not receive any reward from God, but rather receives his punishment. But let us do just as God teaches so that our good works might be known by wise men, that they may see our goodness and that they may marvel and praise our heavenly Father, God Almighty, who rewards us with a hundredfold what we do for poor men for love of him who lives and reigns without end. Amen.[44]

Again, a cluster of biblical images[45] concludes the homily, giving a strong warning against spiritual self-seeking. Fasting and good works are done for the worship and praise of God—for the glorification of God, not self. What of boasting? It is excluded.

While Ælfric's work falls into clearly discernable sections, common themes and common language hold it together. The central theme is the struggle of virtue and vice and Christ's pattern of virtue as the chief exemplar of the Christian life. The temptation narrative is described as a victory of virtue over vice. In the same way the season of Lent is specifically identified as a time to set aside dissolute and inattentive living for the sake of cultivating virtue through good works performed on behalf of the poor for the glorification of God.

In terms of language, two key terms stitch the sections together. The first highlights the theme of redemption as it runs throughout the explication:

---

[43] ÆCHom I, 11, lines 203–13.
[44] ÆCHom I, 11, lines 220–27.
[45] Primarily Matthean images, weaving together Matt 6:1, 5:16, 13:8.

overcoming (*oferswiðan*). The term appears twice in Ælfric's initial summary of the events, at the conclusions of the explications of the first two temptations, and throughout the narrative reversal section—the devil overcomes Adam three times, then Christ overcomes the devil three times as well.

The second repeated term is a little more unusual. It is a vice that Ælfric constantly cautions against: boasting, arrogance, or pride (*gielp*). It occurs in the exegetical section primarily in the discussion of the second temptation but reappears in Adam's temptation to pride and again at the end as the vice that can render fasting invalid or even harmful to the soul. Its constant repetition seems to identify it as a particularly pernicious sin whose remedy is none other than the chief characteristic attributed to Christ—humility.

The Liturgical Context

The chief factor that determines Ælfric's interpretation of this text is its lectionary setting. Matthew 4:1-11 only appears in Ælfric's lectionary on this occasion, and no other text is ever substituted for it; Matthew's temptation narrative is unique to the First Sunday in Lent.[46] As a result, it is inextricably bound with the meaning and the practices of Lent in the early medieval mind. The third section of Ælfric's homily, in fact, flows from this close connection. A discussion of the practices of Lent is an explanation of the passage's practical meaning since the text is inseparable from the season.

The gospel lectionary is not the only cycle of readings that has had a major effect on Ælfric's interpretation of the passage. Equally important is Paul the Deacon's homiliary that appointed Gregory the Great's Homily 14 as the reading for the third nocturn of the Night Office.[47] As Godden's magisterial source commentary amply demonstrates,[48] most of Ælfric's second and third sections are adaptations of Gregory. Ælfric shortens

[46] Luke's parallel does not appear in the lectionary, nor does Mark's verse-long version.

[47] This is numbered as Homily 16 in Migne's *Patrologia Latina*. See p. 64 in chap. 1 on the numbering discrepancies. Gregory's text appears as number 76 in Smetna's list of Paul's original homiliary; it is number 64 in Migne's version.

[48] Malcolm Godden, *Ælfric's Catholic Homilies: Introduction, Commentary and Glossary*, Early English Text Society, supplementary series, 18 (Oxford: Oxford University Press, 2000), 84–94.

Gregory's text, often removing redundant explanations,[49] but largely follows the points that Gregory makes. What Godden does not make clear is that Gregory's text in the portion represented by Ælfric's second section is itself a paraphrase and adaptation of John Cassian's *Conferences* 5.6. While drawing on Gregory directly, Ælfric is remaining securely within the main channels of monastic interpretation of this text.

Ælfric's major change to the shape of Gregory's homily is the introduction of an exegetical section. Gregory's homily on Matthew 4:1-11 is anomalous in this regard; where he usually presents a line-by-line exegesis of the text, this homily is largely thematic. Thus, Ælfric turns to the liturgical homiliaries of Hericus and Haymo for needed amplification and brings in his own material as well.[50]

Three major features of the liturgies appointed for the First Sunday in Lent help contextualize Ælfric's sermon. The first is the dominance of Psalm 90 (Vulgate) within the Propers of the Mass of the Day and its reappearance within the Office materials during Lent. The second is the liturgical placement and interpretation of Adam's Fall in Genesis. The third is the use of the epistle within the Little Hours as a means to stitch together the cycles of Mass and Office and to emphasize the theological point found by medieval liturgists within the epistle.

The sung Propers for the Mass of the Day for the First Sunday in Lent exhibit two unusual characteristics: they all come from a single source, Psalm 90 (Vulgate), and they contain an abnormally long tract, among the longest in the whole gradual.[51] The marginal notes of the Leofric Missal that identify the portions of the Mass not included in the text of the book give neumed incipits—the opening words of the Propers with the

---

[49] For instance, Gregory has several explanations for the number forty—including multiplying the four elements by the Ten Commandments—that Ælfric does not include.

[50] Haymo's Hom. 28 is itself a reworking of Gregory's text.

[51] This statement is certainly true for the Tridentine Gradual and, as noted in chap. 2, although no gradual survives from Anglo-Saxon England, the evidence that does survive and the conservative character of the gradual through time—Vogel calls the Roman Antiphonary "exceptionally stable" (Cyrille Vogel, *Medieval Liturgy: An Introduction to the Sources*, trans. and rev. William Storey and Niels Rasmussen [Portland, OR: Pastoral, 1986], 358) make it likely that this was the case then as well.

notes that begin each melody.[52] The introit antiphon and psalm verse link the last (vv. 15-16) and first verses of the psalm:

> **Ant:** He called upon me and I will hear him, I will deliver him and glorify him. I will fill him with length of days.
> **Ps:** He who dwells in the help of the Most High will remain in the protection of the God of heaven. Glory be . . .
> **Ant:** He called upon me . . .[53]

The gradual that comes between the epistle and the tract contains the very words quoted by the devil to Jesus from verses 11-12:

> **R:** God commanded his angels concerning you, that they will guard you in all of your ways. **V:** In their hands they will bear you, lest you strike your foot against a stone.

This is followed by the massive tract. This tract, which immediately precedes the reading of the gospel, contains virtually all of Psalm 90 (Vulgate), lacking only verses 8-10. The Offertory and the Communion are identical but for a single word: "[The Lord/He] will overshadow you with his wings and you shall trust under his pinions; his truth will encircle you like a shield."[54]

The liturgy makes one major change from the scriptural text—in a number of places it puts into the perfect tense verbs that appear in the psalm as future. Exactly where, how, and why this happens is unclear; the critical apparatus to the psalm notes that while most texts followed the Greek with a future, some manuscripts used the perfect; whether this reflects the liturgy utilizing or affecting the textual tradition is unclear. In any case, the marginal notes of the Leofric Missal contain three shifts from future to perfect: *Invocabit* to *Invocavit* in the introit antiphon and

---

[52] The neumed incipits give the first notes and the first words, assuming that the monks had memorized the full tune and its words.

[53] While the Leofric Missal only contains the incipits: "A. Inuocauit me/PS. Qui habitat" (Nicholas Orchard, ed., *The Leofric Missal*, 2 vols., Henry Bradshaw Society 113 and 114 [Rochester, NY: Boydell, 2002], 129, Item 516), the stability of the antiphonary is confirmed by the correspondence of both the Sarum Missal and the Tridentine Missal in containing the same versions of the referenced verses.

[54] The version of the text in the Communion lacks "Dominus."

tract, *liberabit* to *liberavit* in the tract, and *Scuto circumdabit* to *Scuto circumdedit*. This grammatical shift requires a reassessment of the psalm's meaning. Singing the psalm as written in the future tense would suggest that the primary referent of the "you" in the psalm would be the individual singing it as the saving acts of God described are promised events that would occur in the future. The shift to the past tense does not preclude this possibility and introduces the possibility that Jesus undergoing the temptation may also be the referent. Understood in this fashion, the tense change represents the deliberate introduction of an ambiguity into the psalm's text to expand its exegetical scope.

Similarly, the excision of three verses from the middle of the psalm in the tract renders it both closer to the gospel narrative and simultaneously more reflective of the monastic spiritual experience as described in Ælfric's sermon. The verses removed have a triumphalist tone that assure the ones singing them that "truly your eyes will consider and you will see the retribution of the sinners" (VgPs 90:8) and also that "no evil will approach you" (VgPs 90:10a). Indeed, the last must be repudiated as the gospel narrative directly contradicts it, describing the devil himself approaching Jesus! With these verses removed, the tract portrays the psalm as a strong promise of God's support and comfort, but it no longer promises complete security from evil.

When the entirety of this psalm is thus placed in juxtaposition with the gospel, a number of details from the psalm take on a whole new specificity. Not only is the psalm about the protection that God offers the community in its temptations, but suddenly the "daemonio meridiano" of Psalm 90:6 (Vulgate) is not just any noonday devil but the devil himself; the menagerie of verse 13 are not just the fierce and venomous—they are the downright demonic—especially when cross-referenced with 1 Peter 5:8,[55] Revelation 12:9, and Genesis 3.

This psalm does not, however, only appear in the Mass Propers. Key verses appear in key places in the Office and become seasonal texts, repeated daily through Lent until Passiontide. The Portiforium of St. Wul-

---

[55] This connection between the lion and the devil would be a quite natural one as these two texts are daily juxtaposed in Compline—the 1 Pet verse is the little chapter of the ante-office and VgPs 90 is one of the fixed psalms.

stan has a familiar set of verses as the three versicles and responses that
conclude the psalms of the three nocturns of the Night Office:

> **V.** He has overshadowed[56] you with his wings. **R.** And you shall trust
> under his pinions.
> **V.** His truth will encircle you as a shield. **R.** You will not fear the
> terror of the night.
> **V.** In their hands they will carry you. **R.** Lest you strike your foot
> against a stone.[57]

From this point forward, the first versicle and response become the daily
versicle and response that opens the Office of Lauds; the protection promised by this psalm becomes a daily reminder throughout Lent. Similarly,
the set versicle and response after the hymn each Vespers are the very
words quoted by the devil: "**V.** He has commanded his angels concerning
you. **R.** To keep you in all of your ways."[58] The words intended as a temptation in Matthew now function as a reminder to the community of divine
assistance during their Lenten temptations.

Thus, when Ælfric explains how Satan has misused Scripture, the correct reading of the psalm is derived directly from the liturgy. He refers
to it when he states, "This was not written concerning Christ—as he had
said—but is written concerning holy men."[59] Monastics following the
Rule would have had an intimate familiarity with this psalm, since it was
one of the three invariable psalms used daily at Compline.[60] Furthermore,
its use and repetition at key points throughout Lent would have further
cemented its application to the gathered worshipping community.

Turning to the biblical lectionary for the Night Office, Ælfric's second
section that parallels the temptation of Adam with that of Christ would
have found fruitful ground in the soil of his monastic hearers. According
to the schedule that he presents in the *LME* (and following the older

---

[56] Note the shift from future to perfect again.

[57] Anselm Hughes, *The Portiforium of Saint Wulstan*, Corpus Christi College
Cambridge MS. 391, Henry Bradshaw Society 89 (London: Henry Bradshaw Society,
1958), 27, 28. Items 443–45, 465.

[58] Ibid., 27, 28, 29. Item 439.

[59] ÆCHom I, 11, lines 64–65.

[60] See RB 18.19.

tradition of *OR* XIII),[61] the monks would have begun reading Genesis just three Sundays before at Septuagesima;[62] the temptation narrative would have remained fresh in their minds.

Furthermore, the responsories of Sexagesima place a spin on the Adam and Eve narrative that underscore Ælfric's fundamentally monastic reading of this text. As Genesis was read, a set of responsories was repeated throughout the week of Sexagesima that interpreted the events of the creation and fall of humanity. Responsories for nonsanctoral liturgical occasions were almost invariably direct Scripture citations. The selection and repetition of certain passages would then frame the narrative, providing the monastic hearer with a premade set of biblical lenses through which to view the biblical narrative. A representative set[63] of ten responsories for Sexagesima contain four that conflate the creation of the cosmos with the creation of Adam and describe God placing Adam in the garden.[64] The next two introduce the need for Eve—based in finding a companion for Adam—and her creation from Adam.[65] The Fall story itself is entirely absent from the responsory texts: there is no serpent, Eve never appears as a character, fruit never appears to be plucked or eaten. Instead, the liturgy moves directly to three responsories that describe the aftermath of the Fall. The first describes Adam hiding himself from God.[66] The second describes God's curse of humanity and contains the only nonbiblical interpolation within this set:

[61] On the nature and relationship of these two biblical lectionaries for the Night Office see chap. 2.

[62] Christopher A. Jones, *Ælfric's Letter to the Monks at Eynsham* (Cambridge: Cambridge University Press, 1998), 145. *LME* 70: "in Septuagesima we should read Genesis until mid-Lent" (Exodus begins at mid-Lent). See *OR* XIIIa.1: "In the beginning of Septuagesima they place the Heptateuch until the fourteenth day before Easter."

[63] Since no antiphoners for the Night Office survive from Anglo-Saxon England, we must rely on other representative books from a similar time and milieu. St. Gallen, Stiftsbibliothek, Cod. Sang. 390 is exactly contemporary with Ælfric, having been written between 990 and 1000 and intended for a Benedictine monastery like Ælfric's. Also, its contents match the incipit cues to the required responsories in the *LME*.

[64] René-Jean Hesbert, *Corpus Antiphonalium Officii* (henceforth *CAO*). 6 vols. (Rome: Herder, 1963ff.), 6925, 6928, 6739, and 7798.

[65] *CAO* 6473 and 6883.

[66] *CAO* 6537.

In sudore vultus (CAO 6937)
R. "In the sweat of your brow you will feed on your bread," said the Lord to Adam. "When you work the ground it will not give you its fruits, but it will grow spines and thorns for you."
V. "Because you obeyed the voice of your wife more than mine, cursed be the earth regarding your works. It will grow . . ."[67]

A pastiche of Genesis 3:19, 18, and 17, it introduces the idea that the Fall was fundamentally about obedience and whom Adam obeyed. Note what the responsory does and does not say: it does not blame Eve for the Fall. Nor does it blame the serpent or Satan. Instead, the fault is clearly located with Adam. Adam chose disobedience. This understanding—that disobedience is the root of the Fall—is a consistent theme throughout Ælfric's writings[68] and has a tremendous impact on his thought and his construction of Christ as the New Adam.

The epistle, 2 Corinthians 6:3-7, plays a role beyond its use at Mass. While it is read in its entirety only at Mass, it enters into the fabric of the Office as well, and the Office's selection of verses from it help focus exegetical attention on a certain set of Paul's sufferings that become programmatic Lenten disciplines. Godden notes one point in particular[69] where Ælfric draws in 2 Corinthians 6:3-7, but this is the only overt appearance the passage makes in the homily. In the liturgy, however, it appears as the little chapters for Vespers I,[70] Terce,[71] Sext,[72] and therefore at Terce and

---

[67] *CAO* 6937.

[68] A clear example is his explanation of the Fall in Homily *De initio creaturae*, in *Ælfric's Catholic Homilies: The First Series, Text*, ed. Peter Clemoes, Early English Text Society, supplementary series 17 (Oxford: Oxford University Press, 1997), lines 155–59 (hereafter ÆCHom I, 1). "[The Fall] was not fated by God nor were [the first parents] forced to break God's command but God gave them freedom and gave them their own choice so they could be obedient [*gehyrsum*] or disobedient [*ungehyrsum*]—but they were obedient [*gehyrsum*] to the Devil and disobedient [*ungehyrsum*] to God. They entrusted themselves and all humanity after this life to hell-dwellers and the Devil who led them astray."

[69] This appears at ÆCHom I, 11 lines 200–202: "after the apostle's teaching in great patience and in holy vigils, in fasting, in chastity of mind and body."

[70] 2 Cor 6:1-2a; Hughes, *Portiforium*, 27. Item 436.

[71] 2 Cor 6:2b-3; Ibid. Item 454.

[72] 2 Cor 6:4; Ibid. Item 457.

Sext through the week. It appears in versicles for Vespers I,[73] and the antiphon for Prime.[74] Again, three of the common responsories adapted passages from the epistle. The first combines verses 2b, 4b, 5b, and 7b:

> *Ecce nunc tempus acceptabile* (*CAO* 6600)
> **R.** Behold, now is the acceptable time; behold, now is the day of salvation. Let us commend ourselves with much patience, with many fasts, through the weapons of righteousness of the power of God.
> **V.** In all things let us present ourselves as servants of God that our ministry may not be slandered. Through the weapons of righteousness of the power of God.[75]

The second utilizes verses 4a, 3b, 2b, and 3a:

> *In omnibus exhibeamus* (*CAO* 6920)
> **R.** In all things let us present ourselves as servants of God with much patience that our ministry may not be slandered.
> **V.** Behold, now is the acceptable time; behold, now is the day of salvation. Giving no one any offense. That our ministry may not be slandered.[76]

The last incorporates verses 2b and 3a:

> *Paradisi portas aperuit* (*CAO* 7348)
> **R.** The time of our fasting opened the gates of heaven; let us receive them, praying and supplicating, that on the day of resurrection we might rejoice with the Lord.
> **V.** Behold, now is the acceptable time; behold, now is the day of salvation. Giving no one any offense. That on the day of resurrection we might rejoice with the Lord.[77]

When the Genesis connection is read christologically, Genesis 3:15 in particular stands out, referring back again to a physical overcoming of Satan that illuminates the language of *scuto*—"shield"—in Psalm 90:5 (Vulgate) which, in correspondence with the idea of *sagitta* (arrows) in the following

---

[73] 2 Cor 6:6b; Ibid. Item 437.
[74] 2 Cor 6:7; Ibid. Item 453.
[75] *CAO* 6600.
[76] *CAO* 6920.
[77] *CAO* 7348.

verse, conjures up both Ephesians 6:11-18 (especially v. 16) and 2 Corinthians 6:7. The 2 Corinthians passage, in turn, is reconceptualized not as a description of the hardships that Paul and his companions suffered for the sake of the Corinthians to establish the trustworthiness of their mission against other traveling missionaries and preachers. Rather, the list of hardships are not literal hardships but ascetic practices to be undertaken at this specific time—preeminent among them "much patience . . . in vigils and fastings," practices that are themselves the "arms of righteousness" used to conquer the devil, his minions, and their temptations.

Indeed, following this logic, connecting the first of the three responsories above with a passage from the third section of Ælfric's homily is most instructive. Responsory *CAO* 6600 shares more than a passing resemblance to lines 196–201:

> Just as God's law commands that we should give a tenth of all things from our year's toiling to God, so we should also in these tithing-days tithe our bodies with restraint to the praise of God. We should prepare ourselves in all things just as God's thanes after the apostle's teaching in great patience and in holy vigils, in fasting, in chastity of mind and body . . .[78]

Ælfric, like the responsory, begins with a discussion of time. He then transitions to the necessary preparations of ascetical activity, reminding his hearers that they should be God's thanes. Within Anglo-Saxon religious discourse, "thanes" typically refers to apostles—the Twelve—but is borrowed from secular language in which a lord's thanes were his retainers, usually armed retainers who followed him into battle.[79] From that point, Ælfric continues with the 2 Corinthians passage into a discussion of chastity. While Ælfric may or may not be consciously quoting the responsory, there is no doubt that a common interpretive method lies behind both.[80]

The liturgy simultaneously grounds and transmits this interpretive method. The major themes of the foregoing discussion are neatly

---

[78] ÆCHom I, 1 lines 197–201.

[79] See, for example, the twenty-seven references to *þegn, -as* in Mitchell and Robinson's edition of *Beowulf*.

[80] It is both interesting and suggestive—but again not conclusive—that a few lines later Ælfric quotes Isa 58:7 which is also used on this occasion as the responsory *Frange esurienti panem tuum* (*CAO* 6744).

summarized in a single liturgical text, the episcopal benediction that ends the Mass set for Lent 1 in the Leofric Missal:

> May the Omnipotent God bless you (pl.), he who consecrated for the fast the number forty through Moses and Elijah and likewise our mediator [Christ], and grant you (pl.) accordingly to steward this present life like the denarius received from the master of the household as a reward,[81] traversing through to the forgiveness of all sins and to the glorious resurrection with all of the saints. Amen.
>
> And may he give you (pl.) the spiritual power of the invincible weapons—which is the example of the Lord—that you may mightily subdue the exceedingly keen[82] temptations of the ancient enemy. Amen.
>
> In regard to him in whom a man may not live on bread alone, but in all the words that proceed from his mouth receive spiritual food, through the observation of this fast and the example of other good works, may we be worthy to attain to the imperishable crown of glory. Amen.[83]

This concluding prayer brings together at least three themes in play between the liturgy and Ælfric's homily: 1) the numerology of the Lenten time span is both literal and typological, echoing the fasts of Moses and Elijah, and consummated in Jesus; 2) in a resounding echo of RB 49.1,[84] the Christian life and hope of salvation is connected with the behavior consistent with a holy Lent; 3) the spiritual weapons of 2 Corinthians 6:7 are interpreted in light of this gospel text and conflated with the imitation of Christ.

Thus, with these liturgical connections between the appointed psalm, epistle, and gospel in mind, Ælfric's third section on the time and ascetical practices of Lent appear much more thematically and exegetically linked to his first two sections. It is not simply an add-on that gives information

---

[81] The reference is to Matt 20:1-16, the parable of the workmen in the vineyard, which was unanimously connected to Septuagesima, the solemnity three weeks earlier that began the pre-Lenten period.

[82] Again, the root of "most keen" (*sagacissima*) is virtually a homonym with "arrows" (*sagitta*), invoking VgPs 90:6 and Eph 6:16.

[83] Orchard, *Leofric Missal*, 130, Item 522.

[84] "The life of a monk ought to be a continuous Lent."

about the liturgical season getting underway; it also presents the practices that allow the community to directly participate in Christ's conquest of the devil through his temptations by linking their common temptations to Christ's.

Discussion

One of the strategies common to both moderns and medievals for making sense of this narrative was casting it in relation to an Old Testament narrative. The response to the mythological is an appeal to the typological. It is interesting, however, that they choose different directions in which to head. While Ælfric sees the narrative as a reversal of the Fall in the Garden of Eden, the modern interpreters identify the temptation narrative as a haggadic midrash on Deuteronomy 8:2-3 and suggest that it engages throughout the story of the Children of Israel after crossing the Red Sea. Luz brings up the notion among his list of possible meanings and chooses to leave all of the possible meanings in play while focusing on the christological meaning.[85] Boring is content to mention the term, "haggadic tale" but also focuses his exposition elsewhere.[86] Hare utilizes this notion broadly, but Davies and Allison provide the copious details that support the hypothesis.

Davies and Allison present an intriguing proposition: that Matthew has consciously modeled Jesus and his temptations as an antitype of Israel wandering in the desert after their escape through the Red Sea. The parallels certainly seem plausible, and the parallel between Israel, the disobedient son of God, and Jesus, the obedient Son of God, is elegant. Using Deuteronomy 8:2-3 as a hermeneutical key makes sense in drawing the key terms together—forty, wilderness, testing, hunger—and it works well as an explanation of the first temptation, when Jesus cites Deuteronomy 8:3b. It only works moderately well for the last, however, as there are a range of other Old Testament texts from which the admonition not to worship other gods could come. Finally, it fails to connect at all to the second temptation. Furthermore, if the parallel were to be exact, it is

[85] Luz, *Matthew 1–7*, 149–50.
[86] Boring, "Matthew," in Keck, 162, 163.

curious that Matthew chooses to have the temptations take place *after* the forty days fast rather during it—as Mark and Luke have it.

There are some very intriguing parallels that commend the connection of Matthew's temptation narrative with the account of Israel in the wilderness from Deuteronomy, but the comparison fails when we try to insist on a strict point-by-point comparison.[87] When taken from a more abstract level, and reading the temptation as Jesus' obedience as opposed to Israel's disobedience, it does make for a compelling parallel.

Ælfric's supposition, an ancient one that leads back from Gregory to John Cassian to Leo to Irenaeus's Adversus *Haereses* 5.21.2, is also mentioned by some of the modern interpreters. Luz cites it, noting that a number of modern authors (including Bultmann and Tuckett among others) have continued to champion this interpretation. Luz labels it the parenetic interpretation.[88] Without referring to Genesis, Boring mentions an interpretation that foregrounds vice and virtue, labeling it "the ethical interpretation" and damns it with faint praise, warning against a too-quick turn from the text to personal experience in a "quest for relevance."[89] Davies and Allison offer the unusual suggestion that Mark's temptation narrative did indeed proceed from a parallel with the Garden narrative, but that Q rejected that approach in favor of the wandering Children of Israel.[90] In an interesting twist, Davies and Allison do return to the notion of Jesus as New Adam during the discussion of the ministering of the angels to Jesus in verse 11 and explore pertinent parallels.[91] Hare, however, does not mention this possibility at all.

With Luz, it seems that a both/and approach would be more profitable than a strict either/or. That is, in the temptation narrative, we see Jesus facing the devil in a testing/tempting process that has strong parallels to several texts in the Hebrew Bible including the Fall and the wandering in the desert. Weaker parallels could be drawn to other narratives including David's temptation by his urges toward Bathsheba, and Israel's temptation

---

[87] In particular, Hare's attempt to fit the second temptation with the presence/absence of God comes across a bit strained; see Hare, *Matthew*, 24–25.

[88] Luz, *Matthew 1–7*, 149.

[89] Boring, "Matthew," in Keck, 165.

[90] Davies and Allison, *Gospel According to Saint Matthew*, 1:356–57.

[91] Ibid., 1:374.

to a king despite Samuel's remonstration. Both the stronger and weaker parallels pit obedience toward God—God's commands and words—against disobedience. In each case these groups and people, though beloved of the Lord, fail. Where they fail, however, Jesus does not.

Simply abstracting a meaning of "obedience," however, misses the greater import that Ælfric's connection makes. Ælfric's typology goes beyond the level of typology. He does not simply argue that Jesus is an antitype of Adam, succeeding where Adam failed. Rather, he presents Jesus' replaying the temptations of Adam as fundamentally redemptive. Adam's narrative is not just a shadow whose meaning is found and fulfilled in Christ. It was, rather, for Ælfric, a literal event with palpable consequences. Christ's conquest of the devil is not only an idea coming to fruition but also a redemptive act in and of itself on the literal level. For the modern interpreters, typology is a convention that presents Matthew with literary models on which to construct his narrative of Jesus; in Ælfric's worldview, Adam, Eve, Satan, Jesus, and the monks are all equally real people participating in the grand drama of fall and redemption.

The comparison between Ælfric and the modern interpreters is perhaps most fruitful when we examine where they do not connect. The modern interpreters all relate this story back to its immediate context and the preceding pericope—the baptism of Jesus by John and the declaration that Jesus is God's Son. Ælfric, reading within a lectionary situation, works with the text as a discrete block. Its immediate context for him is not the baptism of Jesus by John but rather Mark's story of walking on the water (Mark 6:47ff)—the gospel reading for the Saturday after Quinquagesima—followed by the gospel for the Monday after Quadragesima, the parable of the sheep and the goats (Matt 25:31ff). The modern interpreters, following their contextual clues, all privilege doctrine generally and Christology specifically as interpretive categories. Ælfric does not. Of the moderns, Luz remains the most open to a nondoctrinal interpretation; Hare seems the most doctrinal.

The moderns, then, look at the temptations as a series of acts that Jesus is challenged to perform by the devil. Thus, to determine its meaning, each act is weighed to ascertain what concept or doctrine is being tested and how that fits into a first-century doctrine of the messiah. The foremost question for each temptation, it seems, is whether it is a specifically messianic temptation. This method of focusing on the act has parallels to

modernist approaches to ethics that seek to determine morality by analyzing actions and the motivations that lead to them.

Ælfric, on the other hand, does not read the temptations as acts. Rather,
he approaches them from a position of monastic pragmatism that asks
less about each act than about the virtue or vices that underlie it and what
the action reveals about the actor's character. In essence, Ælfric presents
a character-ethic reading of the temptation narrative rather than an act-
ethic reading.

Christology, however, is just as possible in Ælfric's view as the other;
there is no reason to separate a "moral" interpretation of the temptation
narrative from a "christological" one. To speak about the acts, the morals,
and the virtues of Jesus *is* to speak christologically. Ælfric's understanding
of redemption is specifically tied to the "morality" or, rather, to the character of who Christ revealed himself to be through the actions described
in the gospel narratives. The actions describe a life of perfect humility
and therefore perfect virtue; the character of this life is of the utmost
importance in order to speak of Christ as both a redeemer and as an
exemplar because, again, these two categories are inextricably bound.

MATTHEW 5:1-12

Introduction

The Beatitudes stand as the great introduction to Matthew's Sermon
on the Mount. As the Sermon on the Mount is one of the preeminent and
most quoted set of dominical teachings, the Beatitudes occupy a privileged place within the history of Christian thought. Chapter 5 begins
with a narrative frame. A disjunctive "When" (*de*) signals a shift from the
narrative summary in 4:23-25 to a new set of actions where Jesus gathers
his disciples and prepares to speak. At that point, the text moves into a
parallel set of eight elements beginning with "Blessed are," (*makarioi hoi*)
and containing a "for" (*hoti*) clause. A ninth element also begins "Blessed"
(*makarioi*) but then diverges from the pattern and expands on the eighth
element. While a "for" (*hoti*) clause is present, the expansiveness of this
ninth element shows a definite break from the earlier pattern. A shift
away from parallelism and a direct address in the second person plural
in verse 13 confirms the end of the literary unit.

The heart of the material is Double Tradition, coming from Q 6:20-23, but Matthew has altered and expanded it. Both Eusebius and Aland note the parallels with Luke 6:20b-23 and the liberties that Matthew takes. Eusebius's Canons alternate between Double Tradition material and material unique to Matthew. Thus, the first verse is canon X, verses 2 through 4 are canon V, Double Tradition Matthew-Luke, verse 5 is canon X, verse 6 is canon V, verses 7-10 are canon X, and verses 11-12 are canon V. The only disagreement between Eusebius and Aland concerns verse 4; Eusebius sees a thematic parallel between Matthew 5:4 and Luke 6:21b that Aland does not, probably because of the lack of overlap in the Greek text.

It should be noted that the Eusebian divisions reflect an issue in the transmission of the text: Eusebius reverses the order of verses 4 and 5. Nor is this simply an issue in his text. Within several translation traditions—the Latin, Syrus Curetonianus, and at least one Bohairic Coptic manuscript—verses 4 and 5 are transposed. This transposition also appears in Origen and in the Western fathers who follow the Latin text, most notably Augustine in his influential commentary on the Sermon on the Mount. The Old English cited by Ælfric follows the transposition found in its Vulgate parent.

Modern Interpreters

Ulrich Luz

Luz frames the Beatitudes as an interpretive trajectory of the Jesus tradition frozen in a moment. His explication considers their origins, their state as they entered Matthew's hands, their state as they left them, and their reception by the church through the ages. Rather than focusing on either end of the process, though, he deftly uses both the prehistory and the interpretive history to shed light on Matthew's text, always returning to the canonical text and focusing on what is found therein.

Luz proposes a three-stage transmission history as the text came to Matthew: a) the first three beatitudes (Q 6:20b-21a, b=Matt 5:3, 6, 4) may go back to Jesus; b) Q adds a fourth beatitude (Q 6:22-23=Matt 5:11-12); c) in light of Isaiah 61, the original three beatitudes were reformulated, and a new fourth beatitude (Matt 5:5) was added to create a series all beginning with the letter "π," and two other beatitudes were also added (Matt 5:7-9). Thus Matthew received a set of seven beatitudes which he then further developed. This separation of layers is essential for Luz as each layer represents a different adaptation of the original. The "unconditional assurance of salvation to people who are in a hopeless situation is decisive"[92] for the first layer that comes from Jesus himself. These authentic beatitudes share "a paradoxical character . . . the apocalyptic hope for a total reversal of conditions."[93] They are not wholly future-oriented, though, because of the person and action of Jesus; their proclamation and Jesus' action toward the poor and marginalized enact the kingdom as a present event. This layer is fundamentally eschatological.

By the time the text leaves Matthew's hands, this orientation has changed. Luz contends that Matthew's changes have altered the original meaning by "*mov[ing] the sense of the Beatitudes in the direction of paranesis.*"[94] Matthew's approach is "characterized by an 'ethicizing' tendency; the Beatitudes become a kind of mirror for a Christian life." The original eschatological meaning of the words of Jesus have been transformed and altered.[95]

Although Matthew "ethicizes," Luz suggests that the evangelist does not calcify a purely ethical meaning. Rather, he enables the interpretive trajectory of this teaching to continue, assuring its continued survival by opening up the language:

> The terms that designate those who are pronounced blessed are very general. They permit the hearers to fill them with their own associations and interpretations. It was precisely the openness of the Matthean formulations that repeatedly makes it possible for the church's interpreters to discover what for them was basic and central in these beatitudes.[96]

Thus, the open-ended character of the Beatitudes allows each generation to inhabit them anew as shifting theologies find traction in the simple and multivalent words that Matthew uses.

[92] Luz, *Matthew 1–7*, 189.

[93] Ibid.

[94] Ibid., 190. Emphasis in the original.

[95] Ibid. I hesitate to go so far as to say "domesticated." While I think it is clear that Luz prefers these sayings to have an eschatological force, he does not reject their ethical meaning, either.

[96] Ibid.

Luz's own interpretation is one that pays attention to these later inter-pretive traditions and chronicles various interpretive approaches. Luz creatively engages these historical interpretations to gain a better insight into Matthew's own text. Most striking is his use of patristic material. He contends in a minor (typographically identified) excursus that the Refor-mation exegetes came closer to the original meaning intended by Jesus but in so doing depart from Matthew's: "The Reformation's interpretation has somewhat eliminated the ethicizing and to that degree has come closer to the original meaning (but not to Matthew's meaning!)."[97] While the Reformation finds the eschatological meaning, the early and medieval church cleaves to Matthew's meaning because of their tendency toward the ethical; their interpretive spin matches and therefore illuminates Mat-thew's. Luz sides with the early interpreters on the meaning of "righteous-ness" in verse 6, a key term for him: "In my judgment, without question the decision is to be made in favor of the first, the early church/Catholic interpretation."[98] Furthermore, in asking whether the ethicizing tendency goes too far, Luz looks to the early church to understand how grace plays into Matthew's message and substantively uses the arguments he finds there to absolve the Beatitudes of the fault of works-righteousness.[99]

As far as the actual content of the Beatitudes goes, Luz states that the structure of the passage determines much of its meaning; the bracketing formed by the appearance of "kingdom of heaven" in verses 3 and 10 sets the agenda for the other beatitudes: "With this first promise Matthew sets brackets around all the Beatitudes (vv. 3, 10); the remaining concluding clauses develop what 'kingdom of heaven' means."[100] Not only does king-dom of heaven appear in strategic locations—so does righteousness. Matthew introduces his "key concept"[101] in the middle and at the end of the sequence. This concept further grounds how the Matthean beatitudes should be understood. Luz understands Matthew's righteousness as:

> a human attitude or conduct. One can be persecuted only because of that conduct, not because one merely longs for (divine) righteousness.

[97] Ibid., 200.
[98] Ibid., 195.
[99] Ibid., 199–202.
[100] Ibid., 193.
[101] Ibid., 195.

> Righteousness is characterized by Christian practice and confessing
> Jesus. . . . Confessing Christ manifests itself in deeds (7:21-23;
> 25:31-46).[102]

Thus, Luz reads the Beatitudes as enjoining a set of actions that jointly
constitute righteousness and set the agenda of the kingdom of heaven.

Davies and Allison

While Davies and Allison begin with looking at the structure of the
Beatitudes (where they decided they are formed from three triplets, given
the Matthean love of threes), their argument proper begins in an excursus
on beatitudes in general. In this excursus, they distinguish between two
fundamental forms of beatitudes: wisdom and eschatological. No absolute
method of discerning the difference between the two is offered, but certain characteristics identify the eschatological form. The most fundamental is the literary function:

> The eschatological makarism, it is important to observe, is usually
> addressed to people in dire straits, and the promise to them is of
> future consolation. So in contrast to the wisdom beatitude where
> moral exhortation is, despite the declarative form, generally the
> object, assurance and the proffering of hope are the goal: eyes be-
> come focused on the future, which will reverse natural values and
> the present situation; fulfillment is no longer to be found in this
> world but in a new world. The dismal status quo of those addressed
> is taken as a given for the present and is only to be altered by the
> eschatological intervention of God.[103]

Thus, the eschatological beatitude is about a "future consolation" while
the wisdom beatitude is about "moral exhortation."[104] Additionally, the
eschatological beatitude is found in series as well as pairs while the moral
is only found in pairs, and the eschatological blessing is sometimes paired
with an eschatological woe. They note that both kinds of blessings are
found within the New Testament writings and that the Beatitudes are quite
typical—only their brevity is exceptional, particularly in their Lukan form.

---

[102] Ibid., 199.

[103] Davies and Allison, *Gospel According to Saint Matthew*, 1:432.

[104] Ibid.

Drawing their observations about structure and beatitudes together, Davies and Allison posit four stages of development for the Matthean beatitudes; the key is that the first stage, coming from Jesus, consists of three eschatological beatitudes (blessed are the poor, blessed are those who mourn, and blessed are those who hunger).[105] The rest of the beatitudes and their later form came at the hands of Q compilers and evangelists. An eschatological quality therefore grounds the series—the precise nature of the Matthean beatitudes is open for question, especially by modern scholars. Davies and Allison present the question with a section titled "Entrance requirements or eschatological blessings?"[106] While confirming the "initial plausibility" of the first and majority position and granting it "an element of truth,"[107] eight points challenge this view and the conclusion disavows it:

> In conclusion, it would be foolish to deny the imperatives implicit in 5.3-12: there is no going around this. (This is also true of the woes in Mt 23, which, although not primarily exhortation, offer such implicitly, even to Matthew's Christian readers.) But the question is whether the primary function of the Matthean beatitudes is moral, and whether a moral dimension excludes a promissory or conciliatory dimension. The answer in both cases is negative. 5.3-12 serves firstly to bless the faithful as they are now. When Jesus speaks, the drudgery and the difficulties of day-to-day life fade away and the bliss of the life to come proleptically appears. Time is, however briefly, overcome, and the saints are refreshed.

Thus, Davies and Allison offer an answer that privileges the eschatological but, upon reflection, is a veiled acceptance of the moral as well. The negative affirmation denies a solely moral meaning and, while straining toward the eschatological, reluctantly acknowledges the presence of the moral.

The exegesis of the beatitudes themselves follows this pattern: eschatological qualities are privileged. Moral meanings are not denied but are not at the forefront either. Thus the addition of "in spirit" to the first beatitude does make a religious turn toward a quality that can be cultivated but does not negate the economic meaning of "the poor" as "the

[105] Ibid., 1:435.
[106] Ibid., 1:439.
[107] Ibid.

two go together."[108] In taking up 5:4 they note "It is difficult to see how [this verse] can be understood as paranesis."[109] Possessing the earth in 5:5 is "an eschatological promise."[110]

While Davies and Allison point out the eschatological character of the verses, however, they do not impose eschatology as a rigid framework nor seek to discover it where there are no warrants. Thus 5:6 is a "recognizable behavior" that must be "earnestly and habitually sought."[111] A moral meaning and presence is neither denied nor denigrated—but neither is it actively advocated.

Five concluding observations round out their treatment of the Beatitudes. In the first, Davies and Allison note that these makarisms are "blessings, not requirements."[112] Like the healings at the end of Matthew 4, these are the breath of grace before the hard words of Matthew 5–7. The second point continues this theme:

> According to Mt. 5:3-12, the kingdom of God will bring eschatological comfort, a permanent inheritance, true satisfaction, the obtaining of mercy, the vision of God, and divine sonship. In brief, it will in every way bring the *telos* of the religious quest. Thus the word "kingdom" serves to foretell the eventual realization in human experience of the fullness of God's bounteous presence. "Kingdom" is indeed almost a surrogate for God, and it is rightly considered the *summum bonum* of Matthew's gospel.[113]

The third point is christological in that the Beatitudes—particularly their earlier layers that may well go back to Jesus—are based on Isaiah 61:1-3. Thus, in his blessing of the poor and mourning in these beatitudes, Jesus is functioning in his messianic role. And yet—point 4 notes that Jesus himself fulfills the very categories he blesses: meek, mourning, righteous, merciful, persecuted, and reproached. "So the beatitudes are illustrated and brought to life by Jesus' actions. He embodies his own words and

[108] Ibid., 1:443.
[109] Ibid., 1:449.
[110] Ibid., 1:450.
[111] Ibid., 1:453, 452.
[112] Ibid., 1:466.
[113] Ibid.

thereby becomes the standard or model to be imitated (cf. Origen in PG 13.152)."[114] The fifth and final point returns again to eschatology. The beatitudes function as a "practical theodicy"[115] that seeks not to explain the mysteries of why some are poor and mourn but put present circumstances into perspective through the appeal to eschatological consolation.

Douglas Hare

Hare does not treat the Beatitudes as a discrete pericope but includes them in a section that covers the whole Sermon on the Mount, stretching from 5:1–7:29. A brief introduction sets up the sermon as a whole then dives into the text. As a result, Hare's treatment lacks many of the technical considerations specific to the Beatitudes as found in the other treatments, notably questions of tradition history. Indeed, he is concerned more with an overall impression than with a detailed analysis.

Hare's quick treatment of the initial setting in verses 1-2 is fairly cursory and suggestive. While he states that Matthew is connecting Jesus with Moses in the use of mountain imagery for his central teaching, he remains insistent that Matthew does not push the Moses typology because Jesus is greater than Moses. Rather, "he apparently wishes his readers to see the Sermon on the Mount as a definitive interpretation of Torah delivered to Moses on Mount Sinai."[116] He suggests that the key Old Testament character and mountain that should be in the reader's mind is less Moses and Sinai and more David and Zion, highlighting what he finds to be kingly imagery:

> [Jesus] sits like a king on his throne, his disciples approach him like subjects in a royal court, and the king delivers his inaugural address, in which he lays out in considerable detail what life in his kingdom will be like.[117]

Because of the emphasis on interpretation rather than a new law, fulfillment rather than dissolution, and what Hare understands as court ceremonial,

---

[114] Ibid., 1:467.
[115] Ibid.
[116] Hare, *Matthew*, 34.
[117] Ibid., 35.

the initial setting of the sermon is more a christological statement than anything else.

Hare then approaches the Beatitudes (5:3-12), beginning with a brief introduction before proceeding to the text. He notes first the scholarly argument as to whether the Beatitudes are "*eschatological warnings* or *entrance requirements*"[118] and takes the irresolvable nature of the debate to signal that they are both "expressions of eschatological grace and implicit commands."[119] As the commentary will reveal, however, he tends toward the eschatological over the ethical. A short introduction to makarisms orients the reader to the main issues, pointing to Psalm 1:1 as the makarism closest in nature to Matthew's. Hare makes no summary statements concerning the Beatitudes but moves directly into the remainder of Matthew's sermon.

Hare approaches the Beatitudes with Scripture firmly in hand, relying on intertexuality to clarify their meaning almost to the point of embracing a canonical criticism model. That is, his approach to the Beatitudes is to find a related text or texts, preferably from the Old Testament, to clarify the meaning of the passage. A comment in his interpretation of verse 4 presents his agenda: "Here as elsewhere in Jesus' teachings the key to interpretation lies in the Hebrew Scriptures" and also in the remarks on verse 7: "Again we must regard the Old Testament background as constitutive of a correct understanding."[120] Deutero-Isaiah and the psalms in particular are identified often as the source of these statements.

This having been said, Hare's most important dialogue partner is not actually from the Old Testament but is Luke's gospel. Perhaps because of his attention to the Lukan parallels, Hare tends to depart from Matthew's text, preferring the "revolutionary rhetoric"[121] of Jesus which he finds more clearly presented in Luke's versions. Following this path, Hare tends toward economic interpretations of the Beatitudes, preferring whenever possible to turn the text and its meaning back to "the world of economic struggle."[122] Thus the "mourning" of verse 4 is not an internalized mourning for sins

---

[118] Ibid. The emphasis is in the original.
[119] Ibid.
[120] Ibid., 37, 40.
[121] Ibid., 37.
[122] Ibid.

but rather—reading through Isaiah 61—mourning for the desolation of the land of Israel and the economic injustices rampant in the land; the "meek" in verse 5 read through Psalm 37 are the tenant farmers who will receive land of their own rather than working the lands of others.[123] Even the peacemakers of verse 9 are those who seek to restore God's *shalom* defined as "harmonious cooperation aimed at the welfare of all, [that] could not be established by the Roman legions."[124] The Beatitudes read this way, then, are presented as primarily eschatological warnings that presage the reversal of the current economic and imperialistic system retaining a subdued ethical note on behalf of social justice.

Eugene Boring

Boring's interpretation of the Beatitudes can only be described as relentlessly eschatological. As a hermeneutic, eschatology is dominant and at times seems to dominate the text itself. Boring begins his exegesis of the Beatitudes with a section that lays out the nature of Matthean makarisms, then produces seven hermeneutical corollaries that flow from this definition. His introductory framework carries through his verse-by-verse treatment. In particular, the seven corollaries lay out the importance of eschatology, which the exegetical section then implements.

The emphasis on eschatology begins with Boring's presentation of makarisms as a form. He asserts:

> The Matthean beatitudes were originally a wisdom form filled by early Christianity with prophetic eschatological content. Matthew's beatitudes are not practical advice for successful living, but prophetic declarations made on the conviction of the coming-and-already-present kingdom of God.[125]

This definition presents two strong themes that will carry throughout the interpretation: 1) the Beatitudes are fundamentally eschatological, and 2) they are not about ethics or virtues. The successive corollaries and exegetical remarks clarify this.

---

[123] Ibid., 37–39.
[124] Ibid., 42.
[125] Boring, "Matthew," in Keck, 177.

The eschatological orientation is clear from the literary form of the text, from the verb tense utilized, and from their very nature. Making a distinction between paranetic wisdom beatitudes and eschatological prophetic beatitudes, Boring strongly asserts the prophetic eschatological nature of Matthew's Beatitudes. He does not spend much time demonstrating this assertion but makes an observation based on form: wisdom beatitudes "declare present happiness and reward"[126] while "in the Prophets, makarisms declare the present/future blessedness of those who are presently in dire circumstances but who will be vindicated at the eschatological coming of God's kingdom."[127] He goes on to note: "In the New Testament outside the Synoptics, most beatitudes are found in the prophetic book of Revelation."[128] As far as Boring is concerned, then, New Testament beatitudes are most likely if not necessarily eschatological in nature.

As Boring proceeds through the text, he notes a number of times the presence of the future passive tense in the second half of various beatitudes. He dissuades readers from seeing these as future rewards for specific behaviors but identifies them as the "eschatological divine passive."[129] The verbs in the second halves of verses 4, 6, 7, and 9 in particular are identified as utilizing this grammatical construction.

Furthermore, Boring flatly asserts the eschatological nature of the Beatitudes in his corollary 6: "The beatitudes are not historical but eschatological."[130] The Beatitudes' structural bracket also feeds into the eschatological interpretation: "The first and last of the formally identical series 5:3-10 refer directly to the coming kingdom, and all the others express some eschatological aspect of it."[131] In the body of corollary 6, Boring interprets the verbal phrases in the second halves of verses 4, 5, 6, 7, and 9 to clarify their eschatological meaning and that therefore all of these blessings "are not this-worldly practical realities, but elements of the eschatological hopes of Israel."[132] By the time the reader gets to the

---

[126] Ibid.
[127] Ibid.
[128] Ibid.
[129] Ibid., 179.
[130] Ibid., 178.
[131] Ibid.
[132] Ibid.

interpretation proper, then, its eschatological character has been prede-
termined.

Corollary 3, though, is Boring's acknowledgement of the moral dimension of the Beatitudes. In this brief corollary he notes that, "there is,
however, an ethical dimension to the beatitudes."[133] The ethical is aligned,
however, with the eschatological: proper ethics are defined as "act[ing]
in accord with the coming kingdom," and Boring notes that the life of
the blessed is elaborated later in the sermon in 5:17–7:12.[134]

A more direct challenge to views of the Beatitudes as either entrance
requirements or a code of ethics comes through Boring's appeal to the
communitarian nature of the text. He begins by stating in corollary 2
that: "they do not directly lay down demands for conversion, but declare
the *notae ecclesiae*, the 'marks of the church.'"[135] His strongest statement
on the matter is in corollary 7:

> The nine pronouncements are thus not statements about general
> human virtues—most appear exactly the opposite to common wis-
> dom. Rather, they pronounce blessing on authentic disciples in the
> Christian community. All of the beatitudes apply to one group of
> people, the real Christians of Matthew's community. They do not
> describe nine different kinds of good people who get to go to heaven,
> but are nine declarations about the blessedness, contrary to all ap-
> pearances, of the eschatological community living in anticipation
> of God's reign. Like all else in Matthew, they are oriented to life
> together in the community of discipleship, not to individualistic
> ethics.[136]

Here Boring cuts to the heart of his opposition to an ethical or ethicizing
interpretation of the Beatitudes. For him, the turn to the ethical is also
the turn to the individual and the interior. Rather, he states, these are the
marks of a community as a whole with various elements embodied at
various times by various members.

---

[133] Ibid., 177.
[134] Ibid.
[135] Ibid.
[136] Ibid., 178.

Finally, Boring also speaks of an implicit Christology in the Beatitudes that pervades all of the Sermon on the Mount. Two of his convictions provide a sense of how this implicit Christology is at work. In corollary 4, Boring states that the Beatitudes are fundamentally performative:

> The beatitudes are written in unconditional performative language. They do not merely describe something that already is, but bring into being the reality they declare. The form is not "if you will x, then y" or "whoever x, then y," but unconditionally declare that those who are x will be y. Like the patriarchal and priestly blessings, and like the prophetic word of the Scripture, the beatitude effects what it says, bringing into being what it states.[137]

Boring does not explicitly tease out the implications that necessarily follow from this set of statements. If the Beatitudes are both highly eschatological and performative, then it must follow that their Christology reveals Jesus as the eschatological power person *par excellence*. He does, however, develop the implicit Christology in the next corollary:

> Understood as a prophetic pronouncement, the truth claim of the beatitude is not independently true but dependent on the speaker. . . . In the narrative context of the Sermon on the Mount, the speaker is more than a prophet, he is the Son of God and the Lord of the church, already seen from the post-Easter perspective. The beatitudes, therefore, are not observations about reality that others of lesser insight had simply overlooked, such as truths of mathematics or logic. They are true on the basis of the authority of the one who speaks. Thus for Matthew Jesus' beatitudes are related to the theme of the authority (ἐξουσία *exousia*) of Jesus (see 7:29; 8:9; 9:6; 21:23; 28:18). In the first words of the Sermon on the Mount, we do not meet general statements, the truth of which we can investigate on our own terms, with our own criteria, but a veiled, implicit, christological claim that calls for taking a stand with regard to the speaker, not merely the content of his speech.[138]

---

[137] Ibid., 177.
[138] Ibid.

Thus, the Christology that Boring finds is not simply that of a wise ethical teacher, rather he discovers a teacher—yes—but more than that, a being of eschatological power whose very word shifts the nature of reality.

While Boring's interpretation tends to extremes with his relentless pursuit of the eschatological, he does so to provide what he understands as a necessary counterbalance to flatly ethical readings that have pervaded the church for centuries. Boring's point is not to repudiate ethics altogether but to present an interpretation that does not give in to either ethicizing or internalizing tendencies. In response, he highlights the eschatological and communal aspects of the Beatitudes to present a better rounded understanding of this central text.

Ælfric's Interpretation

The Homily Proper

I. Treatment of the Epistle (lines 3–146)

  A. Introduction (lines 3–7)

  B. Translation of the Epistle (lines 7–15)

  C. Classifying the Saints and Angels (lines 16–136)

    1. The Angels (lines 16–35)

    2. The Patriarchs (lines 35–41)

    3. The Prophets (lines 41–51)

    4. John the Baptist (lines 52–55)

    5. The Apostles (lines 55–70)

    6. The Martyrs (lines 71–88)

    7. The Priests/Confessors (lines 89–103)

    8. The Hermits (lines 104–17)

    9 The Blessed Virgin Mary (lines 118–29)

    10. Virgins (lines 130–36)

  D. Conclusion/Transition (lines 137–46)

II. Treatment of the Gospel (lines 147–291)

  A. Introduction (lines 147–52)

  B. Translation of the Gospel (lines 152–66)

C. Exposition of the Gospel (lines 167–281)

    1. Narrative Frame (lines 167–79)

    2. 1st Beatitude (lines 180–97)

    3. 2nd Beatitude (lines 198–204)

    4. 3rd Beatitude (lines 205–10)

    5. 4th Beatitude (lines 211–18)

    6. 5th Beatitude (lines 219–21)

    7. 6th Beatitude (lines 222–27)

    8. 7th Beatitude (lines 227–35)

    9. 8th Beatitude (lines 236–79)

D. Conclusion (lines 280–91)

Ælfric's sermon[139] for the feast of All Saints[140] is a bipartite treatment of the epistle and gospel appointed for the occasion. He engages both texts through the lens of the liturgical event, shaping his exposition of the texts specifically for the occasion. This homily is an orderly one, logically constructed and amenable to a structural analysis (see figure 1). In each half of the homily, Ælfric presents the text in English translation after a brief introduction, then explicates the text.

After presenting the appointed epistle, Revelation 7:9-12, Ælfric systematically describes the various categories and classes of angels and saints whom the faithful venerate on this day. He is prompted by the question immediately following this pericope from Revelation 7:13; the elder asks the visionary St. John, "Who are these dressed in white robes

---

[139] The homily for the feast of All Saints is found in *Ælfric's Catholic Homilies: The First Series, Text*, ed. Peter Clemoes, Early English Text Society, supplementary series 17 (Oxford: Oxford University Press, 1997), 486–96 (hereafter ÆCHom I, 36).

[140] The feast of All Saints is celebrated on November 1 following the date of Gregory III's consecration of a chapel in St. Peter's to all saints on that date. Given the large number of saints already venerated by the early medieval church—with more being added almost daily—this festival was an opportunity to properly propitiate all of the saints, even those unknown or forgotten, so that no heavenly intercessors would be overlooked. Among other things, it represents a movement on the part of a heavily monastic clergy to allow the laity to share in the veneration of the saints while recognizing the impracticality of lay attendance at Sanctoral Masses and Offices.

and from whence have they come?" Just as the elder answers the question, so too does Ælfric.

In his response, Ælfric utilizes categories drawn from his periodization of history familiar from the eschatological epic.[141] After briefly mentioning angels and highlighting the dangers of focusing too much on things unknown, Ælfric begins with the biblical saints—patriarchs, prophets, John the Baptist, and the apostles. He moves naturally to postbiblical times and discusses the martyrs; then, alluding to the cessation of official persecution of Christians, to priests/confessors. At this point Ælfric seems to continue his chronological scheme, moving to hermits and the anchorites of the Egyptian desert.[142] A sudden shift to a vocative address of the Blessed Virgin breaks the chronological schema. After an encomium highlighting the virginity of Mary, Ælfric moves to his final category—the virgins and widows. A concluding paragraph returns the focus to the liturgical celebration, reminding the congregation that they are here to honor and venerate these saints and angels, trusting in the strength of their intercession.

While a great number of holy beings are explicated, this half of the homily focuses the most attention on the holy state of martyrdom. While Ælfric heaps praise on all of the holy beings—both angels and humans— the most effusive praise and the most certain picture of glory goes to those who died for their faith:

> After the "army of the apostles" we honor the triumphant host of
> God's martyrs[143] who through great tortures manfully conformed to
> the suffering of Christ and through their martyrdom entered the
> heavenly kingdom. Some were slain with weapons, some consumed
> by fire. Others were beaten with scourges, others thrust through

---

[141] See the discussion of Æflric's conception and construction of the span of history as an eschatological epic in chap. 1.

[142] While the previous transition is clearly temporal, Ælfric's thinking is not as clear here. He begins with an ambiguous "Ðysum fyligð [After these followed]," ÆCHom I, 36, line 104. The notion of following could be temporal in a chronological sense or metaphorical in a categorical sense; Ælfric gives no clear signals but the context urges a temporal reading.

[143] The Old English phrase "heap godes cyþera" appears to be a direct reference to the "Martyrum . . . exercitus (army of the martyrs)" from the *Te Deum*.

with stakes. Some hung on crosses, some sank in the wide sea. Others were flayed alive, others torn with iron claws. Some were overwhelmed with stones, some afflicted with winter's cold, some tormented with hunger. The hands and feet of some were, on account of their faith and the holy name of Christ the Savior, cut off as a spectacle for the crowds. These are the triumphant friends of God for whom the wicked governors had contempt but now they are crowned with the victory of their sufferings in eternal joy. They may have been killed bodily but they would not turn from God despite any torture. Their hope was fulfilled in immortality though they were tortured before men. They were afflicted for a short time but cheered for a long time because their God tested them just as gold in an oven and he found them worthy and, just as a holy offering, he received them into his heavenly kingdom.[144]

The martyrs, then become the "gold standard" for sanctity. The post-Constantinian period became problematic because of a lack of active persecution. As a result, Ælfric explains how the confessors could attain to sanctity through following the path of spiritual martyrdom even if they do not achieve it physically. That is, even though they do not receive martyrdom, their achievements are weighed in relation to it:

> though [the confessors] did not experience the persecution of the sword, yet through the merit of their lives they were not deprived of martyrdom because martyrdom is accomplished not in blood alone but also in abstinence from sins and in the application of God's commands.[145]

The message is that sainthood comes through the persecution and endurance of martyrdom. Even if there are not accommodating heathen rulers about, it may be simulated through asceticism and obedience to God in the face of diabolic temptations.[146]

---

[144] ÆCHom I, 36, lines 71–88.
[145] ÆCHom I, 36, lines 99–103.
[146] See the discussion in the seventh- to eighth-century monastic Irish Cambrai Homily of the ascetical "white" and "blue" martyrdoms contrasted with literal "red" martyrdom. Ælfric makes no references to such a color scheme here or elsewhere.

Ælfric then turns to the gospel reading for the day, Matthew 5:1-12. He introduces it with a segue from the section on the categories of saints by explaining that this gospel tells how the faithful become saints. A translation of the gospel into English follows. Ælfric begins his treatment by explaining that he presents Augustine's teaching and dives into an explanation. The events within the narrative frame preceding the Beatitudes are interpreted as enigmas with doctrinal solutions: the height of the mountain contrasts the height of Jesus' teachings above that of Moses; sitting as a teacher, Jesus called the disciples spiritually to himself as well as physically; the one who opened his mouth was also the one who opened the mouths of the prophets.

Each beatitude is taken in turn. Ælfric gives predominantly moral interpretations of the Beatitudes. That is, each of the predicate nominatives placed apposite to the blessings is interpreted as a manifestation of a concrete virtue. The second half of each line presents a reward granted to those who enact the named virtue. Both the predicate nominatives and the contents of the subordinant clause are treated as enigmas; Ælfric's practice is to present the plain meaning, identifying the virtues inherent in each and its proper reward. Following standard patristic practice, Ælfric's interpretations often contain a passage of Scripture that back the selected solution to the enigma. The first seven blessings are treated in a spare fifty-six lines (lines 180–235)—an average of six lines per blessing.[147]

The first and sixth beatitudes represent Ælfric's treatment of this text. The first receives the longest treatment of any of the first seven beatitudes—eighteen lines (lines 180–97). The treatment begins with the citation of the beatitude itself (lines 180–81). Then, the term "gastlican þearfan [spiritually poor]" is specifically defined: "What are the spiritually poor except the humble who have the fear of God and do not have any arrogance" (lines 181–82).[148] This interpretation returns to the interpretation of the "mountain" in lines 167–73 where the height signifies the lofty commands leading to the filial fear of God as opposed to the old law

---

[147] The first beatitude receives eighteen lines (lines 180–97); the second, seven (lines 198–204); the third, six (lines 205–10); the fourth, eight (lines 211–18); the fifth, three (lines 219–21); the sixth, five (lines 222–26); and the seventh, nine (lines 227–35).

[148] ÆCHom I, 36, lines 181–82.

rooted in servile fear. From this definition, the two key concepts—the fear of God and arrogance—are then clarified by means of two scriptural warrants: "'The fear of God is the beginning of wisdom' [VgPs 110:10; Prov 1:7; 9:10; Sir 1:12] and 'pride is likewise the beginning of sin' [Sir 10:15]."[149] Once the words are defined, Ælfric moves to clarify the concepts represented by the text.

The conceptual explanation draws distinctions through two dichotomies of poverty proceeding from the definitions: a material dichotomy between the rich and poor and a spiritual dichotomy between the humble and the proud. The four possible combinations are described through the use of paradigms. Ælfric begins with the materially poor but spiritually proud; the paradigm operates at the general level of the categorical (encompassing all poor but proud people) and is for the sake of restraint. Their poverty is not commendable because while they are materially poor they wish for wealth. The materially wealthy but spiritually humble are commended. Abraham, Jacob, and David are identified as individual examples for encouragement and emulation. The third category, the materially wealthy and spiritually proud—made explicit as "ðe modigan rican [the proud rich]"—are also are kept at the categorical level of generality and are presented as a negative example. The final category is that which most completely matches the Gospel teaching in Ælfric's eyes and is therefore most worthy of emulation: the materially poor and spiritually humble. Here too the paradigm used is more specific than the category itself; the group selected for emulation are monks. Ælfric explains that for their poverty in both wealth and spirit, monks will receive great glory afterward. At this point, however, the exposition of the first beatitude ends without an explication of the kingdom of God—the reward of the spiritually poor.

The sixth beatitude is an example of Ælfric's more typical brief treatment of the Beatitudes. Spanning only seven lines (lines 222–27) made up of two sentences, Ælfric begins by citing the beatitude, then denying a potential literal reading of the passage: "They are foolish who wish to see God with a fleshly eye for he will be seen with the heart."[150] In essence, he has identified the passage as a metaphor where the action of the eye has been trans-

---

[149] ÆCHom I, 36, lines 182–83.
[150] ÆCHom I, 36, lines 222–24.

The Temptation and the Beatitudes 169

ferred to the heart (which is itself a metaphor for the seat of virtue within a human). He finishes the sentence by restating the beatitude in such a way as to define clean heartedness: "but they who are clean from vice are those who may see God."[151] The concluding sentence is an example drawn from the world of science: "Just as earthly light may not be seen except with a clean eye so also God will not be seen except with a clean heart." With this statement, Ælfric moves on to the next beatitude.

The eighth beatitude receives almost the same amount of material as all of the other beatitudes put together—forty-four lines (lines 236–79). This emphasis is quite deliberate; for Ælfric, persecution is the surest sign of fidelity to Christ in both words and works. Explicating the beatitude through a thick tapestry of Scripture references, he brings in the *climax* from tribulation to hope from Romans 5:3-5, then moves to explicit citations from James 1:2-3[152] and Sirach 27:6 that point to the necessity of testing. He concludes with John 15:18, 20:

> It is fitting that the faithful glory in tribulation because tribulation brings forth patience and patience, endurance [*afandunge*], and endurance [*afandung*] hope. This hope is truly never confounded because the love of God is poured into our hearts through the Holy Ghost through whom we are forgiven. The apostle James spoke concerning this: "Ho, my brothers, endure in all joy when you are in various sufferings because the endurance [*afandung*] of your faith is more precious than gold which has been tried [*afandod*] by fire." Also the holy writings say: "Earthen vessels are tested [*afandode*] in the oven and righteous men in the tribulation of their suffering." Furthermore, the Savior spoke about this to his disciples in another place: "If the earth hates you, know that it hated me before you, and if they persecuted me, then they will also persecute you."[153]

---

[151] ÆCHom I, 36, lines 224–25.

[152] His citation here is more a loose paraphrase of Jas 1:2-3 as filtered through Haymo than a formal quotation. Godden, *Commentary*, 307.

[153] ÆCHom I, 36, lines 262–74. The terms "endurance," "tried," and "tested" in this passage are all forms of the Old English root *afandian*. Modern English does not have a comparable word that covers the range of meanings that this single Old English word captures, thus the logic of the passage which follows the different uses of the term is obscured by my translation.

In this way, Ælfric suggests that true Christianity can be measured. If his hearers are under attack either physically or spiritually, then they are doing something right. Suffering is a true sign of righteous action whether these persecutions be from the visible or invisible forces of Satan.

In his concluding statement on this beatitude, Ælfric makes the crucial link between the two halves of his homily—a link quite natural to him but not immediately apparent to modern readers:

> Christ himself was killed by lawless men—and so too were his disciples and the martyrs. All those who wish to conduct themselves virtuously within the faithful church shall endure persecution either from invisible devils or from the visible lawless "limbs of the devil."[154] However, we should endure these temporary persecutions or tribulations for the name of Christ with joy because he thus commanded all patience: "Rejoice and exult because your reward is manifold in heaven."[155]

The beatitude spoken here by Christ was enacted by Christ on the cross. Those who followed most closely in his footsteps were joined to him in a fate like his: the apostles, all of whom died for their faith (with the sole exception of John) and the martyrs who followed them. Returning to the section on the martyrs (cited in full above), the same words and concepts are utilized: persecution, endurance, death, and the comparison of the righteous with gold tried in the fire. The persecution beatitude is fulfilled most perfectly by the martyrs and those who follow in their footsteps.

A brief conclusion states that much remains unsaid concerning this text. Ælfric then moves toward the traditional trinitarian doxology by praising God for the abundance of his saints. He touches on major points of the theology of the saints—their intercession on our behalf, our rejoicing with them, and the veneration due them—while remaining in a doxological mode leading to the final trinitarian ending.

[154] This is a well-known trope drawn from the seventh interpretive rule of the Donatist Tychonius, handed on to the orthodox church by Augustine in Book 3 of *De Doctrina Christiana* (*De. Doc. Chr.* 3.37.55.). Just as the church is the visible limbs of the body of Christ, so in parallel evil men are considered the limbs of the devil.

[155] ÆCHom I, 36, lines 274–81.

The Liturgical Context

Although the feast of All Saints appears late in Western lectionaries,[156] Matthew 5:1-12 was first connected with feasts of multiple martyrs.[157] Ælfric's emphasis on the eighth beatitude readily locates the interpretive center of gravity for this text within the early medieval period; while all saints are in view throughout Ælfric's work, special emphasis is placed throughout on martyrs and the blessedness accorded to the state of martyrdom. The last beatitude, which focuses on persecution, sets the tone for the homily as a whole.

Ælfric's work is guided once again by the liturgical suggestions given in Paul the Deacon's homiliary. In fact, referring to Paul's homiliary as received by Ælfric gives us important insight into both Ælfric's compositional technique and the context for which he intended his sermons. As the feast of All Saints was not widely celebrated until after the compilation of Paul's homiliary, there is no entry for it in the original collection. In the expanded version of the homiliary, printed in PL 95, one text is appointed for the Vigil of All Saints (a section of Bede's commentary on Luke)[158] and three for the feast of All Saints proper: one attributed to Bede beginning *Hodie, dilectissimi, omnium sanctorum*,[159] one attributed to

---

[156] Readings for All Saints do not appear within Anglo-Saxon lectionaries until the latter half of the tenth century. Lenker reports that Matt 5:1-12 appears as the All Saints' reading in manuscripts Qa, Qb, Qc, Sx, Vb, Vx, Wa, Wb, and A. The only Anglo-Saxon lectionaries that have All Saints but do not appoint this reading for the feast are the Type 3 alt group—Sa, Sb, Sd, and Se. All of them do, however, appoint it for the vigil of the feast. The feast itself receives Luke 6:17-23, which is the Synoptic parallel to Matt 5:1-12 according to both modern and medieval reckonings.

[157] This reading is appointed for the feasts of the Seven Brothers, martyrs (July 10) in a wide number of lectionaries reflecting a widespread assignment going back to Chavasse's stage 2 (Oa, Pa, Pb, Pc, Pg, Ph, Qa, Qb, Qc, Sa, Sb, Sc, Sd, and Se). One ninth-century capitulary (Qe) uses it as the reading for Sts. Tiburtius, Valerianus, and Maximus, martyrs (April 14), Sts. Felix, Simplicus, Faustinus, and Beatrix, martyrs (July 29), Sts. Cosmus and Damian, martyrs (Sept 27) as well as the Common for Plural Martyrs. The eleventh-century New Minster Missal (Wa) uses it for Sts. Marcus and Marcellianus, martyrs (June 18) and Sts. Dionysius, Rusticus, and Eleutherius, martyrs (October 9). It also appears as the Common for Plural Martyrs in Vb, Wh, and Ya and as the Common for Plural Confessors in Ph and Vb.

[158] Paul the Deacon, *Homiliae de Sanctis* LXI (PL 95:1535c-d).

[159] Paul the Deacon, *Homiliae de Sanctis* LXII (PL 95:1535d).

Bede beginning *Legitur/Legimus in ecclesiasticis historiis*,[160] and Leo the Great's Sermon 95 on the Beatitudes.[161] Furthermore, the expanded version includes a section from Augustine's *De Sermone Domini in Monte*, treating the Beatitudes for the feast of Several Martyrs.[162]

Ælfric's sermon falls neatly into two parts, the first utilizing *Legimus in ecclesiasticis historiis*, the second drawing from Augustine's *De Sermone Domini in Monte*.[163] He has thus created a sermon by combining two elements of the Night Office—the *sermo* of the second nocturn that gives general information about the feast day, and the *omelia* of the third nocturn that provides an exegetical explanation of the gospel of the day. There is no doubt, then, that the liturgical experience of the Night Office is directly responsible for the shape of this sermon.

Ælfric then uses a clever sleight of hand to fit the sermon to a new context, however, accomplished by altering the beginning of the Pseudo-Bedan *Legimus*. Ælfric reproduces the text relatively faithfully but for one major exception. The sermon in all of its variations invariably begins with a historical account of the consecration of the Pantheon as a church dedicated to Mary and all saints. It then glorifies the God who enabled these humans and angels to become saints, then moves into the various categories. This kind of introduction is not an uncommon one for early medieval sermons about liturgical feasts with a particular history. Classic examples include sermons for St. Michael and All Angels and the Rogation Days; both anonymous Old English sermons and Ælfric's own sermons for these occasions begin with this historical data.[164]

---

[160] Paul the Deacon, *Homiliae de Sanctis* LXIII (PL 95:1535d-1536a).

[161] Paul the Deacon, *Homiliae de Sanctis* LXIII (PL 95:1535d-1536a). Paul's selection begins at Serm. XCV.2 rather than the start of the sermon.

[162] Paul the Deacon, *Homiliae de Sanctis* LXXXI (PL 95:1550d-1551a).

[163] See Godden, *Commentary*, 199 and Cyril Smetana, "Ælfric and the Early Medieval Homiliary," *Traditio* 15 (1959): 194–95.

[164] See Richard J. Kelly, ed. and trans., *The Blickling Homilies* (London: Continuum, 2003), Homily 16. Blickling describes the historical events surrounding the dedication of the church to St. Michael in Garganus, Italy; see also Vercelli's "Homily 19," in *The Vercelli Book Homilies*, ed. Paul Szarmach, trans. Jean Anne Strebinger, Toronto Old English Series 5 (Toronto: University of Toronto Press, 1981), which describes the origins of the Rogation days in Vienna. Ælfric's ÆCHom I, 18 on the Rogation days and ÆCHom I, 29 on the feast of St. Michael do the same thing.

Here, however, Ælfric has stripped out the historical material and has replaced it with the epistle reading. Where the original sermon begins with a historical incident referring to all of the saints, both angelic and human, which then prompts the author to describe the various types, Ælfric introduces the Scripture passage that mentions all the saints. He has taken a sermon that explains an occasion and has turned it into an exegetical explanation of the epistle simply by replacing the introduction.

This change removes the sermon from the context of the Night Office—where the epistle was not read—and suits it for use in the Mass of the Day—where the epistle was read. Through this clever adaptation, Ælfric has redirected and retargeted his composition and once again demonstrated the fundamental fluidity that marks early medieval preaching. It is not enough to consider a single context—liturgical or otherwise. Rather, the whole scope of the liturgical lifecycle should be considered to properly assess its impact on any given homiletical text.

Both Ælfric's sermon and *Legimus* are fundamentally structured by their liturgical environments. This may be demonstrated by examining their structure and order. From a modern perspective, they seem to follow a natural order—that is, a historical progression from the earliest times to the most modern.[165] While this is true, the order is far more deeply invested in and reinforced by liturgical categories than historical ones. The way that the saints are grouped is fundamentally reflective of liturgical categories. After all, there are other ways that they could have been grouped; by class: saints who were kings, saints who were soldiers, and saints who were commoners; or by people/language: Greek saints, Egyptian saints, Roman saints, Germanic saints. But they are not.

Instead, this sermon participates in a standard liturgical schema for categorizing the saints and utilizes it as a catechetical tactic for instructing the laity. First, the saints presented after John the Baptist are both in the categories and order found in the *commune sanctorum*. In a standard sacramentary, lectionary, or homiliary, the entries for the Temporale and Sanctorale would be followed by a group of generic templates for use in

---

[165] Ælfric would seem to participate in this by identifying historical eras which his source does not do. Rather than seeing this as a sign of an incipient historicizing mind-set, it is far more plausible to see it as yet another expression of the "six ages of the world" motif so popular among Anglo-Saxon exegetes.

celebrating local or, at least, nonuniversal saints. They were arranged in order of their liturgical importance and came with both singular and plural versions—Common of One Apostle, of Many Apostles, of One Martyr, of Many Martyrs, of One Confessor, of Many Confessors, of One Virgin, and of Many Virgins. The *commune sanctorum* was never a completely formalized set, however. While there is no unanimous agreement between the sources, the general order and classes of saints are consistent with one another and with the categories sketched by both sermons.

The order then appears in a host of materials designed to communicate and reinforce these classes of sanctity. The *Te Deum*, a foundational canticle used in the Night Office on every Sunday and feast, uses the same key groups:

> To thee [God] all Angels cry aloud; the Heavens, and all the Powers therein
> To thee Cherubim and Seraphim continually do cry:
> Holy, holy, holy Lord God of Sabaoth,
> Heaven and earth are full of the Majesty of thy glory.
> The glorious company of the Apostles praise thee.
> The goodly fellowship of the Prophets praise thee.
> The noble army of martyrs praise thee.
> The holy Church throughout all the world doth acknowledge thee.[166]

The groupings are then taken up and found scattered throughout the liturgy. For instance, one of the psalm antiphons used in some communities for Lauds on All Saints rehearses the full list:

> Angels, archangels, thrones and dominions, principalities and powers, virtues: cherubim and seraphim, patriarchs and prophets, holy doctors of the law, all apostles, martyrs of Christ, holy confessors, virgins of the Lord, anchorites, and all saints, pray for us.[167]

Similarly, the hymns appointed in the Winchester Hymnals used by Ælfric and his teachers, *Festiva saeclis colitur*[168] and *Christe, redemptor*

---

[166] Translation from *The Book of Common Prayer* (New York: Church Publishing, 1928), 10.

[167] CAO 1398—expanded form.

[168] Inge B. Millful, Hymn 98, in *Hymns of the Anglo-Saxon Church* (Cambridge: Cambridge University Press, 1997), 358–60.

omnium, conserva,[169] praise in turn the Virgin Mary, angels, patriarchs, prophets, John the Baptist, Apostles, martyrs, confessors, virgins, and monks. Inspired by *Legimus*, Ælfric turns this monastic commonplace into a catechetical tool to teach the laity about the various classes of angels and saints venerated by the church.

Within the corpus of commonly used responsories, three proceed directly from the Beatitudes. Of these, the most common and most widely used across the early manuscripts focuses on the same beatitude Ælfric does:

> *Beati qui persecutionem* (*CAO* 6183)
> **R:** Blessed are those who suffer persecution on account of righteousness, for theirs is the kingdom of heaven; blessed are the peacemakers, for they shall be called sons of God.
> **V:** Blessed are the pure in heart, for they shall see God. Blessed are the peacemakers . . .[170]

Another frequently seen conclusion to the responsory was to repeat the response at the end of the verse beginning with "for theirs is the kingdom of heaven."[171] Exegetically, the latter form reinforces that all of the beatitudes are ultimately oriented toward attaining the kingdom.

The recapitulation of the reception of the kingdom of heaven is a feature of another responsory that utilizes the same beatitudes (and adding one) in a different configuration:

> *Beati mundo corde* (*CAO* 6180)
> **R:** Blessed are the pure in heart, for they shall see God; blessed are the peacemakers, for they shall be called sons of God. Blessed are those who suffer persecution on account of righteousness, for theirs is the kingdom of heaven.
> **V:** Blessed are those who hunger and thirst for righteousness. For theirs is the kingdom of heaven.[172]

---

[169] Ibid, Hymn 99, 361–63.
[170] *CAO* 6183a.
[171] See *CAO* 6183b, c.
[172] *CAO* 6180.

Again, receiving the kingdom is emphasized. The other responsory utilizing the Beatitudes simply presents the makarisms in the order of the Matthean Latin text not present in these two.[173]

Thus, looking at the liturgical context of Ælfric's sermon for All Saints, we see once again the fluidity of function that existed concerning early medieval homiliaries. While modern scholars may prefer to assign some to the Night Office and others to the Mass, actual texts like Ælfric's show that such a rigid categorization was not kept in early medieval monasteries. Signs of a context wherein a particular sermon originated and where it was intended to be delivered, however, can indeed yield useful clues to the compositional process.

The liturgical background places emphasis on two points specifically addressed by Ælfric, the first being the categorization of the holy ones that Ælfric transforms into a catechetical tool, the second being the exegetical emphasis on the final beatitude. As the responsory rearranges the Beatitudes to put the last in first place, so Ælfric awards pride of place to the blessedness of persecution when it is for the sake of righteousness.

Discussion

Surveying the modern works on the Beatitudes, a single issue consistently rises to the fore: ethics or eschatology. Martin Dibelius was the first major proponent of an eschatological understanding of the Sermon on the Mount in his 1940 book of the same name.[174] Current scholarship wrestles with the proper place of eschatology and ethics in the sermon as a whole and the Beatitudes in particular, and the authors we have surveyed participate in that struggle. All four of the modern interpretations acknowledge that both ethics and eschatology are in view; in all of them, the eschatological dimension is foregrounded, the ethical receding into the background. In short, they programmatically present an inclusive

---

[173] *CAO* 6181. **R.** Blessed are the poor in spirit, for theirs is the kingdom of heaven; blessed are the meek, for they shall possess the earth; blessed are those who weep, for they shall be consoled; blessed are they who hunger and thirst for righteousness, for they shall be filled. **V.** Blessed are the merciful, for they shall be shown mercy. Blessed are those who hunger . . .

[174] Martin Dibelius, *The Sermon on the Mount* (Philadelphia: Fortress Press, 1940).

both/and rather than an exclusive either/or—but practically prefer the eschatological over the ethical.

Historically speaking, if one option needs to be stressed, then the eschatological deserves it—the history of interpretation has greatly emphasized the ethical and the spiritual. Certainly Leo and Augustine understood the Beatitudes to be describing a set of discrete steps to holiness. Leo describes the purpose of the Beatitudes thus: "that they who wish to arrive at eternal blessedness may understand the steps of ascent to that high happiness."[175] Augustine refers to the sermon as a whole as "a perfect standard of the Christian life"[176] and describes the sequence of makarisms as a set of stages (*gradu*) that lead to completeness and spiritual perfection.

While Ælfric refers to the Beatitudes as being ordered (*geendebyrd*)[177] and uses the term grade or step (*stæpe*)[178] he does not present Augustine's theory of the Beatitudes. Rather than presenting them as steps in a system, he simply elucidates each makarism with an explanatory gloss. It is worth considering whether Ælfric knew of Augustine's strategy and chose not to follow it (especially given his concluding notice: "We might treat this holy reading much more following Augustine's interpretation but we doubt whether you may profitably understand more depth"),[179] or if the portion included in his edition of Paul the Deacon concluded before Augustine's elaboration.[180] Nevertheless, Ælfric consistently lifts up the ethical implications, understanding them not only as describing proper Christian behavior but also identifying monasticism as the preferred state for Christians.[181] Looking, therefore, at the texts of patristic and early medieval interpreters, the ethical is well represented—the eschatological seems absent.

Is there anything that an early medieval reading of the Beatitudes could contribute to the modern scholarly discussion? One of the difficulties

---

[175] Leo the Great, Sermon 95.2, *NPNF*² 12.203.

[176] Augustine, *Sermon on the Mount* 1.1, *NPNF* 6.3.

[177] ÆCHom I, 36, line 150.

[178] ÆCHom I, 36, line 250.

[179] ÆCHom I, 36, lines 282–84.

[180] It is worth remembering whenever dealing with early medieval citation of patristic authors that they were citing from excerpts far more frequently than from whole texts.

[181] ÆCHom I, 36, lines 192–97.

flowing from the modern interpreters surveyed here is understanding how to hold the ethical and the eschatological in a creative tension. Can the medievals suggest an alternate paradigm for holding these two meanings together? Leo and Augustine contain such a paradigm implicitly; Ælfric moves toward making it more explicit through his utilization of the *Legimus* sermon. The liturgical context is the catalyzing element.

Sanctity or holiness within the early medieval period was not fundamentally about pious moralism but about the manifestation of eschatological power. Saints were not venerated because they were ethical people or followed scriptural rules; their veneration was directly related to their ability to provide supernatural benefits—especially healing—to their suppliants. Attempting to communicate to modern medievalists the Anglo-Saxon conception of sanctity, Lapidge draws a vivid picture taken from the writings of Lantfred, a monk visiting Winchester in the 970s:

> [Lantfred] shows us the inside of the Old Minster crammed with persons afflicted with appalling physical deformities, festering wounds, blind, paralytic, deaf, dumb, mutilated indescribably by the just process of law or by self-imposed penitential torture, all clustered around the shrine of St. Swithun, lying there day and night, moaning in pain and praying aloud for deliverance from their suffering. On occasion, Lantfred reports, the church's precincts were so plugged with diseased persons that they periodically had to be cleared to make way for the clergy.[182]

But the presence of the diseased is not the end of the story for Lantfred. The incumbent of Winchester responsible for the translation of St. Swithun's relics to the Old Minster was the reforming Bishop Æthelwold, Ælfric's teacher. Lantfred recounts that when Æthelwold would leave his seat on official business, the monks would ignore his command to sing a solemn *Te Deum* at each miraculous cure—since they were being roused three to four times every night on account of Swithun's power![183]

---

[182] Michael Lapidge, "The Saintly Life in Anglo-Saxon England," in *The Cambridge Companion to Old English Literature*, ed. Malcolm Godden and Michael Lapidge (Cambridge: Cambridge University Press, 1986), 243.

[183] Lantfred's "Life of St. Swithun" is translated in pages 252–322 in Michael Lapidge, *The Cult of St. Swithun*, Winchester Studies 4.2 (Oxford: Clarendon, 2003).

One of the responsories appointed for the feast of All Saints in the early antiphonaries specifically references miraculous cures at the tombs of the saints:

> *Laudemus Dominum in beati* (*CAO* 7082)
> **R:** Let us praise the Lord on account of the glorious merit of blessed bishop N. The sick came to his sepulcher and were healed.
> **V:** Truly wondrous is God who made blessed N. to shine forth continuously with miracles. The sick came . . .[184]

While moderns may be rightfully skeptical concerning the historicity of the miraculous healings recounted in the lives of the saints and the responsories, these texts present a clear expectation that the miraculous is an inextricable element of sanctity. Indeed, as a regularized process became universal within the Western church, the bar for canonization was set at two documented miracles—a criterion still followed today by the Roman Catholic Church.

At the end of the day, the modern and the early medieval monastic approaches to the Beatitudes yield different results. The modern perspective identifies the presence of eschatology within the pages of the text. The early medieval monastic finds a moral program to inhabit. But the early medieval perspective offers the modern a broader scope than just the content of the text, locating an eschatological meaning as the result of the embodiment of the text; the eschatological is in the enacting of the text, not just its reading. Thus, the early medieval offers the modern scholarly endeavor the possibility of eschatological force in the results of embodying the text. Eschatology follows from the ethical.

---

[184] *CAO* 7082a. The version of the antiphon in the *CAO* is also used for the common of bishops; the incipit in the referenced manuscript (Paris lat. 1085) presumably refers to a more generic formula for All Saints.

Chapter 4

Two Healings and the Parable of the Wise and Foolish Maidens

INTRODUCTION

Matthew 8:1-13 falls into two natural sections, each containing a miraculous healing. While the stories are clearly related by the similarity of their content, the lack of an organic connection between them has often been noted by interpreters. Eusebius, the ancient Greek chapter divisions found in the earliest manuscripts called *kephalai,* and the majority of the early Western chapter divisions separate the two parts into different units.

The first is a relatively brief account of Jesus healing a leper (Matt 8:1-4). Eusebius identifies it as Triple Tradition and modern editors concur, placing it parallel to Mark 1:40-45 and Luke 5:12-16. Matthew edits Mark's account down slightly, reducing the emotional content and dropping the ending that has the healed man disobey the injunction to silence. Perhaps Matthew's most significant editorial decision is to use this as the point at which he returns to following the Markan storyline after inserting the Sermon on the Mount.

The second unit (Matt 8:5-13) is broken by Eusebius into three sections. The first (Matt 8:5-11a) is identified as an alternate Triple Tradition—his heading III—that identifies material common to Matthew, Luke, and John. He places Luke 7:1-9 and John 4:46b-54 in parallel. Matthew

181

8:11b-12 and 13 are identified as Double Tradition and paired with Luke 13:28b-29 and Luke 7:10, respectively. Aland's *Synopsis* concurs.[1] Clearly not a straightforward miracle story, the passage hovers between apothegma—a story with a saying attached to it—and a miracle.

MODERN INTERPRETERS

Ulrich Luz

Luz begins his analysis with an overview of Matthew 8–9 in which he compares Matthew's interweaving of themes in this section to a braid. There is a narrative movement in this section of Matthew reinforced by the repetitious character of the story: "Above all, the miracles of Jesus of which 4:23 already spoke are repeated, as are the idea of discipleship and the emerging conflicts with Israel's leaders."[2] Luz sees a great climax coming at the end of chapter 9 that creates the first major rupture in Jesus' mission to Israel; chapters 8 and 9 set the stage for that event.

But something else is going on as well: "In chap. 8 we have the beginning of a story of Jesus on two levels."[3] Luz proposes that chapter 8 begins an allegory that underlies the material, though he does not say here how far it extends. The allegory does not reveal a deeper moral or spiritual meaning but rather a historical one:

> The surface structure of our text describes a succession of miracles and controversy dialogues that are geographically and chronologically connected. They are part of a story of Jesus with his people that will end with his execution and resurrection. It is a story of increasing conflict and of a rupture among the people. Beneath this surface level there is a deeper dimension. On this second level Matthew begins to tell the foundational story of his own church. It is a story that began with the activity of Jesus in Israel, that continued with the formation

---

[1] Kurt Aland, ed., *Synopsis Quattor Evangeliorum*, 13th rev. ed. (Stuttgart: Deutsch Bibelgesellschaft, 1985), 113–16.

[2] Ulrich Luz, *Matthew 8–20: A Commentary on the Gospel of Matthew*, trans. James E. Crouch, Hermeneia (Minneapolis, MN: Fortress Press, 2001), 2.

[3] Ibid.

there of the community of disciples and with its separation from Israel, and that will end with its mission to the Gentiles.[4]

Thus the allegory chronicles the tensions that arose between Matthew's post-resurrection community and their Jewish neighbors that would eventually become an inevitable split. Reading this allegory, the second level of the text, is an important part of Luz's interpretation of this pericope.

Luz places Matthew 8:1-17 under the heading "Jesus Heals in Israel" and notes that the three stories here are tied together by the main words. The quotation in verse 17 "concludes and interprets" the story cluster. The healing of the leper is treated succinctly; using only two and a half pages, Luz moves through the narrative with some dispatch, with only a few details given much attention. He notes in verse 1 that "The phrase 'follow after' characterizes [the people] as potential church, but the evangelist will not develop this thought until vv. 18-27."[5] The use of Lord in verse 2 is significant and points to the sovereignty by which Jesus heals without appeal to the Father. The command to keep the Law is given some attention because it is closely related to the meaning toward which Luz is driving.

Speaking of Jesus' command to the leper to show himself to the priest, Luz uses the command to make a statement about how Matthew constructs Jesus' messiahship:

> For Matthew it is important that the person who is healed keep the Torah of Moses at the command of Jesus (cf. 5:17-19!). The key word [*katharizō*] ("to be clean") that is used three times also shows that we are now dealing with Israel and its law. Until modern times [*marturion*] ("testimony") was interpreted, probably incorrectly, as a sign of judgment on Israel; but it is more likely that what is meant is a positive witness initially for the priests, but then for all the people who are listening: As Israel's Messiah Jesus keeps the Torah.[6]

As the first sequence in a story of increasing conflict with the religious authorities, Luz sees Jesus making an entirely open and honorable first move that should please those authorities.

---

[4] Ibid.
[5] Ibid., 5.
[6] Ibid.

Summarizing the meaning, Luz makes reference to a "curious double quality," functioning for him as a signal that the allegorical level is at work. On the one hand, he sees the leper as a sympathetic character in whom the readers see themselves:

> the leper addresses Jesus as "Lord" and falls at his feet. He acts, in other words, like a disciple and Jesus stretches out his hand over him as he does over the disciples (12:49; 14:31). He thus becomes for the readers of the Gospel, who of course are also disciples, a figure with whom they can identify.[7]

Luz does not, however, refer to the leper as an exemplary character. His main focus is on the second level meaning: "The healed leper embodies, in a way, the basic unity between discipleship and Israel and thus is a witness for the people."[8] This is crucial: in an emerging struggle over negotiating identity, Luz sees this first miracle as a sign that there need not be a choice between being a faithful member of the Jewish people and a follower of Christ. Christianity need not be a repudiation of Jewish identity. This has been ignored throughout the history of Christian interpretation, though, and Luz finds possibilities here for a post-Shoah understanding of "the potential meaning of Jesus' love for Israel."[9]

Moving to the healing of the centurion's son,[10] Luz identifies it as a mixed form story sharing characteristics of an apophthegm (a saying with a context) and a miracle story.[11] He understands John 4:46-53 as a secondary version of the same story which might have an historical kernel; the apophthegm in verses 11-12 might also go back to Jesus.

As with the first miracle, the second functions on both of Luz's levels and he moves through the story with an eye to arriving at his final interpretation. Operating with Jesus' concern for the Law in mind, Luz sees verse 7 as "an astonished question" that Jesus would so break the Law; the centurion's reply indicates a reverence for the Law despite not falling

---

[7] Ibid.

[8] Ibid.

[9] Ibid., 7.

[10] In distinction to many interpreters, Luz insists that παῖν here means "son" rather than "servant"/"slave" with particular reference to the use of δοῦλον in v. 9.

[11] Luz, *Matthew 8–20*, 8.

under it.[12] Verses 10-12 intimate the first signs of the struggle on the narrative horizon.

Luz begins his summary by referring to the story's multidimensional character. It is the story of a miracle that demonstrates the miraculous sovereignty of Jesus. The main meaning, though, refers to the Gentile identity of the centurion and its implications for the mission to Israel and the future direction of Matthew's community. The Gentile who stands outside of the Law yet respects it and possesses faith in Jesus is both the trigger for a warning to Israel and Matthew's own experience:

> Matthew has experienced both Israel's no to Jesus and the destruction of Jerusalem. He has seen many Gentiles turning to Jesus, and he challenges his own church to become involved in the Gentile mission. The threatening word is for him also a prediction that exactly describes his own situation. . . . The centurion of Capernaum is a marginal figure with a future perspective. . . . This perspective is important for readers in Matthew's church, for in the story of Jesus they recognize their own way. It is a way that, after Easter, leads them into conflict with Israel, out of Israel into the gentile world, and then in that world to the proclamation of the gospel to the Gentiles.[13]

The presence of this character at this point in the story foreshadows how the conflict will develop and serves as a call to mission for the Matthean community.

The other meaning refers to the example of the centurion, and Luz affirms the interpretation of this character often found within the church:

> [Our story] emphasizes the faith of the centurion and gives the readers courage in their own faith. The centurion becomes for them a figure with whom they can identify. The church's interpretation has always correctly understood it this way when the centurion became either the type of true humility or a model of faith. The story thus becomes transparent for the reader's own experience. The granting of the centurion's request becomes the promise to the church that lives by virtue of its Lord's support (28:20).[14]

---

[12] Ibid., 10.
[13] Ibid., 11, 12.
[14] Ibid., 12.

Matthew intends the righteous, God-fearing, Law-respecting centurion as a model for all of his readers, Jew and Gentile.

In conclusion, Luz acknowledges the plain fact of the healing miracles in each episode. They perform a narrative role in setting up the coming conflict, but the greater significance in these stories points to Luz's historical allegory where the conflict referred to in the narrative is a lived reality. These stories affirm for Matthew's community that there does not need to be a choice between Jewish and being Christian. Because most of the Jewish people will not grasp unity, however, the community must bring into the fold those Gentiles who respect the Law and have faith in Israel's Messiah.

Davies and Allison

Davies and Allison begin by locating the whole complex of Matthew 8–9 in complementary parallel with Matthew 5–7. These two sections represent "a two panel presentation which typifies Jesus' ministry. In 5–7 Jesus speaks. In 8–9 he (for the most part) acts. It is thereby shown that God in Christ heals by both words and by mighty deeds."[15] Furthermore, the characters that appear in this second section "are generally recognized to be either from the margins of Jewish society or to be without public status or power."[16] Despite this common characteristic, though, there is no general agreement on the main themes of the block and they rehearse eight main options for how the structure of the two chapters should be understood. Their solution is to see it as a set of three triads of miracle stories. Our pericope forms the first part of the first section which they extend to 8:22.

The function of Matthew 8–9 as a whole, however, is best understood within the complex of Matthew 5–10. This six chapter block "depicts the mission to the lost sheep of the house of Israel"[17] and furthermore communicates the central paradigm of discipleship:

---

[15] W. D. Davies and Dale C. Allison, *A Critical and Exegetical Commentary on the Gospel According to Saint Matthew*, 3 vols. International Critical Commentary 26 (London/New York: T & T Clark International, 2004), 2:1.

[16] Ibid.

[17] Ibid., 2:5.

chapters 5–7 and 8–9 prepare for chapter 10, in which Jesus instructs his missionaries on what they should preach and how they should act. The many parallels between what Jesus has already said and done and what the disciples will say and do demand that one function of the miracle chapters is to set up an example: like master, like disciple (cf. 10.24f.). The Jesus of Mt 8–9 is a model. One must not only learn his words (5–7) but copy his acts, that is, imitate his behaviour. As pupil with rabbi, the disciple of Jesus learns by normative precept (5–7) and by normative example (8–9).[18]

As a result, what occurs in 8–9 should be seen in continuity with and illustrative of the teachings recorded in 5–7. Davies and Allison understand the imitation of Christ to be an overarching theme found in the narrative.

The actual analysis of the first triad of miracle stories that includes Matthew 8:1-13 begins by noting the structure—three miracle stories (8:1-15) and buffer material (8:16-22)—then moves quickly to sources. A longer analytical unit identifies this section split between Double and Triple Tradition material as a typical knot of the Synoptic problem rather than part of its solution.[19] A preface to the exegetical phrase-by-phrase unit provides guidance about what will be uncovered:

> Two themes are highlighted by 8.1–22. First, the three healing stories and the summary in vv. 16–17 show forth Jesus' rôle as compassionate healer and extraordinary miracle worker. Secondly, those healed all belong to the fringes of Jewish society: a leper, a Gentile youth, a woman, demoniacs. This fact reflects the universalism of Matthew's Jesus: the salvation he offers is for all. It is not for any privileged group.[20]

Having identified these emphases, Davies and Allison only occasionally reference them, preferring them to stay in the background and exert a subtle influence over the rest of the interpretation. That is, they are consistent themes, not hermeneutical agendas.

---

[18] Ibid.
[19] Ibid., 2:7.
[20] Ibid., 2:8.

Davies and Allison see the first miracle as having a number of significant facets, most of them revolving around leprosy: the miracle illustrates what came before it, sets up what will follow it, and makes a christological statement. This miracle immediately follows the Sermon on the Mount "primarily because of the reference to the law Moses commanded. Jesus' injunction to follow the Penteteuchal legislation happily illustrates one of the central themes of the Sermon on the Mount: Jesus did not come to do away with Moses (cf. 5.17-19)."[21] Likewise, it looks ahead to chapters 10 and 11 where the healing of lepers is a sign of eschatological expectation fulfilled (11:5) and where Jesus, in a move unique to Matthew, specifically grants his disciples power to heal leprosy as well as other ailments (10:8). Last, the combination of eschatological expectation fulfillment with the intertextual recognition that only powerful prophetic figures were able to cure leprosy in the Old Testament—particularly Moses and Elisha—makes Jesus' healing of leprosy a sign of his christological power.

In contrast to other interpreters (Chrysostom is specifically mentioned) Davies and Allison take Matthew 5:17-19 to be determinative regarding Matthew's belief about Jesus touching a leper; such a touch did not break the Mosaic Law. Further, they believe it is unlikely that Matthew believed such a touch would have made Jesus ceremonially unclean.

A certain amount of space is spent on the question of the historicity of the episode. Of the five encounters with lepers listed in the New Testament,[22] they judge the first, second, and fifth convincing enough to state that: "Jesus was accurately remembered as a man whose healing ministry encompassed even lepers."[23]

The second miracle story (8:5-13), is identified as "more a pronouncement story than a miracle story."[24] At the outset it is placed in parallel with John 4:46-54. The question at hand is historical: do the two accounts—Q and John—reflect two different episodes or one episode, and what conclusions can be drawn concerning its historicity? The coherence of elements between the two and the fact of its early multiple attestation

---

[21] Ibid., 2:10.
[22] Matt 8:1-4 and parallels; Matt 11:5=Luke 7:22; Luke 17:11-19; Matt 10:8, and the mention of Simon the Leper (Ibid.).
[23] Davies and Allison, *Matthew*, 2:12.
[24] Ibid., 2:17.

lead them to conclude that "Mt 8.5–13 par. preserves a concrete memory from the ministry of Jesus."[25] A historical kernel lies at the root of the tradition but its precise details cannot be determined.

Davies and Allison note two meanings of the centurion. First, he is a Gentile. As a character, he foreshadows what will occur later in Matthew and in history. In connection with the magi he helps maintain a minor but consistent Gentile presence in the gospel even during the mission to Israel. Second, he is "a paradigm for the believer in so far as he exhibits true faith. . . . This is why his faith is mentioned not once but twice."[26] Thus another character in addition to Jesus is put forth as a model for imitation.

The heart of the interpretation weighs questions of ethnicity and geography. The presence of a Gentile character within a block specifically identified as the mission to the lost sheep of the house of Israel forces some interpretive choices. As a result, Davies and Allison take Jesus' speech in verse 7 as interrogative rather than indicative; the reflexive "I myself" (*ego*) signals that it should be understood as a question, not a statement.[27] Also, while they note that verse 8 could follow either a statement or a question, the implication (probably correct) is that it more naturally follows a question.[28] As in the case of the Canaanite woman, though, faith is what gives the centurion a hearing and prompts Jesus' miraculous response. Perhaps the most curious part of the interpretation, taken in accord with their overarching theme, is the argument that the phrase "many from the east and west" refers to Jews of the diaspora rather than Gentiles.[29]

In conclusion, Davies and Allison take the two healing miracles that begin Matthew 8 as episodes that both confirm the Sermon on the Mount and provide examples of the works that the disciples will later accomplish in imitation of Jesus. While part of the larger mission to Israel, they represent Jesus' care and concern for those on the margins of Israel, which includes both the unclean and foreigners.

---

[25] Ibid., 2:18.
[26] Ibid., 2:19.
[27] Ibid., 2:21–22.
[28] Ibid., 2:22.
[29] Ibid., 2:27–28.

Eugene Boring

Boring offers brief commentary on the pericope, letting it speak for itself as a narrative. In a lengthy excursus after Matthew 8–9, Boring discusses the interpretation of miracles for the modern context in some detail. This effective section seeks to reframe their interpretation, insisting that a belief in the factuality of the miracles recorded in Matthew is not an adequate yardstick for Christian or biblical faith;[30] rather, their importance—and value to modern Christian communities—lies in the christological claims inherent within them. Because of this section, he does not engage here issues of miracles and meaning—the christological meaning is implicit in the form.

Boring places the Matthew 8–9 block in direct relationship with Matthew 5–7, stating that it has "been constructed by Matthew as a single integrated unit presenting Jesus as 'Messiah in deed' (cf. 11:2), corresponding to 5:1–7:29 as 'Messiah in word' (7:28 and Introduction). The picture of Jesus speaking and acting with 'authority' binds together the two sub-sections."[31] Boring sees the structure of three triads of miracles plus one as "another reflection of the Moses typology that shimmers through Matthew's compositional strategy."[32] There are more than just miracles here, though; discipleship material is an integral part of the block "which underscores the Matthean conviction that Christology and discipleship (ecclesiology) are inseparably related."[33] Thus, the section as a whole he entitles "Miracles and Discipleship"; the pericope 8:1-13 is contained in the first of three subsections, the one entitled "Christ Acts in Power for the Marginal and Excluded."

Though Boring's treatment of the healing of the leper receives only two long paragraphs, he deftly packs a number of exegetical observa-

---

[30] He reminds his readers that all first-century people believed in miracles and believed that Jesus did them. Not all of these people, however, believed in Jesus as Christ. In this way he effectively divorces a belief in the facticity of miracles from the confession of Jesus as Christ, enabling him to place an emphasis on the latter rather than the former.

[31] Eugene Boring, "Matthew," in *The New Interpreter's Bible: Matthew-Mark*, ed. Leander E. Keck, vol. 8 (Nashville, TN: Abingdon, 1995), 222.

[32] Ibid., 223.

[33] Ibid.

tions into the brief space. Noting that the rabbis equated leprosy and its healing with death and resurrection, Boring states that "Matthew has rearranged the sequence of his source to begin with this story, which symbolizes the human situation and the saving work of God in Christ, who restores people to life and community, and also to emphasize Jesus' respect for the Torah."[34] Boring's deliberate ambiguity in referring to "the human situation and the saving work of God in Christ" provides ample space for modern readers to find theological meaning in the story. He draws attention to the leper's use of "Lord," his confession of "faith appropriate to the post-Easter exalted Lord" and dependence on "Jesus' sovereign will" and, furthermore, that Jesus' response is commensurate with these things.[35]

A discussion of Jesus' command focuses on both Jesus' obedience to the Law and the social aspects of the priestly pronouncement of cleanliness. The Markan secret is now a Matthean urging to hasten and perform the Law. A sudden twist on Jesus' attention to the Law concludes the section: "In this pericope Jesus both upholds the Law (as in 5:17) and transcends it, technically violating it (in touching the leper, 8:3; cf. Lev 5:3; 14–15). The pericope thus has the same dialectical attitude toward the Law as do the antitheses (see 5:21-48)."[36] Boring supplies no motive on the part of either Matthew or Jesus for the violation of the Law.

Boring's treatment of 8:5-13 is more lengthy and, following Matthew's own tendencies, focuses on the dialogue rather than the narrative. Boring understands verse 7 as a "question expressing hesitation"[37] that underscores Jesus' commitment to following the Law. The centurion receives the question as "a test of faith—which he passes with flying colors."[38] Boring reminds his readers that "the note of disappointment that such faith has not been found in Israel"[39] is proleptic—Jesus has just started his acts of ministry and subsequent tour of Israel. Boring is at pains to point out that while the "'many from east and west' refers to believing

---

[34] Ibid., 224.
[35] Ibid., 225.
[36] Ibid.
[37] Ibid., 226.
[38] Ibid.
[39] Ibid.

Gentiles . . . this is not, however, necessarily a negation of the promises to Israel, for all Jews are not excluded."[40] Finally, the miracle's effect is described briefly since the emphasis is not on the miracle itself but on the faith of the centurion.

In the "Reflections" section (which does not encompass the healing of the leper), Boring explores what is said and left unsaid concerning the centurion and his faith. He reminds his readers that a Roman officer is "an unlikely candidate for faith, and even more so for the other characters in Matthew's story."[41] He is not only a Gentile but also a direct enforcer of an oppressive system. Furthermore, certain qualifications we might expect are left unsaid in Matthew:

> One who is looking for evidence of faith in this man may first be struck by what is not said: There is nothing at all about his creed. So far as the story is concerned, we do not even know whether he was a theist, not to speak of monotheism. Yet Matthew speaks of him as a model of faith. What does Matthew want to say to us in this story about the contours of real faith? The man feels compassion for someone else who depends on him. Matthew does not novelistically speculate on the details of the boy's illness or his relationship to the centurion. The story focuses on the centurion's concern for him, a concern that impels him to make a potentially humiliating request. He is not embarrassed to seek out an itinerant Jewish preacher and healer, confess his unworthiness to receive a personal visit, and ask him only to speak the authoritative word of healing for the child.[42]

Jesus is the one who certifies the centurion's faith and points it out to those who follow. Whatever its limits, Matthew's Jesus finds the centurion's faith acceptable. As a result, Boring leaves a certain ambiguity open in both stories. In the first Jesus both keeps and breaks the Law—enjoining its performance but engaging in a technical violation. In the second, the faith of the Gentile is accepted but the scope and nature of that faith is not defined.

---

[40] Ibid.
[41] Ibid., 227.
[42] Ibid., 227.

Douglas Hare

Hare treats Matthew 8:1-11 within the context of the larger block of miracle stories. He identifies a series of ten miracle stories that follow the Sermon on the Mount and, within those, puts the first three healings together into a block, noting that verses 16 and 17 serve as summaries that offer transitions to the next block. These ten miracles serve two purposes. On a very basic level, they establish Jesus as a miracle worker. The second and potentially more important purpose is to make a christological point about who Jesus is and the nature of his messianic ministry: these miracles demonstrate that Jesus does not perform miracles for his own glorification but rather in obedience to the will of his Father. Obedience is paramount.

Within this overarching schema, Hare sees the first three miracles as a single interpretive unit, drawing out an element common to all three, then discussing how each of the miracles embodies and adds depth to the common theme. He has titled this block of three "Healing the Excluded," and this title encapsulates his interpretive approach to these texts. He begins his interpretation by making his position explicit: "Matthew's selection of the first three miracles seems to be dictated by the fact that in each case the recipient is excluded from full participation in Israel: the leper is excluded as unclean, the centurion's servant as a Gentile, and Peter's mother-in-law as a woman."[43] Thus these miracles, occupying an important place in Matthew's story of Jesus, signal the importance of the theme of inclusion as a whole. They make a christological statement about Jesus as Messiah: "Jesus is the Messiah by whose power and authority the excluded are included."[44]

Taking up the healing of the leper, Hare draws three main points from it in addition to its overall meaning of inclusion. First, it verifies Matthew 5:17-19 that Jesus has not come to abrogate the Law. Since Jesus sends the leper to see the priests, he is supporting the practice and fulfillment of the Law. (Hare takes no position on the legality of touching a leper.) Second, the leper serves as a paradigm for the Matthean community. The

---

[43] Douglas Hare, *Matthew*, Interpretation (Minneapolis, MN: Fortress Press, 1995), 88.

[44] Ibid., 90.

leper's faith is an important part of the story because it shows that the point of the miracle is not to awaken faith but rather to confirm it. Similar to the leper, the readers of Matthew already come to Jesus and his story with faith. Third, the leper offers an example of the bold suppliancy needed by Christians. The leper approached Christ boldly, disregarding the usual distance requirements to come into the presence of Christ and ask for his healing. Hare exhorts his readers to act with similar boldness in beseeching Christ's gifts.

Rather than offering a comprehensive discourse on the healing of the centurion's servant, Hare prefers to let the episode speak for itself and highlights a few elements for his readers' consideration. He does mention the contrast in the modes of presence in the first two miracles—healing in proximity by touch and at distance with a word—he draws no further attention to the fact on the basis that Matthew does not seem to highlight it either.

While Hare suggests that the Gentile readers of Matthew's community would have been encouraged by the prominent placement of a Gentile in the narrative, Hare warns against misreading this fact. He sees the same reluctance present here as in 15:23-24 (the story of the Canaanite woman) and interprets the words of Jesus in verse 7 as a question rather than a statement. Only the centurion's faith overcomes the Messiah's reluctance. The centurion has rightly perceived that Jesus stands within a chain of authority and, in obedience to God, is entrusted with issuing orders to the angels. Presumably, this facet of the story connects with the overarching theme of obedience that Hare sees connecting the whole of the miracle block.

Finally, Hare finds in Jesus' statement on behalf of the Gentiles not only a Matthean reproach to the Jews who did not follow Jesus but also a warning to all who are complacent in their faith. Transcending the boundaries of the Matthean narrative, Hare warns his comparatively affluent North American and European readers not to trust in their birthright, for many will come from the modern East and West—Asia and Africa—as a judgment against those who confess the faith but do not follow it.

In the main, Hare prefers to offer collected observations on the narrative, pointing out particular elements of the stories for the edification of his readers. His liberation hermeneutic grounds his reading of the pericope and is augmented with both historical and spiritual interpretations of the text. His spiritual interpretations tend to focus on qualities for emulation within the characters and by means of these offer applications of the text to the modern world.

ÆLFRIC'S INTERPRETATION
Homily Proper

Ælfric's interpretation of Matthew 8:1-11 is a clearly structured exposition that moves methodically through the Matthean text.[45] The two miracles within the pericope are treated separately; functionally speaking, these are two homilies here compressed into a single text. While there are thematic consistencies between the two, Ælfric does not put the two sections into direct relationship with one another.

Ælfric understands the miracle stories like other narrative passages of the gospels—they are moral discourses to be parsed for virtues to be imitated by the faithful. As far as Ælfric's interpretation is concerned, the chief point of contact between these two healings is that the characters model the same virtues. In both cases, Jesus models humility while the one requesting the healing models faith. As a result, the fundamental message of the passage as a whole is the importance of humility and the centrality of faith to the Christian life.

Following his usual practice, Ælfric begins with a translation of Scripture. Rather than rendering the whole gospel, however, he only translates the initial verse and the first miracle story, Matthew 8:1-4. After the translation, he makes reference to Haymo, tacitly identifying him as a source. While within Matthew's narrative 8:1 serves as a transition between the Sermon on the Mount and a cluster of miracle stories, Ælfric sees it operating in a different way. From his perspective, this line is the beginning and introduction to what follows and serves as a statement of purpose rather than transitional material. Reading it allegorically, the descent

---

[45] This is the homily for the Third Sunday after Epiphany in *Ælfric's Catholic Homilies: The First Series, Text*, ed. Peter Clemoes, Early English Text Society, supplementary series 17 (Oxford: Oxford University Press, 1997), 241–48 (hereafter ÆCHom I, 8).

from the mountain and the following crowd refer to the incarnation and the company of the faithful:

> The teacher Haymo said about this teaching that the mountain on which the Savior stood signified the kingdom of heaven from which the Son of the Almighty God came down when he received our nature and became enfleshed incarnate to men that he might redeem mankind from the power of the devil. He was invisible and impassible in his nature, then he became visible and sensible in our nature. The great many who followed him signified faithful Christians who with their conduct follow the steps of their Lord. Naturally we follow Christ's footsteps if we imitate his examples with good works.[46]

Reading this as an introduction to these two miracles, the good works to be imitated by the faithful naturally refer to the miracles or at least the virtues displayed and admonitions contained therein.

Instead of moving line-by-line, Ælfric then cites the first half of the miracle that describes the healing itself. This allows him to address the concepts within this thought complex rather than restricting him to the literal phrases themselves. He begins with a general statement of the miracle's purpose: "In this deed is manifested God's might and his humility."[47] Thus, Ælfric identifies two general ideas around which the rest of the interpretation will turn: the power of God (which we will see is the power to cleanse from both sickness and sin) and the central virtue displayed by Christ, once again the key monastic virtue of humility. Within these stories, humility is defined as counting one's status for naught and thus the willingness to engage people of all stations and conditions, in particular those who fall below one's station by virtue of sickness or status. For the humble, there is no one below them with whom they are ashamed to associate.[48]

Ælfric addresses a number of items in relation to the healing portion of the story. He understands Jesus touching the leper as a violation of

---

[46] ÆCHom I, 8, lines 15–24.

[47] ÆCHom I, 8, lines 29–30.

[48] See the seventh step of humility described in RB 7.51-54: "The seventh step of humility is that a man not only admits with his tongue but is also convinced in his heart that he is inferior to all and of less value." (RB 7.51).

Mosaic Law that simultaneously demonstrates his mastery over it, and the humility to reach out to a leper when his word alone could have healed the man:

> The law of Moses forbade anyone from touching a leper, but the humble Christ would not scorn him though he was repulsive. He also manifested that he was master of the old law and not its servant. Mightily, he could have cleansed him with his words but he touched [him and] thus he manifested that his touch is exceedingly saving to the faithful.[49]

Ælfric then uses the leper's pleas as evidence for his faith: "Faithful was the leper when he said, 'Lord, if you will, you could cleanse me.'"[50] Not Christ alone, but both characters provide models for imitation.

Ælfric then moves from an investigation of the moral qualities embedded in the literal/historical actions to an allegorical and intertexual reading of the significance of the event. The leper symbolizes all humanity who labor under the disease of sin while Jesus is the one prophesied by Isaiah in the suffering servant songs:

> In a spiritual sense, the leper signifies all mankind who are repulsively leprous with manifold sins in the inner man, unless it submits to belief in Christ and prudently perceives that it may not receive soul cleansing except through the Lord who worked no crime nor was any deceit found in his mouth. Hateful is the leprous body with many ulcers and swellings and with manifold eruptions, but the inner man—that is, the soul—is more repulsive if it is steeped in manifold sins. We should rightly believe in Christ that he may heal our souls from the eruptions of sins and we should constantly bid his will to progress. His hand signifies his might and his fleshliness. Just as Christ healed the leper by touching with his hands, so he redeemed us from the offenses of our souls through taking on our flesh. Just as the prophet Isaiah said: "Truly he himself carried our infirmities and he himself bore our afflictions."[51]

---

[49] ÆCHom I, 8, lines 30–34.
[50] ÆCHom I, 8, lines 35–36.
[51] ÆCHom I, 8, lines 40–53.

Both the act of healing and the act of touch have christological implications through the fulfillment of Isaiah's prophecy. The Isaiah citation is a
silent reference to Matthew's own citation of this passage to explain these
healing miracles in his summary in Matthew 8:17.

The healing proper concluded, Ælfric moves to the meaning of the commands of Jesus to the newly restored man without citing them. He draws
from the injunction to silence one of his favorite moral meanings:

> With this then he forbade the healed leper that he should speak of
> this to anyone; with this he gave us an example that we should not
> celebrate our good deeds but we should shun with an inward heart
> idle boasts if we do a little good. Naturally, if we do good in order
> to boast we will not be rewarded with any other reward except hell-
> fire because the boast is a deadly sin.[52]

His attention is focused on the second command of Jesus, however. He
explains the process described in Leviticus for the examination of the
leprous and a declaration of their cleanness, then identifies this procedure
as a type of sacramental reconciliation and the need for priestly absolution. He joins into a debate of the time concerning who the true actor is
in sacramental absolution—if God is the one forgiving, what is the role
of the priest? Affirming that God is the one who absolves, Ælfric understands the priest to play a social role in admitting penitents back into the
fold or leaving them excommunicated until their condition improves,
following the lead of Leviticus:

> So shall each who is leprous inwardly with deadly sins come to God's
> priest and open his secrets to the spiritual healer and by his counsel
> and his help treat, by repenting, his soul's wounds. Certain men think
> that it will suffice completely for healing if they confess their sins with
> a contrite heart to God alone and they do not need to confess to any
> priest if they wander into evil. But, if their belief was true, why would
> the Lord send him whom he himself healed to the priest with any
> sacrifice? For another example of the same, he also sent Paul to the
> priest Annais whom he himself spoke to from heaven saying thus:
> "Go into the city and there it will be said what it is fitting to be done."

---

[52] ÆCHom I, 8, lines 54–60.

The priest does not make a man leprous or unleprous, but he deems that he should be separated from the society of men if his leprosy is getting worse or to dwell with men if his leprosy is getting better. Thus shall the holy priest do. He shall rectify God's people and separate them and excommunicate from Christian men the one so leprous in evil deeds that he will defile others with his evilness. Concerning this the Apostle Paul says: "Expel the evil one from you; lest one ill sheep defile the whole herd." If his leprosy gets better, that is, if he wandered into evil but his habits are rectified through fear of God, he will have a dwelling among Christian men once he is fully healthy in his way of life.[53]

Here, therefore, Ælfric sees the gospel narrative recommending a specific ecclesial practice, the function of which is the preservation and protection of the moral and spiritual life of the community, not just the individual.

Ælfric then takes up the rest of the pericope, translating 8:5-13. At the conclusion of the translation he dives directly into its interpretation. Throughout the interpretation of this second miracle, Ælfric mentions social issues pertinent to his day, perhaps in continuity with the social function of penance and excommunication above. He begins with a moral assessment of the centurion who is found to be a paragon of virtue:

The leader of a hundred approached the savior; he did not do so partially but completely. He approached with great faith and with true humility and wisdom and true love. He had great faith when he said, "Lord, say the word and my servant will be healed." Truly he manifested great humility with this when he said, "Lord, I am not worthy that you should come under my roof." He had great wisdom when he understood that Christ is present everywhere through his divinity when he went bodily and visibly among men. Nor did he lack true love when he bid the Lord for the health of his servant. Many other men asked the Lord, some for their own health, some for their children, some for beloved friends but this thane asked for his servant's health with true love because he did not discriminate according to his own kinsmen. The Lord saw this thane's manifold goodness and said, "I will come and heal your servant."[54]

---

[53] ÆCHom I, 8, lines 60–86.
[54] ÆCHom I, 8, lines 104–17.

The analysis of the centurion's humility and love touches on issues of standing and social relations. In both cases, embodiment of the Gospel virtues
allows the centurion to transcend socially located values for the sake of right
action. He pleaded for the healing of his servant although the man lay
outside his kinship group and thus had no social claim on him. In addition,
the centurion was willing to forgo his rightful place within the human social
hierarchy in recognition (in Ælfric's eyes) of the divinity of Jesus.

Ælfric then brings in a parallel account of the distance healing of a
high-status individual's relation to once again speak to the humility of
Jesus. Ælfric paraphrases John 4:46-53, then draws a comparison with
the Matthean passage. Noting that Jesus heals the prince in John with a
word yet offers to come into the presence of the servant in Matthew,
Ælfric connects humility with a disregard for human status conveyed by
wealth and power, and a recognition of the intrinsic worth of the poor
derived from the image of God:

> Though invited, the Lord would not go bodily to the king's unhealthy
> son but—not present—healed him with his word yet he was ready,
> though uninvited, to go bodily with the centurion. He knew well
> that the king had more might than any centurion, but the son of
> Almighty God manifested with this act that we should not honor
> the rich for their riches but for their [common] human nature. Nor
> should we scorn the poor for their poverty but we should honor
> God's likeness in them.[55]

Moving to the action and speech of Jesus, Ælfric briefly notes that Christ's
words apply to the particular generation within which he lived rather
than Israel historically in order to exempt the prophets and patriarchs.
Without explanation, a quotation from Mary and Martha on the ability
to heal Lazarus follows. Then Ælfric presents another Scripture block—
Matthew 8:11-12—taking up after it those who will come from east and
west to rest with the patriarchs. He gives a spatial and temporal interpretation of these words seeing them both as the Gentiles and as those who
convert in the morning and in the evening.[56] An interesting later addition

---

[55] ÆCHom I, 8, lines 127–34.

[56] Note the similarity of this interpretation with the explanation of the times to which
workers come to the vineyard in his homily for Septuagisima on Matt 20:1-16.

to the homily (only found in manuscripts N and Q) but coming from Ælfric's hand seeks to resolve the potential contradiction between the "many" mentioned here and the "few" referred to elsewhere:

> My brothers, understand this: many will come from east and west and they will rest with Abraham and Isaac and Jacob in the heavenly kingdom. No earthly king may live like a king unless he has thanes and so arranges his household in a manner befitting his kingship. What do you think? Would not the Almighty King who shaped the heavens and the earth have a boundless household who rule with him? He will have many from humanity for his heavenly household and whoever holds this honor there has it on account of what he has earned here in this world.[57]

Anglo-Saxon court convention drives this interpretation; the more powerful a lord is, the more retainers he can support at his hall. Followers are a sign of status. It is perfectly natural to Ælfric, then, that the Lord of All should have a well-filled hall as a sign of his power and status.

The next section offers a curious interpretation based on a deliberate misreading of the passage. Ælfric writes:

> The saying that follows after is very dreadful. The rich sons are cast into the outer darkness where there is weeping and tooth biting. The rich sons are the Jews. God ruled over them through the old law but they rejected Christ and scorned his teaching and he cast them into the outer darkness where there is weeping and tooth biting. Many rich men may do good if they may be righteous and merciful. The patriarch Abraham, David the great king, and Zaccheus (who gave half his possessions to the poor and with half repaid fourfold what he had earlier unrighteously stolen) were all rich men. These rich men and their like came to the eternal kingdom through conversion to God and did not weary him.[58]

The "rich sons" appear nowhere in the Greek text of the passage—or the Vulgate. Ælfric has introduced a deliberate change in order to move away from a literal reading that is of little interest to him and his community

---

[57] ÆCHom I, 8 (App) lines 1–8.
[58] ÆCHom I, 8, lines 166–76.

to secure a moral reading in line with the rest of his homily. The Old English noun for kingdom (*rice*) is a homophone for the adjective for rich or wealthy (*rice*). They are, however, declined differently: "sons of the kingdom" would be *rices bearn*, but Ælfric, both here and in the translation above, consistently offers *rican bearn*, "rich sons." Godden finds the error unaccountable since Ælfric was following Haymo's text to this point and Haymo's interpretation makes much of the distinction between Jews and Gentiles. Ælfric omits most of this material, retaining only a brief note identifying the "rich sons" as the Jews, and focusing, rather, on the issue of how the rich and powerful may be righteous as well, referring to the *topos* of the righteous wealthy to which he appealed in his reading of Matthew 5:2.[59]

This passage adds circumstantial evidence to Lenker's suggestion that the purpose of the West Saxon gospels—written in Old English—was exegetical preparation for homilies.[60] Ælfric's change must have been suggested by looking at an Old English text of the passage. The most secure conclusion that can be drawn is that the change, however it happened, was deliberate and served the advancement of Ælfric's moral reading of the text.

Ælfric then turns to a discussion of the outer darkness, suitably expanded by references to Mark 9. A brief vice list establishes that those with similar sins shall share in similar torments. Ælfric touches on the paradoxical nature of the torments—hell's dark fire which does not dispel the extreme cold—but does not elaborate on them or offer explanations.

The final line of the passage leads Ælfric into a brief summarizing statement on the importance of faith that concludes with the homily's benediction exhorting its hearers to faith in the Trinity:

[59] While it would be nice to attribute Ælfric's changes to Haymo to a rejection of Haymo's anti-Semitism, it seems more likely that he and his community had little or no contact with Jews at all. His explanation of circumcision in his homily for the feast of the Holy Name seems to assume a complete unfamiliarity with Jews and Jewish customs on the part of his hearers. Thus, Ælfric may have considered exhorting his congregation to "pious" anti-Semitism as less edifying then exhorting them to moral reflection on the proper disposition of wealth.

[60] Ursula Lenker, "The West Saxon Gospels and the Gospel-Lectionary in Anglo-Saxon England: Manuscript Evidence and Liturgical Practice," *Anglo-Saxon England* 28 (1999): 141–78, here 172–74.

Belief is the foremost power of all without which no man may please God and the righteous man lives by his faith. Let us come to believe in the Holy Trinity and in the true unity that is the Almighty Father and his Son (who is his wisdom) and the Holy Ghost (who is both their love and will); that they are three in person and in name yet one God in their divinity, ever living without beginning or end. Amen.[61]

Liturgical Context

The season of Epiphany was, according to the early medieval lectionaries, a clearly defined period with its own theological integrity.[62] Following temporally on the heels of the Christmas season, it also follows it theologically; Epiphany represents the working out of themes established by Christmas. The key to the season is the feast of Epiphany itself. Known as both *Epiphania* ("the manifestation") and *Theophania* ("the manifestation of God"),[63] it celebrates the signs and wonders that pointed to the manifestation of God in Jesus. John's Prologue (heard on the feast of the Nativity) provided further guidance for the lectionary's selection of passages for the season, particularly John 1:10-15. The Epiphany season readings group around three major themes of manifestation described in the Prologue: the early miracles of Jesus ("the glory, full of grace and truth," of John 1:14), the rejection of Jesus at Nazareth ("his own people did not accept him" of John 1:11), and the calling of the first followers ("those who believed in him, who believed in his name, who became the children of God," from John 1:12).

The playing out of these themes begins with the distribution of biblical events originally clustered on Epiphany itself. In addition to the Vespers antiphon discussed above in chapter 2, the gospel antiphon appointed for the Lauds of Epiphany by the Portiforium of St. Wulstan identifies the

[61] ÆCHom I, 8, lines 205–10.

[62] The modern Revised Common Lectionary has effectively suppressed the season by making it the first block of Ordinary Time marked by the start of readings in course through the gospel of the year. Only vestiges remain: it retains the traditional themes and emphases for the first two Sundays after Epiphany and—oddly—in the last Sunday after Epiphany/before Lent which it calls the feast of the Transfiguration. This celebration was moved from August 6 in service of the traditional Epiphany theology which was then suppressed.

[63] Both titles are found in Anglo-Saxon lectionaries and missals.

three clustered themes and simultaneously places them under a broader interpretive frame: "Today the heavenly Bridegroom was joined to the Church for in the Jordan Christ himself washed away her guilt, the magi ran with gifts to the royal wedding, and the guests were gladdened by wine made from water, alleluia."[64] The reference to the magi was retained for the feast of Epiphany itself (Matt 2:1-12), with baptismal narratives next placed on the Octave of Epiphany (John 1:29-34) and the Wednesday following the First Sunday after Epiphany (Matt 3:13–17). While the First Sunday after Epiphany completed the biblical account of Jesus' boyhood and the first manifestation of his knowledge of God (Luke 2:42-52), the Second Sunday after Epiphany begins a period of time focused on the first manifestations of Jesus' miraculous powers: the wedding at Cana (John 2:1-11), identified as the first of Jesus' signs (John 2:11),[65] was appointed for the Second Sunday after Epiphany; the Capernaum exorcism (Luke 4:31-37), the first miracle narrative in Luke was appointed for the Friday after the Second Sunday after Epiphany; the healing of the leper and the centurion's servant (Matt 8:1-13) the first miracle narrative in Matthew was appointed for the Third Sunday after the Epiphany. While Matthew 8:1-13 is the first block of miracle narratives, the occurrence of prior miracles is noted in a summary of Jesus' postbaptismal and pre–Sermon on the Mount activity in Matthew 4:23-25—and this passage was appointed for the Friday after the Third Sunday in Epiphany.

As a result of these lectionary mechanics, Ælfric encountered Matthew 8:1-13 as part of a cluster of stories all recounting the first manifestations of God and divine power in the person of Jesus Christ. This liturgical context pushes to the forefront the notions of manifestation and physical incarnation, and Ælfric follows these leads.

In his various English discussions of the seasons of the liturgical year, Ælfric uses the Old English term "*Swutlode*" to refer to Epiphany; this is a direct translation of the Greek term as the root "+*swutl-*" means "manifest." It is therefore no accident that forms of this root appear eight times throughout this homily. Although Ælfric not infrequently uses words

---

[64] *CAO* 3095. By the time of the *Golden Legend* in the 1260s, a fourth had been added: the feeding of the five thousand. See the discussion above in chap. 2.

[65] Note that this verse explicitly collects themes laid out in the prologue—the sign "revealed his glory and his disciples believed in him" (ibid.).

from this root, its occurrences are higher on the average in two homilies: the homily for Epiphany itself and this text. As a result, the season not only has helped determine a theme of the homily (manifestation) but also has shaped Ælfric's choice of words.

The liturgical texts appointed for this time both ground Ælfric's main moral/spiritual interpretation and reveal another theme in the homily, a latent one that Ælfric brought in from his sources. He retained it but did not appreciably expand or draw further notice to it. When the homily is placed in relation to the liturgical Propers, though, this theme appears.

The material that would be repeated throughout the following week matches Ælfric's main thrust. The morning Benedictus antiphon for the third Sunday and the rest of the week that followed is essentially Matthew 8:1-3: "But when Jesus had come down from the mountain, behold a leper coming worshiped him, saying: 'Lord, if you wish, you can cleanse me.' And extending his hand he touched him saying: 'I wish, be made clean.' "[66] The liturgical use of this text again focuses interpretive weight on this verse that describes the physical action of Christ. The healing is implied but not stated in the text; rather the text describes Jesus receiving the leper's request and touching him. The meaning and significance of the actions are left open. The evening Magnificat antiphon from Matthew 8:12 stating, "Many shall come from the east and west, and recline with Abraham, Isaac and Jacob in the kingdom of heaven"[67] serves as an exhortation to join the company coming from east and west and complements the Magnificat's own themes of eschatological reversal. The collect for the occasion, repeated in the weekly masses, directly relates to the gospel text as well: "Almighty and eternal God, deliver us from our various infirmities and extend the right hand of your majesty to protect us. Through Jesus Christ our Lord."[68] It focuses attention on the spiritual meaning of the act of healing, placing the praying community in the place of those beseeching healing. It is very specific about the means by which the healing occurs: "extend the right hand of your majesty." This reference, in turn, leads to the second theme in the liturgical materials.

---

[66] *CAO* 1985.

[67] *CAO* 3832.

[68] Nicholas Orchard, ed., *The Leofric Missal*, 2 vols., Henry Bradshaw Society 113 & 114 (Rochester, NY: Boydell, 2002), 117, item 426.

206 Reading Matthew with Monks

The Offertory in particular focuses on the image of the right hand: "The right hand of the Lord has exerted power; the right hand of the Lord has exalted me. I shall not die but live, and I will recount the works of God" (VgPs 117:16, 17).[69] The Introit and Alleluia both draw on Psalm 96 which connects the notion of God's kingly rule and the manifestation of God's glory to his presence on the earth: "The Lord reigns; let the earth rejoice, let many islands be glad" (VgPs 96:1).[70] The Communion cites an otherwise unconnected phrase from Luke 4:22: "All marveled at this, which proceeded from the mouth of God"[71] that takes on a new meaning when placed in relation to the healing word spoken by Jesus in the second half of the gospel.

Haymo's homily on Matthew 8:1-13 contains a doctrinal discussion of the power of Jesus in relation to the boundaries of the incarnation and the literal and spiritual meaning of the healing power of the hand of Jesus. Haymo essentially argues that the image of the hand (or right hand) is a metaphor for God's might—Jesus' might—and that the distance healing of the centurion's servant demonstrates the continued omnipresence of Jesus while maintaining the localized presence required by the incarnation.[72] Godden notes that these are the aspects of Haymo that Ælfric borrows most, not taking up Haymo's other major theme contrasting Jews and Gentiles.[73]

Taking these liturgical sources back to Ælfric's homily, a deeper level of meaning emerges that had previously been overshadowed by Ælfric's attention to the moral meaning. Ælfric and his sources notice the unusual

---

[69] This is the offertory in the majority of sources in Hesbert's *Antiphonarium Missarum Sextuplex* and in the *Leofric Missal*. (n.b.: the *Leofric Missal* displaces the Epiphany materials by one Sunday so this offertory appears with the usual gradual Propers and gospel for the Fourth Sunday after Epiphany rather than the Third.)

[70] See Hesbert and the *Leofric Missal*.

[71] See Hesbert and the *Leofric Missal*.

[72] Though Ælfric puts up no red flags, Haymo seems on dangerous ground here doctrinally; this view of the omnipresence of Jesus' divinity and the localization of his humanity seems rather Nestorian, crossing the bounds of the Chalcedonian understanding of the two natures of Christ.

[73] Malcolm Godden, *Ælfric's Catholic Homilies: Introduction, Commentary and Glossary*, Early English Text Society, supplementary series, 18 (Oxford: Oxford University Press, 2000), 60.

contrast between the first two miracle stories: that Jesus touches in the first yet heals from a great distance in the second. The juxtaposition of the two miracles becomes a two-step argument concerning the nature of Christ's healing power. The first miracle emphasizes the bodily presence of Christ and the salutary nature of his touch. Ælfric—in line with the collect—connects the literal events of the touch and the healing with the spiritual realities of healing made possible through the incarnation:

> Mightily, Jesus could have cleansed [the leper] with his word, but he touched him: thus he manifested [*geswutelode*] that his touch is exceedingly saving to the faithful. . . . His hand signifies his might and his incarnation.[74] Just as Christ healed the leper by touching him with his hands, so he redeemed us from our souls' sins by taking our flesh just as the prophet Isaiah said: "Truly he himself carried our infirmities and he himself bore our afflictions."[75]

Thus, the incarnation enables Christ to redeem humanity and grants him the touch that heals both body and soul. The second step explores the issue of the presence of Christ and how the healing reveals truths about the mode of Christ's presence even during the incarnation.

The doctrinal aspects of the second miracle are placed within the story's frame by attributing them to the centurion's perceptive wisdom: "[the centurion] had great wisdom when he understood that Christ is present [*andwerd*] everywhere through his divinity when he went bodily [*lichamlice*] and visibly among men." The terms "presence" (*andwerd*) and "bodily" (*lichamlice*) are closely connected here in a manner that will occur again in the homily. Their relation is the issue at stake: must Christ—and his healing right hand—be bodily present in order to be truly present? Ælfric's answer is that the second miracle provides a negative answer. The healing power of the word demonstrates that Christ's healing right hand is independent of his bodily location.

The two terms occur again in Ælfric's comparison of the Johannine parallel but here the doctrinal meaning is suppressed in favor of the moral:

---

[74] Literally, "fleshliness" (*flæsclinysse*). This is linguistically paralleled by Ælfric's use of "taking our flesh" (*anfenge ure flæsces*) in the Isaiah quotation below.

[75] ÆCHom I, 8, lines 32–34, 49–53.

The Lord, though invited, would not go bodily [*lichamlice*] to the king's unhealthy son but, not present [*unandwerd*], healed him with his word. And yet, he was ready although uninvited to go bodily [*lichamlice*] with the centurion. He knew well that the king had more might than any centurion but the son of Almighty God manifested [*geswutlode*] with this deed that we should not honor the rich for their riches but for their [common] human nature nor should we scorn the poor for their poverty but should honor God's likeness in them. The humble son of God was ready to go to the servant with his presence [*andwerdnyss*] yet he healed the prince with his command. Concerning this the prophet said: "The exalted Lord observes the humble, and he knows the haughty from afar."[76]

In essence, this interpretation seems to overturn the first, denying Christ's presence to the prince. The moral meaning, then, is drawn from the literal level; Christ could have healed the leper, the centurion's servant, or the prince whether present or absent but deployed his bodily presence to give an example to be followed on the treatment of rich and poor. The humility manifested in the bodily example should be imitated, supernatural capabilities aside.

The doctrinal focus on presence also clarifies an otherwise confusing comparison between the centurion and the two sisters Mary and Martha. In treating Jesus' comment on the surpassing greatness of the centurion's faith above all of the Jews of his generation, Ælfric mentions Mary and Martha. By placing the reference here, Ælfric clearly intends his hearers to see how they are surpassed by the centurion's witness, but no explanation is given as to how this occurs: "Mary and Martha were two sisters exceedingly faithful to God; they said to Christ: 'Lord, if you had been present [*andwerd*] here, our brother would not have departed.' This thane [the centurion] said to Christ, 'Say the word and my servant will be healed.'" All three characters are identified as having powerful faith—the centurion having "great faith" (*micelum geleafan*),[77] while Mary and Martha are "exceedingly faithful" (*swiþe belyfede*).[78] The comparisons appear positive; there does not seem to be a defect in their faith. Viewed from

---

[76] ÆCHom I, 8, lines 127–38.
[77] ÆCHom I, 8, lines 105 and 106.
[78] ÆCHom I, 8, lines 147–49.

the liturgical emphasis on presence, though, it appears that the sisters' defect was not in their faith *per se* but in their understanding of the omnipresence of Christ. They failed to perceive, as the centurion had, that Christ was present even when not there bodily.

The doctrinal focus on the presence or absence of Christ in relation to the bodily presence of the man Jesus diminishes (if not effectively bypassing altogether) the centurion's statement on authority. Because Ælfric is attempting to communicate that it is Christ's divine presence accomplishing the healing, he makes no reference to angelic or supernatural mediators through whom Jesus accomplishes healing.[79] While Anglo-Saxon Christians firmly believed in the role of supernatural beings causing illness as shown by the numerous references to and charms against elf-shot in the healing manuals, Ælfric gives no hint at all that that supernatural beings outside of the Trinity are involved in the distance healings.[80]

Discussion

The modern commentaries emphasize the marginal nature of the individuals healed in this pericope; Ælfric makes no reference to this common characteristic. If anything, he seems to flatten the distinction between Jew and Gentile, regarding the centurion as socially equivalent to a minor secular lord of his own day and therefore a person of social power and influence rather than an outsider. Luz contends in his brief survey of the history of interpretation of the healing of the leper that the social aspect of the text has been missing until recent times: "The leper is a type of the believer who comes to Christ and receives a gift from him. As a rule his gift was understood figuratively; one is freed from 'spiritual leprosy,' from mortal sin. Seldom was the physical and social dimension of Christ's help

---

[79] Smaragdus cites two unattributed but presumably patristic passages that both discuss the angelic beings located in Jesus' control in the divine chain of command. Ælfric is not ignorant of this reading. Rather, he chooses to suppress it.

[80] See Karen L. Jolly, *Popular Religion in Late Saxon England: Elf Charms in Context* (Chapel Hill/London: University of North Carolina Press, 1996), and Richard S. Nokes and Kathryn Laity, eds., *Curing Elf-Shot and Other Mysterious Maladies: New Scholarship on Old English Charms* (University Park, PA: Penn State University Press, 2009).

taken seriously."⁸¹ Ælfric's interpretation confirms the truth of the first part of Luz's statement but calls into question the second.

Ælfric's discussion of the healing of the leper does make the ready turn to a spiritualizing interpretation. It holds, however, the spiritual meaning in tension with the literal meaning of the passage, placing the two in parallel: "Just as Christ healed the leper by touching [him] with his hands, so he redeemed us from the offenses of our souls by taking on our flesh."⁸² The spiritual truth does not cancel out the literal truth though Ælfric clearly considers the spiritual to be of more relevance to his congregation.

Ælfric refutes Luz with his attention to the social dimensions of the text. Ælfric offers his hearers a brief recap of the Levitical laws concerning leprosy that includes the social penalties of the sickness. Furthermore, Ælfric went beyond speaking of the text as text and offered a concrete discussion of how the text was to be acted out in the community of his day by reference to specific ecclesial practices embodying Christ's healing inclusion.

The patristic and early medieval church took sin seriously. The consequence of mortal sin was eternal damnation in the torments of hell—torments described frequently and in laborious detail by the anonymous Old English homilies as well as more orthodox material. The church did not regard sin solely as a problem for the individual sinner. The presence of unrepentant sinners within the community threatened the whole community's eschatological standing. An insufficient response on the part of the church authorities risked the spread of sinful behavior. As early as 1 Corinthians (1 Cor 5:1-13) and Matthew's own gospel (Matt 18:15-17), excommunication was the ultimate means of discipline if other methods failed.

Godden notes that Ælfric's connection of "sick sheep" to 1 Corinthians 5:13 suggests that his discussion of excommunication is filtered through the Rule of Benedict where the last resort is expulsion: "For the Apostle says: *Banish the evil one from your midst* (1 Cor 5:13); and again, *If the unbeliever departs, let him depart* (1 Cor 7:15), lest one diseased sheep infect the whole flock" (RB 28.6-7). Intentional communities cannot survive without clear methods of discipline—and monasteries are no exception. Benedict spends seven chapters specifically on excommunication—what faults deserve it and how it should be handled.

⁸¹ Luz, *Matthew 8–20*, 7.
⁸² ÆCHom I, 8, lines 50–52.

When severe offenses occur in the monastery, the process laid out in Matthew 18:15-17 is used; if no reconciliation occurs, the offender is excommunicated. There are two degrees of monastic excommunication, and both are fundamentally social. For less serious faults, offenders were allowed to participate in the community's liturgical life but could not have leadership roles in worship. Furthermore, they were excluded from the common meal, eating alone after the others. For severe faults, offenders are excluded from both the community's liturgical life—including Mass and reception of the Eucharist—as well as the common meal. Furthermore, all contact is cut off: the monastics must work and eat alone and receive no blessings, nor is the food of offenders blessed. Anyone contacting offenders without permission is likewise excommunicated. The only human contact allowed by the Rule is from the abbot/abbess or seniors when they attempt to persuade offenders to reform their ways. If neither remonstrations nor beatings prove effective, offenders are expelled from the community. Those expelled who show sufficient contrition may be received back twice but a third expulsion is final.

Similarly, the excommunication of a lay person cut them off from Christian fellowship. The rest of the community was not to associate with them and they could not receive the sacraments or a Christian burial thus ensuring their eternal damnation. According to the official Canons of the Western church, excommunicates could be reconciled with the church and community by becoming Penitents, a technical term denoting a class of people, some of whom underwent public penitential acts for the rest of their life. This form of penance could only be undertaken once; there was no second chance.

In the early medieval period the practice of private auricular confession gained ground as an alternative to this merciless process.[83] A form known as "tariff penance" arose in Celtic monastic communities and spread from the British Isles to the continent. Rooted in monastic ideals, particularly Cassian's *Insititutes* on the vices and their contrary remedies, sinners could confess their faults, receive a penance (which usually involved fasting for set periods), then receive priestly absolution.

---

[83] While popular in this period, auricular confession did not gain official standing in the Western church until it was mandated by the bull *Omnis utriusque sexus* promulgated by the Fourth Lateran Council in 1215.

While the rabbis compared the social consequences of leprosy to death, early medieval theologians compared the state of mortal sin (including excommunication) to both leprosy and death.[84] Its reversal in auricular confession was thus equivalent to miraculous healing and resurrection: the two proof texts with which it was consistently connected are the healing of the leper and the resurrection of Lazarus.[85]

While Luz contends that the leprosy was spiritualized and the social aspects of this text were therefore overlooked by early interpreters, I would contend that the spiritualization of leprosy and the comparison of confession to the miraculous cure not only capture the concept of the inclusive power of Christ's healing but also literally enact it within the community. Through sacramental absolution, those excluded by their sinful behavior are welcomed back into the community; the repentant sinner, like the healed leper, is reintegrated within the social order.

MATTHEW 25:1-13

Introduction

Matthew 25:1-13 is a parabolic narrative. That is, it appears as a parable in the midst of parables. Its introductory formula is common to several of Matthew's parables of the kingdom,[86] and like them, a narrative follows. However, the narrative is more extended than usual, raising the question of whether the passage is properly a parable, an allegory, or some blend of the two.

This parable is unique to Matthew—Eusebius assigns it to Canon X. Aland notes some minor thematic parallels between the parable and Mark 13:33-37 and Luke 12:35-38; 13:25-28. The final verse of the parable shares a number of textual and thematic parallels to other verses within this discourse, most notably Matthew 24:42 but also 24:50.

---

[84] Indeed, the seventh-century Penitential of Cummean begins with this statement: "Here begins the prologue on the medicine for the salvation of souls." Oliver Davies, *Celtic Spirituality*, Classics of Western Spirituality (New York: Paulist Press, 1999), 230. The Penitential is in Davies, *Celtic Spirituality*, 230–45.

[85] See Peter Lombard's foundational treatment in *Sententiarum Libri Quatuor* 3.18.1.

[86] Matt 13:24, 31, 33, 44, 45, 47; 18:23; 20:1; 22:2.

Modern Interpreters

Luz

Luz locates the parable of the virgins as "the third watchfulness parable" that is linked to the preceding parables by a set of catchwords—"wise," "delay," "master/Lord."[87] Overall, he posits a fairly complicated structure to make sense of all of the elements of the parable; it "follows the classical three steps of a dramatic narrative" and also contains a title and an ending refrain.[88] Thus, we have the title in verse 1, background exposition in verses 2-5, the conflict appears in verses 6-9, and the denouement encompasses verses 10-12. Luz refers to verse 13 simply as "a refrain-like call to watch" and passes over how or if this verse is integrated with the larger whole.

Luz devotes a substantive section of his treatment to the source of the text. He attacks the question by considering whether or not the narrative is culturally plausible based on a knowledge of first-century marriage customs, apart from any metaphorical or allegorical meaning. The two central points that he must explain are these: where the virgins are sleeping, and what the "lamps" are, where they are, and whether they are ignited while the virgins sleep; these are the elements that seem least plausible (for what sort of women fall asleep—outside—with lit oil lamps?). After making a compelling argument that the *lampadēs* were lantern torches rather than simply oil lamps and suggesting that the virgins were inside rather than outside when the call comes, he concludes that verse 1 is a title. In light of these interpretations, he decides that this narrative is a plausible story reflecting ancient Palestinian life and could indeed go back to Jesus rather than necessarily being a creation of the early church.

As a result, Luz offers three interpretations: one for the parable as told by Jesus, another for the parable as told by the church, and the third as Matthew understood it. The first is rather simple and straightforward; Luz believes that Jesus' original parable had no reference to the Parousia—the second coming of Christ—but was about recognizing the "*kairos* of joy" in

---

[87] Ulrich Luz, *Matthew 21–28*, trans. James E. Crouch, Hermeneia (Minneapolis, MN: Fortress Press, 2005), 227.

[88] Ibid.

the presence of Jesus. At the second level, however, the bridegroom was no longer the earthly Jesus but the exalted Jesus, and the delay of the bridegroom is now related to the delay of the Parousia. The third level leads into Luz's verse-by-verse exposition. He moves briskly, covering the twelve verses in just two and a half pages, utilizing a reader-response perspective that envisions how Matthew's readers understand the tragic drama unfolding before them and attending to how Matthew creates tension, introduces reversals, and (in v. 11) shifts from bridegroom to Son of Man-World Judge. At this point he chooses to take the same tack as he sees Matthew taking, and leaves the meaning of the story and the significance of the oil open.

While Luz typically includes a "History of Interpretation" section, in this case he launches into a (comparatively) lengthy eleven-page examination of the church's use of this text, complete with a manuscript illumination and three photographs of sculptures that depict the parable. In defense of this extreme treatment, he notes that "no parable of Jesus was painted or portrayed in the plastic arts as frequently" and examines the interpretations embedded within medieval artistic depictions of the parable. Following his usual method he breaks the potential meanings into general categories, identifying five:

1. *The spiritual interpretation in terms of the individual.* This is a predominantly early and Alexandrian reading where the virgins are the senses that must be kept unstained from evil. It is noneschatological, and Origen is the chief exemplar.[89]

2. *The ecclesiastical eschatological interpretation.* These interpretations see the virgins as representative of individual Christians who live their lives, die, then appear at the Great Judgment. The virgins function in two ways in this strand:[90]

   a. *Wise women as positive models.* Especially in the Eastern church, the wise virgins were models for Christian female ascetics. Bride mysticism may be a component of this interpretation as well. Western medieval illustrations also teach this perspective and the parable becomes an encouragement to virginity.

---

[89] Ibid., 235–36.
[90] Ibid., 236–40.

b. *Preaching of penitence.* This interpretation focuses on the foolish virgins as negative models; Luz refers to both medieval plays featuring the virgins but also to the inclusion of the virgins into the depictions of the Last Judgment carved into high medieval cathedrals.

3. *Parenetic interpretations.* Parenetic readings were the most common, though, and these fall into three types:[91]

   a. *The classic Catholic interpretation.* Here the lamps of the virgins represent faith while the oil represents good works.

   b. *The Augustinian type.* This is focused on the believer's attitude. The lamps refer to faith; as for the oil, "The information that Augustine and his followers give is somewhat unclear."[92] The main point is the attitude or motive that produces the good works.

   c. *The anti-ascetic type.* John Chrysostom and others deny that asceticism alone will get one into the banquet, rather the crucial oil is "human kindness, alms, aid to the needy."[93]

   d. *The pictorial interpretations.* In the Gothic style, many depictions of the foolish virgins present them in overly elaborate clothing, suggesting that wasteful and immoral behavior is the key to their guilt.

4. *Interpretations with salvation history tendencies.* Starting with Jerome, some saw the wise virgins as Christians or representatives of the church and the foolish as Jews or representatives of the Synagogue. This interpretation also appears in some of the Gothic cathedral carvings.[94]

---

[91] Ibid., 240–42.

[92] Ibid., 242. The truth of this comment will become quite clear in the following modern and medieval interpretations. However, Luz makes matters more complicated than he should have as he attempts to harmonize Augustine's two major treatments into a single reading. In my view, Augustine actually gives two completely different readings, one of which was taken up by the tradition, as will be discussed later in Ælfric's treatment of the text.

[93] Ibid.

[94] Ibid., 242–43.

5. *Matthew 25:1-13 in the confessional conflict.* In the Reformation and post-Reformation periods, the oil was either faith or the Holy Spirit. This interpretation was a conscious reversal of the classic Catholic parenetic interpretation, insisting that works without faith are worthless.[95]

Surveying all of these options, Luz dismisses interpretations 1 and 4 as being furthest from the original meaning of the text. He approves the bride mysticism of number 2 as legitimately within the bounds of the text. While number 5 has roots in Paul, it contradicts the emphases of the Matthean text. Numbers 3b and 3c, with their emphasis on love, are "not far removed" from the original intent.[96] Luz finds the emphasis on virginity in 2a and on judgment in 2b as quite problematic.

Luz summarizes the parable as parenesis for the church. "Here the readers learn that not everyone who is called to the wedding of the bridegroom will actually share in it."[97] The final note on watching is a call to constant obedience to the will of the Father so that believers are fully prepared and need not worry even if they do sleep; the timing of the Parousia is immaterial if one is always prepared for it. However, Luz concludes his summary with a critical reflection, drawing on Kazantzakis's treatment of the parable in *The Last Temptation of Christ*. With Kazantzakis, Luz greatly prefers an alternate ending where the doors are thrown open and all—even the foolish and unprepared—are let into the feast.

Davies and Allison

Structurally, Davies and Allison locate the parable of the virgins within the context of the final discourse of Jesus within Matthew (Matt 24:36–25:30), a discourse treated under the heading "Eschatological Vigilance."[98] The key theme of the discourse is presented in its initial verse, Matthew 24:36: "Its declaration of eschatological ignorance grounds the entire section: one must be ever prepared for what may come at any time."[99] The

---

[95] Ibid., 243.
[96] Ibid., 244.
[97] Ibid.
[98] Davies and Allison, *Matthew*, 3:374.
[99] Ibid.

immediate context is a set of three parables that have much in common: "All three concern the delay of the *parousia*, preparedness for the end, and recompense at the great assize; and in each the concluding emphasis is on those who suffer punishment (24:50-51; 25:10-12, 24-30)."[100]

Following several influential modern commentators, they conclude that "a pre-Matthean parable lies behind 24.1b, 3–10b. "We attribute it to Jesus who taught that although the precise date of God's coming cannot be predicted (cf. v. 5), the present is the time of preparation for its joyful advent."[101] Matthew has adapted the parable and "thoroughly assimilated [it] to its present context: its major themes are all reflected in the surrounding material."[102] These themes are: division into two groups, delay of the *parousia*, ignorance of the hour, suddenness of the end, necessity to watch, and requirement of prudence. The language and style is also distinctively Matthean.

Davies and Allison explain the text's broad meaning succinctly before moving into their phrase-by-phrase analysis; they do so with a citation from Jeremias's work on parables:

> Matthew's text is plainly "an allegory of the Parousia of Christ, the heavenly bridegroom: the Ten Virgins are the expectant Christian community, the 'tarrying' of the bridegroom (v. 5) is the postponement of the Parousia, his sudden coming (v. 6) is the unexpected incidence of the Parousia, the stern rejection of the foolish virgins (v. 11) is the final Judgement" [Jeremias, Parables, p. 51].
>
> The parable and application teach three simple lessons, the first indicated by the behaviour of the bridegroom, the second by the behaviour of the wise virgins, and the third by the behaviour of the foolish virgins. The bridegroom delays and comes at an unforeseen time, which circumstances entail yet again that no one knows the day or hour of the Son of man's parousia. The wise virgins, who stand for faithful disciples, reveal that religious prudence will gain eschatological reward. The foolish virgins, who stand for unfaithful disciples, reveal that religious failure will suffer eschatological punishment.[103]

---

[100] Ibid.
[101] Ibid., 3:393–94.
[102] Ibid., 3:394.
[103] Ibid., 3:392.

Thus they see the passage as both a parable and an allegory with the caveat that not "every detail has an allegorical meaning."[104] There is overlap between the two categories that this text occupies. They also call attention to points where the author slips, as at the end. The repetition of "Lord" is "inappropriate when spoken to the groom";[105] Jesus as eschatological Lord is clearly in Matthew's mind rather than a man getting married. Furthermore the formula "truly, I say to you" is also "out of place in a bridegroom's mouth but not in the mouth of the Son of man."[106] As their analysis will bear out, though, they prefer to stay on the side of parable and move to the level of allegory only when necessary.

For interpretive resources, Davies and Allison return to earlier usages in Matthew. In particular, they highlight sections of the Sermon on the Mount (5:15-16; 7:24-27),[107] the parable of the wedding feast/garment (22:11-14), and earlier sections of the eschatological discourse (24:23-43). The main detail that they discuss aside from those identified in the passage quoted above is discussion about the meaning of "the lamp (and/or its fuel)" two objects which they take together.[108] Drawing on the earlier Matthean parallels, they offer a tentative suggestion:

> In view of 5:15-16 and the parallels with 7:24-27 and 22:11-14 (where the absence of a wedding garment must[109] symbolize the absence of good deeds), one wonders whether Matthew did not identify the lamp (and/or its fuel) as a symbol of good works. Certainly the next parable, that of the talents, has to do with good deeds, and Jewish sources use both lamp and oil as metaphors of the law and virtue. But we are uncertain.[110]

[104] Ibid., 3:392n130.

[105] Ibid., 3:400.

[106] Ibid.

[107] Interestingly, aside from the single bare citation of "Compare 7.23" in the discussion of the end of v. 12 (401), 7:21-23 is not mentioned.

[108] Davies and Allison, *Matthew*, 3:397.

[109] Not all interpreters are of this opinion; Luther understood the garment as faith while Gregory saw it as love—reminiscent of their interpretations of the oil. I would not be surprised to find that most interpreters interpret the garment and the oil as the same thing.

[110] Davies and Allison, *Matthew*, 3:396–97.

A footnote after "good works" offers a number of interpretations from the patristic authors through the present day; it concludes with two that underscore an agnosticism toward any secure identification: "Contrast Calvin *ad loc.*: 'There is great ingenuity over the lanterns, the vessels, the oil: the plain and natural answer is that keen enthusiasm for a short term is not enough.' The great number of differing opinions led A. B. Bruce, *The Parabolic Teaching of Jesus*, London, 1882, p. 502, to remark: the oil is 'anything you please.'"[111]

Throughout the footnotes Davies and Allison maintain a running conversation with Augustine's *Sermo* 93. They note his identification of the oil as love in note 159;[112] mention "patristic tradition" including Augustine on the identification of sleep with death, without approving or refuting it, in note 164; mention in a question his connection of the cry at midnight with the trumpet of 24:31, in note 167; disagree with his identification of verse 9 as reproach, in note 173. This running engagement with a patristic source is relatively unusual for this commentary, and no other premodern source is followed this closely, although Calvin is mentioned multiple times as well. Thus while modern commentators form the major conversation partners for the commentary, in this section that they have identified as allegorical, they engage premodern sources more than usual.

Pointing toward the conclusion of the theme of the discourse as well as the parable, Davies and Allison propose by citing Manson that: "'it may be suggested that the original and essential point of the story is that the ten virgins have one task and one only, to be ready with lamps burning brightly when the bridegroom appears' [Manson, *Sayings*, 243]."[113] Rounding out the editorial conclusion of verse 13, they note the ambiguous note on which the text ends. They end with some ambiguity as well:

> The call to wakefulness—a conflation of 24:36, 42, and 50—has been thought odd given that even the five wise virgins fell asleep (v. 5). But [*gregoreite*] may mean only "be prepared!" And in any case the imperative is addressed to the reader, not the foolish virgins. What

[111] Ibid., 3:397n159.

[112] They also note his alternate identification of the oil with joy in *De Div Quaest.* 83 without citing it.

[113] Davies and Allison, *Matthew*, 3:400, quoting from T. W. Manson, *The Sayings of Jesus* (London: SCM, 1949).

wakefulness precisely consists in—doing the will of God?—is here left unsaid, although it plainly involves looking to the future.[114]

Due to the ambiguity surrounding the lamps, the oil, and the parable's conclusion, they treat the three parables as a unit and stay on the level of the general. Matthew is concerned about spiritual lethargy in the face of the delay of the Parousia and exhorts his readers to moral preparation lest they be caught unaware.

Eugene Boring

After noting that the parable is a continuation of the judgment discourse, Boring blends the question of original authorship (noting that scholars have proposed Jesus, the early church [presumably pre-Matthean], or Matthew) with the question of form: is this a parable or an allegory?[115] Authorship is presumably dependent on the solution of the form. Boring draws a dichotomous distinction between the two: "The key issue is whether the details are realistic (parable) or seem contrived to fit the theological meaning (allegory)."[116] Noting that "the story itself is unclear on the procedures of the wedding celebration,"[117] that "details within the present story seem inherently unrealistic"[118] like the midnight arrival and probability of oil shops open at that hour, and identifying numerous thoroughly Matthean themes, Boring concludes that "it seems likely that the story is an allegory constructed by Matthew to further illustrate and emphasize the theme of being ready for the coming of the Lord, despite the apparent delay."[119] Having identified the story as an al-

---

[114] Davies and Allison, *Matthew*, 3:401.

[115] Boring, "Matthew," 449.

[116] Ibid. In earlier discussions on parables prefacing Matt 13 and on Matthew's notion of the Kingdom in Matt 12, Boring has expressed a general distaste for allegorical interpretation of parables: "Such an interpretation offers fertile ground for the preacher's imagination, but has little to do with the text of the Bible." (Boring, "Matthew," 298); he has observed that "Matthew sometimes misses the parabolic character of Jesus' message" (Boring, "Matthew," 294). These judgments seem to play a role in his conflation of form and authorship and with his findings.

[117] Boring, "Matthew," 449.

[118] Ibid., 450.

[119] Ibid.

legory, Boring treats it with dispatch, presenting a list of element identifications, providing a summarizing paragraph on the allegory, then a summarizing paragraph on the conclusion, then a modern appropriation in his reflections section.

Boring lines up the five key elements, italicizes them, and heads five successive paragraphs with them, identifying each concisely with little discussion and no presentation of alternatives. The bridegroom "is Jesus at his eschatological advent."[120] The bridesmaids "represent the church, the present *corpus mixtum* that will be sorted out at the *parousia*."[121] The bridegroom's delay is the delay of the Parousia while the bridegroom's arrival "is the *parousia*."[122] The oil "or rather *having* oil, represents what will count at the *parousia*: deeds of love and mercy in obedience with the Great Commandment (25:31-46)."[123] The identifications that he provides are broadly traditional, falling in line with many modern commentators[124] as well as ancient, once again corresponding with Augustine's identifications in *Sermo* 93. The only difference is that Augustine understands the oil a little differently based on his analysis of the lamps; Boring does not mention the lamps, nor does he take up why all ten started with lamps and oil. In his summary and reflections, however, he indicates that the foolish began with works of mercy and love but did not persevere in them as the wise did. He does not mention 24:12, but it seems implicit in his explanation.

Boring draws on the surrounding discourse and on the Sermon on the Mount for his identifications. Rather than referring to individual verses within the Sermon on the Mount and constructing a number of oblique connections, however, Boring is quite explicit about them, devoting his post-interpretation paragraph to a direct connection with Matthew 5–7:

> The futile attempt to buy oil after the arrival of the bridegroom, though historically unrealistic, shows the futility of trying to prepare when it is too late. As in other Matthean scenes, there are finally only two groups: those who are ready and those who are not. As in

---

[120] Ibid.

[121] Ibid.

[122] Ibid.

[123] Ibid. Emphasis in the original.

[124] Though not all, of course; as noted above, Davies and Allison reject the notion that the church is the *corpus mixtum*.

the Sermon on the Mount, Matthew is not averse to closing on a negative note, with those who say "Lord, Lord" being excluded if they do not have the corresponding deeds of discipleship (cf. 7:21-27). The Sermon on the Mount has much more in common with the "eschatological discourse" than is generally noticed by those who are fascinated only by the one or the other. Both are thoroughly Christological; both are thoroughly eschatological; both are thoroughly committed to the conviction that having the right confession without the corresponding life is ultimately disastrous.[125]

The connection that Boring makes on literary and thematic grounds is turned to the modern situation in a sizable section of his reflections:

> Readiness in Matthew is, of course, living the life of the kingdom, living the quality of life described in the Sermon on the Mount. Many can do this for a short while; but when the kingdom is delayed, the problems arise. Being a peacemaker for a day is not as demanding as being a peacemaker year after year when the hostility breaks out again and again, and the bridegroom is delayed. Being merciful for an evening can be pleasant; being merciful for a lifetime, when the groom is delayed, requires preparedness.
>
> At the beginning of the life of faith, you cannot really tell the followers of Jesus apart. They all have lamps; they are all excited about the wedding; they all know how to sing, "Lord, lord." Deep into the night, when we spot some persons attempting in vain to fan a dying flame to life, we begin to distinguish wisdom from foolishness.

The meaning of this pericope is, for Boring, inextricably tied to the Sermon on the Mount. His reflections on the judgment discourse as a whole not only acknowledge this but also use it as a means for redirecting a potential overemphasis on the more bizarre eschatological elements back to a central Matthean focus on discipleship:

> Matthew 24 is not an eschatological discourse that presents Matthew's or Jesus' doctrine of the end, but is part of chaps. 23–25, whose aim is pastoral care and encouragement. A synopsis will show that

---

[125] Boring, "Matthew," 450.

by incorporating the "little apocalypse" of Mark 13 into this larger framework, Matthew (affirms but) reduces the significance of apocalyptic per se, subordinating it to other, more directly pastoral, forms of discourse. What Matthew presents, and what is to be preached from these texts, is judgment and warnings on Christian discipleship oriented towards the eschatological victory of the kingdom of God, represented in Christ.

Matthean eschatology is fundamentally then not about the end and its coming but is rather an impetus for authentic discipleship. This passage, despite Boring's misgivings about its form, is an illustration of this fundamental theme.

Douglas Hare

Hare treats the parable within the broader context of the apocalyptic teaching of Matthew 24:1–25:46, which he entitles "The Discourse about the Messiah's Glorious Coming."[126] Its immediate context is within a parable collection in Matthew 24:45–25:30, "Three Parables about Faithful Waiting," which are specifically addressed to three groups of Christians concerning three different kinds of accountability.[127] The first parable, the parable of the slave left in charge (Matt 24:45-51), is directed to church leaders. The third parable, the parable of the talents (Matt 25:14-30), is directed to those who have been given special gifts. This middle parable, the parable of the wise and foolish virgins (Matt 25:1-13) is directed to the rank-and-file Christians—everybody.

Hare states that the parable was intended by Matthew to be read as an allegory: "certain details of the parable are allegorical for Matthew."[128] He does not address the tradition history of the parable, refusing to speculate on its original author or transmission history. Rather, he engages the received text directly. Within the text, he finds a number of obvious identifications: the virgins are Christians, Jesus is the bridegroom, the

---

[126] Hare, *Matthew*, 273.

[127] Ibid., 283. For his groupings to function, he does not recognize Matt 25:31-46, commonly referred to as the parable of the sheep and the goats, as a parable. Throughout its interpretation he mentions it only as a "passage" and applies it entirely to "pagans," denying that it speaks of the judgment of Christians.

[128] Ibid., 284.

bridegroom's delay is the delay of the Parousia (though he avoids the technical term for the sake of his readers), the marriage feast is the life of the age to come, and the closed door is the Last Judgment.

Other elements of the story are less clear, in particular: "the key element in the story—the extra oil that the wise virgins have and the foolish do not—since this is not a stock metaphor."[129] Hare mentions Luther's suggestion of faith and anonymously puts forward Augustine's suggestion of love with his reference to Matthew 24:12 but asserts: "The most popular suggestion is that Mathew regards the oil as standing for good works."[130] Following the work of Susan Praeder, he rejects this option because good works do not burn out or are not consumed before the Last Judgment. He concludes, rather, that "It is better to take the oil not allegorically but parabolically. The main point of the story is that the foolish virgins are not ready when the great moment finally arrives."[131] He then goes on to enumerate a list of passages in the gospel referring to various good works that Matthew may have understood as part of being ready for the moment.

Hare also disagrees with the interpretation of the virgins' sleep as death and the great cry as the general resurrection. He prefers to see the sleep as not allegorical but "simply a narrative detail." He concludes his exposition by reminding his readers, "Despite the attached command 'Watch!' (v. 13), the sleeping of the foolish virgins is not the source of their problem, since the wise sleep also. Being watchful means being ready at all times, whether waking or sleeping."[132] Although he does not state that the concluding verse has been incorrectly attached to the parable, he implies it by his reinterpretation of the word "watch."

Thus Hare presents a reading of the parable that both understands it as allegory but simultaneously refuses to acknowledge it as such. That is, he accepts the presence of certain allegorical elements but denies that other elements—the major ones, in fact—are allegorical.

---

[129] Ibid.

[130] Ibid., 285. Regrettably, he does not mention any of the authors or interpreters who have suggested this option. Augustine, Gregory, and writers following them mentioned good works but identified them with the lamps rather than the oil.

[131] Ibid.

[132] Ibid.

Ælfric's Interpretation

The Homily Proper

Ælfric's homily on Matthew 25:1-13 has a complicated, almost disorganized, structure that reveals his difficulties in negotiating this parable.[133] Standing in continuity with the tradition, Ælfric understands the parable of the wise and foolish virgins to be an allegory elucidating one aspect of the Last Judgment. He does not read it as comprehensively describing the event but rather as an explanation of why some who appear righteous will be rejected from the final consummation on the last day. As a result of this interpretive decision, much of the body of the homily is spent identifying the proper understanding of the elements in the parable. Combined with a typical verse-by-verse outline, the frequent glosses, interpretations, and supporting references result in a frenetic text lacking an effective flow. This is complicated by points when Ælfric returns in later verses to elements he had interpreted earlier and either expands or modifies his previous interpretation.

Ælfric's interpretive method follows standard patristic rules for interpretation—any truth presented obscurely in Scripture is necessarily explained openly somewhere else.[134] Therefore the task of the interpreter is to correctly link the clear with the obscure, links most often established by common language.[135] For the most part, Ælfric follows these principles, demonstrating responsible medieval exegetical technique by citing the various passages from which he draws his interpretation either in Old

---

[133] The text is Homily for the Common of Virgins in *Ælfric's Catholic Homilies: The Second Series, Text*, ed. Malcom Godden, Early English Text Society, supplementary series 5 (London: Oxford University Press, 1979), 327–34 (hereafter ÆCHom II, 44).

[134] A representative example of this teaching is the view found throughout Augustine's *De Doc. Chr.* that "the more open places present themselves to hunger and the more obscure places may deter a disdainful attitude. Hardly anything may be found in these obscure places which is not found plainly said elsewhere" (Augustine, *De Doc. Chr.* 2.6.8, 38).

[135] "When a figurative locution appears, the words of which it is composed will be seen to be derived from similar things or related to such things by association" (Augustine, *De Doc. Chr.* 3.25.34. Augustine, *On Christian Doctrine*, 99). While the wording is ambiguous, Augustine's own interpretive writings make abundantly clear that he means that the "similar things" mentioned here are words used in other passages of Scripture.

English or in both Old English and Latin. Only a few times does he offer identifications not grounded by Scripture citation and these are the elements to which he returns later in the homily to ground scripturally.

The interpretation of the allegory is not haphazard but focuses around three particular blocks of Scripture—one that provides the general interpretive context and two that supply equivalencies for the particular elements. The contextualizing block is also the immediate context of the passage: Matthew's final apocalyptic discourse (Matt 24:1–25:46). While Ælfric makes limited direct reference to this section within the homily, its presence and relevance is assumed; there is not the least suggestion that this allegory could refer to anything other than the Last Judgment.

The meat of the interpretation is drawn from Matthew's Sermon on the Mount (Matt 5:1–7:27) and from a Pauline understanding of the last day centered around 1 Thessalonians 4–5. The different blocks offer solutions to different portions of the allegory. The Sermon on the Mount material provides the overall meaning and therefore fills in details concerning the virgins and their accoutrements while the Pauline materials serve to sketch the eschatological timeline.

The controlling Matthean texts that guide Ælfric's overall interpretation are Matthew 6:1-8, 16-18; 7:7, 21-22. The first section presents Jesus' teaching on good works and practices of piety that requires the proper internal disposition. Those who perform good works for the sake of human adulation have already received their reward and, in doing so, have forfeited their eschatological recompense. Ælfric explicitly cites the statement on rewards (Matt 6:2b and parallels) in both English and Latin:

> Some men are so seduced by frivolous boasting that they do for the praise of men what they ought to do for the love of God; then they are foolish for they seek after frivolous sounds, not the eternal rewards. Concerning such the Savior said in a certain place: *Amen dico uobis. receperunt mercedem suam.* "Truly I say to you, they have received their reward." That is, the frivolous fame which they love. They have this world's fame which they sought rather than the eternal reward which did not interest them.[136]

---

[136] ÆCHom II, 44, lines 71–78.

The second section connects to the act of knocking. In Matthew 7:7 its effectiveness is assured; the knocking implied by Matthew 25:11 fails. Ælfric resolves the apparent contradiction with an appeal to time—knocking now in the time of mercy will be effective. In the last day, however, it will be too little, too late. The third section, Matthew 7:21-22, cooperates with the first to present a coherent plain-sense meaning for the application of the parable. While good works, confession of Jesus as Lord, and deeds of power are marks of discipleship, in and of themselves they do not guarantee entry into the final consummation. Rather, doing the will of the Father guarantees entrance. How these beseeching entrance failed to keep the will of the Father is not revealed—the first section, however, supplies for Ælfric a likely answer. The good works flowed from bad intentions, a desire for human praise rather than the love of God. Two features of this third section recommend it specifically for application to the parable: the dialogue and its result. Matthew 7:21-23 is functionally replicated in the dialogue at the gate in Matthew 25:12—both the request "Lord, Lord" and the response "I do not know you" are the same. Also in both cases, those beseeching entrance are left outside, the spatial difference a clear reference to a relational difference—those who belong are within in the presence of Christ, those who do not are outside.

Based on these texts, Ælfric interprets the allegory in this way: the virgins are all "faithful" of the church who have good works to their credit. The wise are those whose works are motivated by a love for God: the foolish are those whose works are motivated by a desire for earthly acclaim. All will die and be raised together. But in the great judgment when each individual's deeds are judged without reference to how other people perceived them, the foolish will be found wanting; Christ will deny them based on the vice that motivated their externally virtuous acts. The ignorance of humanity concerning the timing of the judgment—referred to under the symbol of midnight and directly by the concluding exhortation—is a warning for Ælfric's hearers to investigate their motives and to recall the proper reason for good deeds.

The Liturgical Context

In the lectionaries of the Benedictine Revival, Matthew 25:1-13 was utilized for a general class of occasions: feasts of multiple virgins. By Ælfric's time, there was a fairly well-defined set of saints venerated in common by the Western church. This sanctoral kalendar was born from attempts to standardize liturgical practice across the West—particularly by Charlemagne and the rulers after him—but does not represent in any way the establishment of a centralized control or process over who was named a saint and how it occurred. As a result, the addition of new saints to the kalendar was not an uncommon occurrence in an early medieval monastery.

As the new saints were added to the yearly round, they required liturgical texts so that they could be properly venerated. Thus a generic set of texts were appointed to cover a variety of saintly classifications: apostles, martyrs, confessors, bishops, abbots/abbesses, and virgins. These appeared in both singular and multiple configurations. Practically speaking, the multiple appeared most often in the case of groups of martyrs who were killed together. The various liturgical books had a set of the most necessary of these—though not necessarily standardized—referred to as the Commons of the Saints.[137] The Leofric Missal, for instance, contains commons for the vigil and feast of one apostle, a feast of multiple apostles, vigils of holy martyrs, a feast of one martyr, a feast of multiple martyrs, vigils of holy confessors, a feast of one confessor, a feast of multiple confessors, a feast of virgins and martyrs, and a feast of several saints in common. Paul the Deacon includes similar categories including materials for a vigil of one apostle, a feast of one apostle, a feast of one martyr, a feast of multiple martyrs, a feast of multiple confessors, and a feast of multiple virgins. Ælfric, in turn, provides in the *Catholic Homilies* for a feast of one apostle, a feast of multiple apostles, a feast of one martyr, a feast of multiple martyrs, a feast of one confessor, a feast of multiple confessors, and a feast of multiple virgins.[138]

The parable of the wise and foolish virgins is appointed for a general kind of liturgical occasion, the common of multiple virgins, and also appears early at the feast of some virgin martyrs, most notably Agatha. The logic here is not too hard to trace—but is more interesting than it first appears. The obvious correlation is that the occasion celebrates virgins who, by virtue of their sanctity, have entered into the final consum-

---

[137] This *Commune Sanctorum* is typically found after the listings for the Temporal and Sanctoral cycles. Sometimes the dedication of a church is included with these as well.

[138] These are homilies ÆCHom II, 33–39.

mation and stand now in the presence of God and the Lamb as intercessors on behalf of the faithful; the passage itself features multiple virgins who enter into the marriage banquet that is surely a symbol of eschatological rejoicing.

This interpretation is well attested in the liturgical variety of the church. Hesbert's great collection of antiphons and responsories from medieval Europe contains four antiphons[139] and twelve responsories[140] that use this passage. Most of them connect it explicitly to virgin saints. Sometimes exegetical decisions are already encoded into these texts. Responsory 7228, which circulated with two different verses, is a prime example:

> You will not be among the foolish virgins, says the Lord, but you will be among the wise virgins; taking up the oil of gladness in their lamps, going out to meet him, they will meet the Bridegroom with the palms of virginity.
> (Verse 1a): But at midnight a cry was made: Behold, the Bridegroom comes, go out to meet him.
> (Verse 1b): But coming they will come with exultation, carrying their sheaves.
> Response: Going out to meet him they will meet the Bridegroom with the palms of virginity.

The interpretation identifying the oil as "the oil *of gladness*" is interesting and has two complementary possible sources. The early medieval church read Psalm 44 (Vulgate) narrating the marriage between Christ and women religious—"the oil of gladness" is mentioned in verse 8. The gloss may be a direct reference to the psalm. Alternatively, Augustine made the connection between the psalm and Matthew 25 in *Eighty-Three Different Questions*.

Verse 1b represents another exegetical option. While verse 1a uses a text from the Matthean parable, verse 1b introduces a passage from the psalms (VgPs 126:6). According to Augustine, the psalm refers to almsgiving; the sowing of the seed is the giving of alms, returning with sheaves speaks of the eschatological rewards of the almsgiving.[141]

---

[139] Antiphons 3730, 4543, 4953a, 4953b.

[140] Responsories 6151, 6760, 6806, 6807, 6809, 7139, 7228, 7496, 7667, 7668, 7803 ["Ecce" is unnumbered].

[141] Augustine, *Enarrations on the Psalms*, NPNF[1] 8.605–6.

Another antiphon also with two options for the verse explicitly cites
Psalm 44 (Vulgate) in one of them while in the midst of using the image
of the lamps from Matthew 25:

> The five wise virgins took oil in their vases for their lamps. But at
> midnight a cry was made: Behold, the bridegroom comes, go out to
> meet Christ the Lord.
> (Verse 1b): Listen, daughter and see, and incline your ear, for the
> king has desired your beauty.
> But at midnight a cry was made: Behold, the bridegroom comes, go
> out to meet Christ the Lord.[142]

This responsory specifically identifies the bridegroom as Jesus and stitches
together Psalm 44:11a, 12a (Vulgate) into a harmonious whole. This move
mutually reinforces the interpretive connections between Matthew 25
and virgin saints and Psalm 44 (Vulgate) as well.

There is, however, a second correlation that could be masked by the
more obvious relationship between the virgins in the passage and the
ascetical class of virgins in the Western church. Indeed, this second correlation only becomes visible when lectionary selections are viewed across
categories. The parables of the gospels are found in various places in the
most prevalent Anglo-Saxon lectionaries, but the parables of Matthew
13 and 24–25 are particularly appointed for the saints. In a representative
Anglo-Saxon lectionary, the gospel list contained in London, BL, Cotton
Tiberius A.ii,[143] Matthew 13:44-52, a cluster of three kingdom parables,
is appointed eight times, all for feasts of virgins and their companions.[144]
Likewise the parable of the industrious servant in Matthew 24:42-47 is
appointed six times, generally for feasts of popes and bishops.[145] Our
parable of the wise and foolish virgins is appointed for five occasions—

---

[142] *COA* 7496.

[143] This is Lenker's Qe.

[144] St. Lucia (December 13), St. Prisca (January 18), Octave of St. Agnes (January
28), St. Pudentiana (May 18), St. Praxedis (July 21), St. Sabina (August 29), and
Sts Eufemia, Lucia, Geminianus (September 16) and for the Common of Several
Virgins.

[145] St. Marcellus (January 16), St. Urban (May 25), St. Eusebius (August 14), St.
Augustine of Hippo (August 28), St. Calistus (October 14), and the Common of One
Confessor.

again, virgin saints.[146] Finally the following parable of the talents (Matt 25:14-23) appears just four times—also on feasts of bishops and popes.[147] Thus there is an overwhelming preference to assign the Matthean parables of the kingdom to saints. As a result, there would be no doubt in the early medieval mind that the protagonists of the parable would be saints of some kind.

Perhaps the most interesting feature of this homily is the way it reveals Ælfric taking part in the conversations of his day, both the critical and the popular. Ælfric explicitly mentions that this passage had been treated by both Augustine and Gregory. The conclusion of his introduction implies that the text to follow is from Gregory: "Moreover Augustine the wise man explains to us its deepness and also the holy Gregory wrote concerning this same text saying thus."[148] To assume along with DeLubac that what follows is simply plagiarism of Gregory is quite incorrect.[149]

By Ælfric's day, Paul the Deacon's homiliary appointed four homilies for feasts of multiple virgins.[150] The first taken from Haymo of Auxerre treats Matthew 13:44-45; the second is Augustine's Homily 93 on Matthew 25:1-13; the third is Gregory's Homily 12 on Matthew 25:1-13; the fourth, also on Matthew 25:1-13, is a homily incorrectly attributed to Chrysostom. Following the expectations and purposes of early medieval homiletics, Ælfric remains within the critical conversation of catholic orthodoxy by dutifully using passages and insights from both Augustine and Gregory but in their combination creates a new interpretation different from both his sources in a number of respects. Furthermore, an excursus within this sermon takes to task a heretical teaching that impacts the passage's meaning current in the popular conversation of his day.

[146] St. Agnes (January 21), an alternate for the Octave of St. Agnes (January 28), St. Agatha (February 5), St. Cecilia (November 22), and the Common of Several Virgins.

[147] St. Leo (April 11), St. Martin (November 11), St. Silvester (December 31), and Common of One Confessor.

[148] ÆCHom II, 44, lines 25–27.

[149] Henri De Lubac, *Medieval Exegesis: The Four Senses of Scripture*, trans. Mark Sebanc, 4 vols. (Grand Rapids, MI: Eerdmans, 1998–2009), 2:120.

[150] In Migne, these are Homilies XCIII–XCVI.

Gregory's Homily 12[151] is a second edition of Augustine's Sermo 93. Augustine's sermon is a longer and more thorough text that works carefully through each of the details in the parable, allegorizing each and identifying the various intertexual cross-references to other biblical passages that ground his reading. Augustine often makes interpretive suggestions, deploying texts in their support that he later dismisses in favor of other equally or more supportable choices, giving this sermon a thick, complex texture that requires careful attention to follow the various threads and possibilities Augustine raises. While there are moments and sections of exhortation, the sermon communicates the feel of an interpretive puzzle slowly worked out in the hearer's presence.

Gregory's version greatly simplifies the work and moves it in different directions. Gone are the interpretive dead ends; reduced are the number of scriptural citations. In addition to creating a leaner text with a cleaner flow, Gregory ratchets up the hortatory character by building on the elements of eschatological urgency. A helpful initial paragraph presents the main thrust of his interpretation up front and a colorful local story of one who repented too late rounds out the conclusion. Indeed, an Augustinian passage that acknowledged the reality of the Bridegroom's continued delay is removed entirely to maintain a sense of imminent expectation.

As most commentators agree, the heart of the parable lies bound up with the lamps and their oil. Augustine presents the lamps as good works. Of the modern commentators surveyed here, Davies and Allison take the whole lamp/oil complex to be good works, Boring does not mention the lamps but considers oil to be good works. Hare states that a majority of interpreters take the oil as good works but he ultimately rejects it. Both Davies and Allison and Hare present Augustine's option of the oil as love. On a strictly literal level this is correct; Augustine says plainly: "charity seems to be signified by the oil."[152] However, this kind of simple identification is not enough to grasp Augustine's argument. After all, most every ambiguous sign in Scripture for Augustine is somehow love! He gives voice to this hermeneutic in *On Christian Teaching*:

---

[151] Note that in the Hurst translation, he relies on an idiosyncratic numbering system; in that edition this text is reckoned as Homily 10.

[152] *Sermo* 93.5.

Therefore a method of determining whether a locution is literal or figurative must be established. And generally this method consists in this: that whatever appears in the divine Word that does not literally pertain to virtuous behavior or to the truth of faith you must take to be figurative. Virtuous behavior pertains to the love of God and of one's neighbor; the truth of faith pertains to a knowledge of God and of one's neighbor. . . . But Scripture teaches nothing but charity, nor condemns anything except cupidity, and in this way shapes the minds of men. . . . Therefore in the consideration of figurative expressions a rule such as this will serve, that what is read should be subjected to diligent scrutiny until an interpretation contributing to the reign of charity is produced.[153]

When Augustine identifies something as love, he often later qualifies it by describing who is in love with what in what manner or to what degree.

Furthermore, when Augustine identifies the oil, he does so with a certain amount of hedging:

By what [do we] make the distinction [between wise and foolish]? By the oil. Thinkest thou that it is not charity? This we say as searching out what it is; we hazard no precipitate judgment. I will tell you why charity seems to be signified by the oil. The Apostle says, "I show unto you a way above the rest. Though I speak with the tongues of men and of Angels, and have not charity, I am become as sounding brass, or a tinkling cymbal." This, that is "charity," is "that way above the rest," which is with good reason signified by the oil. For oil swims above all liquids. Pour in water, and pour in oil upon it, the oil will swim above. Pour in oil, pour in water upon it, the oil will swim above. If you keep the usual order it will be uppermost; if you change the order, it will be uppermost. "Charity never faileth."[154]

However, this is an Augustinian trial interpretation and by the end of the sermon he has settled on a second—different—interpretation. Later on, Augustine returns to the oil:

---

[153] *De Doc. Chr.* 3.10.14, 15; 3.15.23.
[154] *Sermo* 93.5.

> Now those wise virgins had brought oil with them in their vessels;
> but the foolish brought no oil with them." What is the meaning of
> "brought no oil with them in their vessels"? What is "in their ves-
> sels"? In their hearts. Whence the Apostle says, "Our glorying is this,
> the testimony of our conscience" (2 Cor 1:12). There is the oil, the
> precious oil.[155]

Thus Augustine's real interpretation is not love after all. The rest of the
sermon makes clear that this "inner oil of conscience"[156] is fundamentally
about motive—are the good works (the lamps) borne of an intent to please
and garner respect from humans or God?

Gregory operates as a classical early medieval monastic author in that
he takes up the substance of Augustine's work but reorders, restructures,
and repurposes it. Gregory's Homily 12, as an epitome of Augustine, cuts
out the initial interpretive feint altogether. Thus Gregory takes the portion
above from the end of Augustine's sermon and inserts it in his initial
discussion of the oil and flasks. He corrects the potentially misunderstood
reference by removing it altogether.

Ironically, Ælfric misses the fact that Gregory's homily is a simplifica-
tion of Augustine's and attempts to harmonize the two. As a result, he
seizes on Augustine's clear statement about oil as love and the engaging
illustration of oil and water, then immediately follows it up with Gregory's
explanation taken from the end of Augustine's sermon. The result is that
he presents Augustine's two options together without differentiation,
making the oil a love-based motive for good works that should be directed
to God. The rest of his sermon, following on the heels of Gregory, actually
does a better job than Gregory of showing that the whole issue of motive
is rooted in the concept of love and is focused on who and what the virgins
(i.e., Christians) love: God or human praise. Nevertheless, this sermon
shows us Ælfric deeply embedded in the critical conversation. He is
determined to pass on the wisdom of the orthodox teachers even if in
doing so he confounds Gregory's editorial purposes!

Despite his concern for the critical conversation in this sermon, this
is not Ælfric's sole focus. After his discussion of those who are locked out

---

[155] *Sermo* 93.9.
[156] *Sermo* 93.17.

of the marriage feast, Ælfric makes an aside that addresses the popular conversation of his day. As mentioned in chapter 1, one of the motives for this cycle of English language homilies was to counteract the heresies found in earlier English texts.[157] The direct correspondence between Ælfric's description given here and a sermon surviving in a unique copy in the Vercelli Book is nothing short of amazing given the rarity of survivals from the period. Homily XV of the Vercelli Book is an English paraphrase of the longer recension of the Apocalypse of Thomas[158] which describes the rise of the antichrist, the signs wracking creation the week before the judgment, then the events of the day of judgment itself. Included among them is a scene of intercession to which Ælfric is probably referring:

> Then our dear Lady, the Blessed Mary, Christ's mother, will see the heap of the wretched, the sorrowful, and the blood-stained, and then she with a weeping voice will arise and fall at Christ's knees and at his feet, and she will say:
> "My Lord Savior Christ, you humbled yourself so that you were dwelling in my womb. Do not allow the power of the devils to have so great a crowd of your handiwork." Then our Lord will grant to the holy, blessed Mary a third part of that sinful crowd.
> Then, still further, there will be a very great crowd—very sorrowful and bloodstained—ever since they were engendered. And then will arise the holy Michael, and he will creep on hands and feet, and with great grief and many tears, he will bow very humbly at the Lord's feet and at his knee. And he will say thus, "My Almighty Lord, you granted to me authority under you over all heaven's kingdom so that I might be your defender of (tortured?) souls. Now I pray to you, my Lord, never let the devils have power in this way over a great crowd of your handiwork." And then our Lord will grant to the holy St. Michael a third part of the sinful crowd.
> And then, still further, there will be a very great, vast throng of sinful souls. And then will arise the holy St. Peter, His chief thane, very sorrowful and very sad and with many sorrowful tears, and he

[157] See a discussion of the likely candidates for exactly which heresies Ælfric was referring to in Malcolm Godden, "Ælfric and the Vernacular Prose Tradition," in *The Old English Homily & Its Backgrounds*, ed. Paul Szarmach and Bernard F. Huppé (Albany: State University of New York Press, 1978), 99–117.

[158] This text was condemned in the sixth-century Psuedo-Gelasian Decretal.

with great humility will fall at the feet of the Savior and at his knees. And he will say: "My Lord, my Lord Almighty, you gave me and you entrusted to me the key of heaven's kingdom, and also (the key) of hell-torments, so that I might bind as many on earth as I wished and release as many as I wished. I ask you, my Lord, because of your kingly rule and because of your majesty that you grant to me the third part of this poor and sinful band." And then our Lord will grant to the holy Saint Peter the third part of the sinful band.

And then, still further, there will be a very great throng, and that (throng) very hateful to God. Then the trustworthy Judge will took on the right side towards His chosen and holy ones, and He will say thus: *"Venite, benedicti patris mei, percipite regnum quod vobis paratum est ab origine mundi!"* He spoke thus, "Come now, you blessed ones, and receive the kingdom of my Father that was prepared for you from the beginning of middleearth." [Matt 25:41] Then our Lord will look on the left hand at the sinful band. And he will say thus to them, *"Discedite, maledicti, in ignem aeternum qui praeparatus est diabulo et angelis eius."* He spoke thus, "Depart, you wicked ones from me into the nethermost punishment of hell into the eternal fire which was prepared for the devil and for you who obeyed him." [Matt 25:41][159]

The issue at stake is the perennial argument between justification by grace versus the demands of discipleship. The Vercelli homily represents an early medieval form of justification by grace where those deserving punishment receive grace from Christ the eschatological judge through the intercession of the saints. It is worth noting that this vision is probably not too far off from how many understood the role of the saints in salvation. Also, the Vercelli homily notes that not all are saved in this fashion—there is still a large crowd handed over to torment; due to a missing manuscript leaf it is unclear who is in which crowd. Clearly one group is saved while another is damned. Presumably all those within the church are saved by the intercession of the saints. Ælfric condemns a concept much like this on the grounds that it undercuts true discipleship and

---

[159] "Homily 15," in *The Vercelli Book Homilies*, ed. Paul Szarmach, trans. Jean Anne Strebinger, Toronto Old English Series 5 (Toronto: University of Toronto Press, 1981), 98–103, here 101–2.

represents—to use the phrase of Dietrich Bonhoeffer—"cheap grace." Instead, he retains the strong focus on discipleship and obedience (with a special emphasis on chastity) found throughout his works.

Discussion

The modern study of parables inaugurated by Jülicher began with a strict distinction between parables and allegories. Jülicher and the scientific study of the New Testament were legitimately reacting to allegorical excess in the interpretation of the parables that had shaped the church's interpretation for centuries. In Ælfric's interpretation we are able to see a number of factors that led to the Protestant backlash against the traditional Catholic reading of the Scriptures that was then carried on by the scientific study of the New Testament. First, Ælfric never questions whether this text might be anything other than an allegory. He begins from a position of certainty that substituted meanings are at the foundation of understanding this text properly. Second, his interpretation is focused entirely on the moral meaning of the text. Indeed, he goes out of his way to emphasize the need for good works against a contemporary reading that elevated grace. He is therefore guilty of "moralizing," a polemical term used particularly in Lutheran circles to suggest that he is transforming a message of grace into law.

By and large, these critiques are not entirely off base. That is, Ælfric is fundamentally interested in how the meaning of the text can be enacted as Christian behavior. There is no doubt that this text is legitimately an admonition; it is counseling a particular kind of action. Since that action is not entirely clear, Ælfric uses the patristic teaching at his disposal to turn the text into an imperative that he and his community may embody. In his defense, Ælfric has treated this text fully and appropriately based on his understanding of the exegetical task.

Ælfric's reading, however, cannot be considered the authoritative early medieval interpretation of this text. Rather, it is one aspect of the total reading.

Ælfric's sermon—or any early medieval sermon for that matter—is one piece of the liturgy. It is the most discursive piece to be sure, but only one element that makes up the whole. As with the Beatitudes, Ælfric's sermon and the antiphons and responsories of the liturgy utilize different aspects of the text. To use John Cassian's distinctions (which, to be clear,

Ælfric does not), Ælfric's sermon focuses on the tropological meaning of the text, the "moral explanation pertaining to correction of life and to practical instruction."[160] The antiphons and responsories, on the other hand, utilize the text in such a way to expose its anagogical meaning, "which mounts from spiritual mysteries to certain more sublime and sacred heavenly secrets . . . by which words are directed to the invisible and to what lies in the future."[161]

As with the Beatitudes, Ælfric's exposition is primarily moral and focused on practical instruction, but an anagogical and eschatological component to the text is explored within the liturgy contributing to a holistic reading of the text. Through its fusion of the anagogical and eschatological, the early medieval reading invites modern scholarship to reflect on the character and extent of eschatology found within Matthean texts—or any religious texts for that matter. Early medieval interpreters were certainly no strangers to eschatological readings in the modern sense; indeed, one of the hallmarks of Gregory the Great's preaching was an intense focus on the end times and on the radical inbreaking of divine power into the everyday world. Rhetorically, he used eschatology as a spur to move his congregation to enact the moral meaning of the text.

What we find in the antiphons and responsories is of a different character, though. By interweaving the gospel texts with narratives of sanctity and eschatological power—like healings—the antiphons and responsories show how early medieval readers perceived the potential of eschatological participation and power within the embodiment of the texts. For them, eschatology was not just a characteristic of the text but a consequence of it as well. The value in this perspective for modern academics is in the way that it challenges their conceptual categories. They may not find these mechanisms in the text; they may not believe that these reflect the intention of the author. Nevertheless, the early medieval monastic readers of these religious texts found this potential within them. Wrestling with these readings may lead contemporary critical scholars to new possibilities for understanding how religious texts inspire transformation either in relation to or apart from original authorial intent.

---

[160] John Cassian, *Conferences*, 14.8.3, trans. Boniface Ramsey, Ancient Christian Writers 57 (Mahwah, NJ: Paulist Press, 1997), 510.

[161] Cassian, *Conferences*, 14.8.3, p. 511.

Conclusion

Bringing Early Medieval Voices into the Conversation

We opened with a discussion of hermeneutics and microcultures, focusing on a particular question: with whom do we read? Strong readers of Scripture will seek to read with a diversity of voices; by listening to others, we learn far more about the text and from the text than we expect. Modern readers can learn tremendous amounts about the Scriptures from academic scholarship. Over the past four centuries, the scientific study of the New Testament has had profound effects on how these texts have been read and understood. Readers who seek to understand them thoroughly must learn from this body of scholarship. Conversely, readers who reject this material will be the poorer for it. Academic scholarship, however, brings certain questions to the text and avoids others. Those who read the biblical text with and for faith communities must be attentive to which questions academic scholarship is positioned to answer and which it is not. Alternate voices enrich the conversation and bring different questions to the table.

This project has sought to evaluate whether early medieval monastic biblical interpreters can serve as effective conversation partners for modern readers committed to broadening their reading of the Scriptures. The first step was to identify the qualities that would characterize effective conversation partners. The second step was locating a representative interpreter within a known milieu; Ælfric of Eynsham, a key figure of the second generation of England's Benedictine Revival, was an ideal candidate given the size of his extant works and the amount of information available on his time and place. The third step was to understand the relationships, the similarities and differences, between the interpretive projects of early medieval monastics and modern academic interpreters. In the fourth step, Ælfric and his interpretive milieu were put into relation with four modern scholars.

From my perspective, Ælfric and his early medieval colleagues are excellent conversation partners. Their worthiness is based on their deep commitment to engaging Scripture and their faith in its transformative power. By giving attention to this author and his milieu, I am in no way claiming his superiority over other potential interlocutors. Rather, I suggest that whenever modern readers of Scripture seek to understand the potential for moral, spiritual, or formative meanings within the text, the early medieval monastic interpreters would serve as excellent guides, representing actual communities who sought to put those aspects of the biblical text into practice.

In the course of laying these foundations, this project has produced the first full-length study of early medieval monastic biblical interpretation that analyzes homiletical material within its liturgical context. Much yet remains to be done. Specifically, what I have done is only the foundation for the conversation and not the true conversation itself. The true conversation would be creative exegesis informed both by the academy and the early medieval monastics.

To those who would continue on to this conversation, I offer some initial observations concerning the character of early medieval monastic interpretation on the Gospel of Matthew and how it best complements modern exegetical techniques. Rather than reading it as an inferior form of modern scholarship, I read early medieval monastic interpretation within its cultural context. While focused on the same texts, monastic culture had radically different purposes in reading Scripture that required different methods and commitments from the modern academic project which—likewise—should be understood in its cultural context. Once the differences between the two sets of reading practices are understood as fundamentally cultural, then points of comparison and coherence can be found and utilized for cross-cultural dialogue. While there are some cultural similarities between the two, the great difference involves the *telos* of interpretation and the paradigmatic context for encountering the Scriptures. For the early medieval monastics, the *telos* of Scripture study and embodiment was no less than the attainment of sanctity; the paradigmatic context for encountering the Scriptures was the liturgy. Monastic exegetical efforts, especially homiletical ones, must be understood within the full scope of the liturgical setting.

Thus, the critical conversation and the appropriation of patristic wisdom was liturgically governed; homiliaries mediated the wisdom of the past through the liturgical framework. The selection of Scriptures encountered was likewise embedded within a liturgical framework governed by the liturgical year which was itself a harmonization and interpretation of the life, death, resurrection, and ascension of Jesus as recorded in the gospels. This is the broader context of the liturgy. The narrower context requires an understanding of how the various liturgical services themselves served to interpret biblical texts.

By placing scriptural texts in relation to one another without explication—as in the antiphons and responsories of the Office and the sung Propers of the Mass—the liturgy engages its participants in the process of meaning-making that is simultaneously collective, as it occurs within the context of shared communal worship, yet is deeply individual as well, since each participant creates relationships between the texts in light of their own spiritual progress and understanding. The yearly repetition of the liturgical cycles brings the community back to these juxtapositions time and again, offering new opportunities for meaning that build on the previously created collective and individual meanings. A young monk or nun might expect to experience each cycle fifty times or more. Furthermore, the practice of *lectio* played off the liturgically grounded meanings. Monastic interpretation did not seek to move forward but to circle ever deeper into the meaning of the texts.

The more discursive elements of the liturgy—from the collects and benedictions up to and including sermons and homilies—are oriented primarily toward the moral sense of the text and secondarily toward the doctrinal. It is worth noting, however, that there is no clear and easy distinction between them: the moral sense of the text, the doctrine contained within the text, and Christology itself. They all freely shade into one another. Rooted in a robust understanding of 2 Timothy 3:16-17, emphasizing the utility of Scripture for instruction for the accomplishing of good works, the interpretation of Matthew is characterized by a robust imitation of Christ. Already focused in this direction by the Christ-shaped Temporal cycle and augmented by the Sanctoral cycle, the gospel is particularly parsed for the presence of virtues—preeminently humility and obedience. Through this process, readers become attuned to these virtues and to methods of reading that maximize their presence.

Another means of reading, sometimes alongside the moral, sometimes in support of it, is the mystical sense. Most of the strategies that fall under the category of "mystical" involve matching patterns of various sorts. Patterns found in other scriptural passages, in liturgical rites, in the etymology of a name, or in events of everyday life may be mapped on the patterns in the text—meaning is produced through these intersections. However readings are derived, their primarily role is focused on action. Scripture does not consist of texts to be read as much as commands to be obeyed or, in a gentler formulation, oracles to be enacted.

The goal of enacting these moral meanings is portrayed in anagogical readings found in some of the discursive materials, particularly collects and benedictions, but are primarily suggested by antiphons and responsories. These liturgical elements introduce the sanctoral and eschatological elements that may not be located in the sermons alone. As a result, any analysis of early medieval monastic exegesis that looks only at the content of the sermons and homilies will inevitably miss the interpretive aspects of the other liturgical materials that provided the proper context for the homilies and can be assumed to be known by the medieval speakers and hearers.

Although they use different reading strategies for the sake of different purposes, early medieval monastic interpreters can serve profitably as outside voices to challenge the conceptions and constructions of the modern American academy. Scholars are correct that early medieval exegetes have little to offer a New Testament inquiry focused on the history of the ideas of the earliest Christian texts. Similarly, they do little to illumine the intentions of the original author. If, however, the inquiry asks about the meaning potential within the biblical texts—what texts themselves could mean, how they could be used—then the early medieval monastic interpreters provide a valuable and reliable example of how text-centered communities read and embodied the New Testament.

In particular, they offer special promise when readers seek to understand how the texts could be used for the purposes of moral and spiritual formation. While the modern academic community prides itself on reading Scripture as any other text—and rightly so given dogmatic restraints of previous generations—the early medieval monastics will continue to insist that the New Testament writings are self-consciously *religious* texts. Moral and spiritual meanings are intrinsic to their very nature. In this capacity, the spirituality of the early medieval monastics reminds present-day scholars that this fundamental fact should not be ignored. Asking how these texts form the morality and spirituality of the individuals and communities who gather around them are entirely legitimate questions.

Perhaps the best ending note is to recognize the solid commitment of early medieval monastic exegesis to multiple meanings. Meanings and interpretations—whether found in homilies, in liturgies, in illuminations, or in songs—were utilized where and when they were useful. There is a decidedly nonhegemonic character to early medieval monastic interpretation which makes it quite amenable as a conversation partner that offers possibilities but does not insist on one or even a limited selection of readings. A foundational text for this commitment is in John Cassian's *Conferences* 14.11.1-5 where, in the person of Abba Nesteros, Cassian offers no less than five different interpretations of the apparently straightforward command, "Do not commit fornication."[1] Each is appropriate to different circumstances, and each builds to the cultivation of virtue at a different level of meaning.

Furthermore, this commitment to multivalence enables the spirit of exegetical play found especially in the homilies and responsories where intertextual connections between widely disparate texts flow seamlessly into one another and illuminate practices and ideals embodied in the Christian communities. Even within this form of play there were boundaries and constraints, to be sure, but different boundaries than those that constrain present-day academic readers. They were the boundaries of shared liturgical practice and experience and formational boundaries that identified meaningful readings as those that edify the community toward true love of God and the accomplishment of good works.

---

[1] John Cassian, *Conferences*, 14.11.1-5, trans. Boniface Ramsey (Mahwah, NJ: Paulist Press, 1997), 515–16.

244 Reading Matthew with Monks

LEARNING FROM EARLY MEDIEVAL READERS

While much can be learned from placing early medieval monastic interpretations in relation to other readings, there are some direct lessons taught by these reading strategies. For those people who read Scriptures in and with the church, who study the Scriptures for the sake of the church and for its edification (of which their own edification is necessarily a part!), these texts also hold lessons worth learning. In particular, I offer three observations where the church of the twenty-first century can learn from the women and men who struggled toward holiness in their own way, in their own time, separated from us by the space of a thousand years.

First, Scripture interpretation normatively occurred in the midst of the community at prayer. While we might think of biblical interpreters as solitary individuals holed up in their studies surround only by books, the early medieval situation gives us a very different perspective. Yes, there is an interpretive moment when an individual sits alone and writes; certainly we have conjured up the image of Ælfric sitting at a writing desk with the homiliaries of Paul the Deacon, Haymo of Auxerre, and Smaragdus open before him, but this is one step in a greater act of creation. For Ælfric and his kin, Scripture interpretation began in the context of the choir. This is where they heard Scripture whether in the readings of the Mass or the Office, where they heard how the Catholic fathers had read it and discovered interpretive clues and hints in the rhythms of the church year and the antiphons and Propers that embellished the liturgies.

It makes a difference when the Scriptures are primarily encountered within an act of praise. Seeing them as an integral part of the church's prayer and praise provides a different starting place; an act of prayer brings a different perspective than an act of study. Study—particularly in our modern sense—implies that the text is a puzzle that requires solving. The text itself can become the subject of study to the degree that the focus remains on a purely textual level. When the text is normatively encountered in prayer, though, the perspective is different. The text is not—cannot be—an end in itself and is understood to be a vehicle through which the community and God relate to one another. Because that relationship has already been established in prayer, the text can never be an ultimate end but is an aid in better understanding and building up the life of grace.

Also, encountering it in the midst of fellow monastics, Ælfric and his fellow interpreters were literally confronted with the reality that interpretation occurs within a communal body and that interpretation is guided by and for that community. This situation places interpretative constraints on what can be found in the text; the presence of the community invokes communal norms about how the text can be read. These norms restrain the interpreter from excesses of individual enthusiasm. That is, there are some radical directions that an individual might be willing to go in as an individual interpreter that one beholden to a community might not.

Second, liturgy and Scripture were perceived to be part of a continuum, not distinct entities, much less opposites to be pitted against one another. The very notion that the two are separable from one another would have been foreign to Ælfric and his compatriots. Instead, liturgy and Scripture mutually reinforce one another, creating a hermeneutical spiral. That is, the liturgy offers insights into the understanding of Scripture, the Scriptures offer deeper insights into the liturgy and its character, and these insights themselves create new vistas on Scripture.

Modern interpreters should utilize the liturgy as an interpretive resource. Very few modern church environments exist in the same kind of intentional liturgical communities that Ælfric and his companions did; our days are not filled with Scripture and liturgical song the way theirs were. However, for liturgically-based communities, the same principles of selection, repetition, and juxtaposition still occur. The liturgical year still provides a hermeneutic that shapes our readings of the texts that fall within them and that shades those same texts when we encounter them outside of their usual season. Repeated elements of the liturgy—the Lord's Prayer, the Song of Mary (Magnificat), the Song of Zechariah (Benedictus Dominus Deus), Jesus' Summary of the Law (Matt 22:37-40)—still function as hermeneutical touchstones, positions from which to understand and draw meaning from the rest of Scripture.

In addition, the interpretations found within the liturgy still form us and remind us of how our spiritual ancestors have interpreted texts. Sometimes scriptural phrases are incorporated wholesale into liturgical elements, showing us how they were read or used. Hymns in particular serve as transmitters of interpretive traditions, demonstrating within their praise of God how certain texts were incorporated into the spiritual lives of the past. Attentive readers will seek to discover how a text has been treated in both liturgy and hymnody as a way to better understand how it has been read, heard, and lived in the church.

Third, early medieval readers press us to consider the full scope of the act of interpretation. Earlier scholars of biblical interpretation looked for commentaries. Finding none, they concluded that substantive and important biblical interpretation was not being done within this period. In doing so, they failed to understand both the product and the point of the interpretative act as it took place within the monasteries. Exegesis did not end on the written page. A commentary was not the final product of the act of interpretation. Early medieval monastic authors like Ælfric and others did produce texts, but their most important, most intellectually challenging, and hardest works were not commentaries but embellishments of the liturgy. As discussed earlier, the height of the art of letters was the production of poetry in classical meters. It found its fullest expression within the liturgy as hymns to Christ and his saints, reponsories, antiphons, tracts, and all other manner of liturgical song gave the liturgy added richness and depth. Ælfric even tapped into the spirit of the vernacular epic poetry to further his homiletical arts. In the time of Ælfric and in the century after him, tropes and proses would provide even more opportunities for ornate composition to bring beauty and dignity to the liturgy in praise of God.

However complex and figured the liturgical embellishments became, however, even they were not the final product. The final product of exegesis for the early medieval monastics was not written in commentaries or even the liturgy but in human lives. Reduced to its most essential point, the act of interpretation was not complete until someone's habits had changed. Conversion of life was the purpose of monastic life; conforming one's life to the pattern of the biblical text was the ultimate goal. Holiness of life came through the formation of the liturgy but it was in the act of conforming the will to the Scriptures that it achieved its fullest form.

Bibliography

Aland, Kurt, ed. *Synopsis Quattor Evangeliorum.* 13th rev. ed. Stuttgart: Deutsch Bibelgesellschaft, 1985.

Anderson, Rachel S. "Saint's Legends." In *A History of Old English Literature,* 87–105. Edited by R. D. Fulk and Christopher M. Cain. Maldon, MA: Blackwell, 2005.

Andrieu, Michel, ed. *Les Ordines romani du haut moyen âge.* 5 vols. *Spicilegium Sacrum Lovaniense,* 11, 23, 24, 28, 29. Louvain, 1931–1961.

Assmann, Bruno. *Angelsächsische Homilien und Heiligenleben.* Bib. ags. Prosa 3. Kassel: G. H. Wigand, 1889. Reprinted with an introduction by P. Clemoes. Darmstadt, 1964.

Augustine, *On Christian Doctrine.* Translated by D. W. Robertson, Jr. Upper Saddle River, NJ: Prentice-Hall, 1958.

Baird, William. *The History of New Testament Research: Volume One: From Deism to Tübingen.* Minneapolis, MN: Fortress Press, 1992.

Barré, H. *Les homéliares carolingiens de l'école d'Auxerre.* Studi e Testi 225. Rome: Biblioteca Apostolica Vaticana, 1962.

Bately, Janet. "The Nature of Old English Prose." In *The Cambridge Companion to Old English Literature,* 71–87. Edited by Malcolm Godden and Michael Lapidge. Cambridge: Cambridge University Press, 1986.

Bede the Venerable. *Homilies on the Gospels: Book One: Advent to Lent.* Translated by Lawrence T. Martin and David Hurst. Cistercian Studies 110. Kalamazoo, MI: Cistercian Publications, 1991.

Blount, Brian K. *Cultural Interpretation: Reorienting New Testament Criticism.* Minneapolis, MN: Fortress Press, 1995.

The Book of Common Prayer. New York: Church Publishing, 1979.

Boring, M. Eugene. "Matthew." In *The New Interpreter's Bible: Matthew-Mark*, 87–506. Edited by Leander E. Keck. vol. 8. Nashville, TN: Abingdon, 1995.

Boynton, Susan and Diane J. Reilly. *The Practice of the Bible in the Middle Ages: Production, Reception & Performance in Western Christianity*. New York: Columbia University Press, 2011.

Bultmann, Rudolf. *The History of the Synoptic Tradition*. Translated by John Marsh. New York: Harper & Row, 1976.

Cameron, Angus. "A List of Old English Texts." In *A Plan for the Dictionary of Old English*, 25–306. Edited by Roberta Frank and Angus Cameron. Toronto: University of Toronto Press, 1973.

Cassian, John. *The Conferences*. Translated by Boniface Ramsey. Ancient Christian Writers 57. Mahwah, NJ: Paulist Press, 1997.

———. *The Institutes*. Translated by Boniface Ramsey. Ancient Christian Writers 58. New York: Newman Press, 2000.

Cassiodorus. *Explanations of the Psalms*. 3 vols. Translated by P. G. Walsh. Ancient Christian Writers 51–53. New York: Paulist Press, 1990.

Clayton, Mary. "Homiliaries and Preaching in Anglo-Saxon England." *Peritia* 4 (1985): 207–42.

Clemoes, Peter A. M. "Late Old English Literature." In *Tenth Century Studies: Essays in Commemoration of the Millennium of the Council of Winchester and the* Regularis Concordia, 103–114. Edited by David Parsons. London: Phillimore, 1975.

———. *Ælfric's Catholic Homilies: The First Series, Text*. Early English Text Society, supplementary series 17. Oxford: Oxford University Press, 1997.

Clover, Carol J. "The Germanic Context of the Unferþ Episode." *Speculum* 55 (1980): 444–68. Reprinted in *The Beowulf Reader*, 127–54. Edited by Peter S. Baker. New York: Garland, 2000.

Colgrave, Betram, ed. and trans. *The Earliest Life of Gregory the Great*. Lawrence: University of Kansas Press, 1968.

Crawford, Samuel J. *Exameron Anglice or The Old English Hexameron*. Bib. ags. Prosa 10. Hamburg: H. Grand, 1921. Reprinted Darmstadt, 1968.

———. *The Old English Version of the Heptateuch*. Early English Text Society 160. London: Oxford University Press, 1922. Reprinted with additions by N. R. Ker, 1969.

Davies, Oliver. *Celtic Spirituality*. Classics of Western Spirituality. New York: Paulist Press, 1999.

Davies, W. D. and Dale C. Allison. *A Critical and Exegetical Commentary on the Gospel According to Saint Matthew*. 3 vols. International Critical Commentary 26. London/New York: T & T Clark International, 2004.

Day, Virginia. "The Influence of the Catechetical *Narratio* on Old English and Some Other Medieval Literature." *Anglo-Saxon England* 3 (1974): 51–61.

De Lubac, Henri. *Medieval Exegesis: The Four Senses of Scripture.* Translated by Mark Sebanc. 4 vols. Grand Rapids, MI: Eerdmans, 1998–2009.

Dibelius, Martin. *The Sermon on the Mount.* Philadelphia: Fortress Press, 1940.

Elliott, J. K. ed. *The Apocryphal New Testament.* Oxford: Clarendon, 1993.

Epp, Eldon J. and George W. MacRae, eds. *The New Testament and Its Modern Interpreters.* Atlanta, GA: Scholars Press, 1989.

Fehr, Bernhard. *Die Hirtenbriefe. In altenglischer und lateinischer Fassung.* Darmstadt: Wissenschaftliche Buchgesellschaft, 1966. First published 1914.

Feine, Paul, Johannes Behm, and Werner G. Kümmel. *Introduction to the New Testament.* Translated by A. J. Mattill, Jr. 14th rev. ed. Nashville, TN: Abingdon, 1966.

Fish, Stanley E. *Is There a Text in This Class?: The Authority of Interpretive Communities.* Cambridge, MA: Harvard University Press, 1980.

Flynn, William T. *Medieval Music as Medieval Exegesis.* Lanham, MD: Scarecrow, 1999.

Förster, Max. "Über die Quellen von Ælfric's exegetischen Homiliae Catholicae." *Anglia* 16 (1894): 1–61.

Fry, Timothy et al., eds. *RB 1980: The Rule of Saint Benedict in Latin and English with Notes.* Collegeville, MN: Liturgical Press, 1981.

Fulk, R. D. and Christopher M. Cain. *A History of Old English Literature.* Malden, MA: Blackwell, 2005.

Gatch, Milton McC. *Preaching and Theology in Anglo-Saxon England: Ælfric and Wulfstan.* Toronto: University of Toronto Press, 1977.

Gneuss, Helmut. "Liturgical books in Anglo-Saxon England and Their Old English Terminology." In *Learning and Literature in Anglo-Saxon England: Studies Presented to Peter Clemoes on the Occasion of His Sixty-Fifth Birthday*, 91–141. Edited by Michael Lapidge and Helmut Gneuss. Cambridge/ New York: Cambridge University Press, 1985.

Godden, Malcolm. *Ælfric's Catholic Homilies: Introduction, Commentary and Glossary.* Early English Text Society, supplementary series, 18. Oxford: Oxford University Press, 2000.

———. *Ælfric's Catholic Homilies: The Second Series, Text.* Early English Text Society, supplementary series 5. London: Oxford University Press, 1979.

Grant, Robert M. with David Tracy. *A Short History of the Interpretation of the Bible.* 2nd ed. Philadelphia: Fortress Press, 1984.

Green, Joel B., ed. *Hearing the New Testament: Strategies for Interpretation.* Grand Rapids, MI: Eerdmans, 1995.

Grégoire, Reginald. *Homéliaires liturgiques médiévaux: analyse des manuscrits.* Bibl degli studi medievali 12. Spoleto, 1980.

———. *Les homéliaires du moyen âge.* Rerum Ecclesiasticarum Documenta, Series Maior, Fontes 6. Rome, 1966.

Gregory I. *Forty Gospel Homilies.* Translated by David Hurst. Cistercian Studies 123. Kalamazoo, MI: Cistercian Publications, 1990.

Gretsch, Mechthild. *Ælfric and the Cult of Saints in Late Anglo-Saxon England.* Cambridge Studies in Anglo-Saxon England 34. Cambridge: Cambridge University Press, 2005.

———. *The Intellectual Foundations of the English Benedictine Reform.* Cambridge Studies in Anglo-Saxon England 25. Cambridge: Cambridge University Press, 1999.

Hall, Thomas N. "Ælfric and the Epistle to the Laodicians." In *Apocryphal Texts and Traditions in Anglo-Saxon England,* 65–84. Edited by Kathryn Powell and Donald Scragg. Cambridge: D. S. Brewer, 2003.

Hare, Douglas. *Matthew.* Interpretation. Minneapolis, MN: Fortress Press, 1995.

Harper, John. *The Forms and Orders of Western Liturgy from the Tenth to the Eighteenth Century: A Historical Introduction and Guide for Students and Musicians.* Oxford: Clarendon, 1991.

Hayes, John H. and Carl R. Holladay. *Biblical Exegesis: A Beginner's Handbook.* Rev. ed. Atlanta, GA: John Knox, 1987.

———. *Biblical Exegesis: A Beginner's Handbook.* 2nd ed. Louisville, KY: Westminster John Knox, 2007.

Hesbert, René-Jean. *Corpus Antiphonalium Officii.* 6 vols. Rome: Herder, 1963ff.

Hill, Joyce. "Ælfric and Smaragdus." *Anglo-Saxon England* 21 (1992): 203–37.

Hill, Thomas D. "Literary History and Old English Poetry: The Case of *Christ I, II, III.*" In *Sources of Anglo-Saxon Culture,* 3–22. Edited by Paul E. Szarmach. Studies in Medieval Culture 20. Kalamazoo, MI: The Medieval Institute, 1986.

Hornby, Emma. *Medieval Liturgical Chant and Patristic Exegesis: Words and Music in the Second-Mode Tracts.* Woodbridge: Boydell Press, 2009.

Hughes, Anselm. *The Portiforium of Saint Wulstan (Corpus Christi College Cambridge Ms. 391).* Henry Bradshaw Society 89. London: Henry Bradshaw Society, 1958.

Johnson, D. W. "Pelagius." In the *Dictionary of Biblical Interpretation,* 255–56. vol. 2. Edited by John H. Hayes. Nashville, TN: Abingdon, 1999.

Johnson, Luke T. and William S. Kurz. *The Future of Catholic Biblical Scholarship: A Constructive Conversation.* Grand Rapids, MI: Eerdmans, 2002.

Jolly, Karen. *Popular Religion in Late Saxon England: Elf Charms in Context.* Chapel Hill: University of North Carolina Press, 1996.

Jones, Christopher A. *Ælfric's Letter to the Monks at Eynsham.* Cambridge: Cambridge University Press, 1998.

Kissinger, W. S. "Sermon on the Mount." In the *Dictionary of Biblical Interpretation,* 462–66. vol. 2. Edited by John H. Hayes. Nashville, TN: Abingdon, 1999.

Kloppenborg, John S. *The Formation of Q: Trajectories in Ancient Wisdom Collections.* Harrisburg, PA: Trinity, 1999. First published 1987.

Knowles, David. *The Monastic Order in England.* Oxford: Clarendon, 1968.

Kümmel, Werner G. *The New Testament: The History of the Investigation of Its Problems.* Translated by S. McLean Gilmour and Howard C. Kee. Nashville, TN: Abingdon, 1972.

Lapidge, Michael. "The Saintly Life in Anglo-Saxon England." In *The Cambridge Companion to Old English Literature,* 243–63. Edited by Malcolm Godden and Michael Lapidge. Cambridge: Cambridge University Press, 1986.

———. *The Anglo-Saxon Library.* Oxford: Oxford University Press, 2008.

Leclercq, Jean. *The Love of Learning and the Desire for God: A Study of Monastic Culture.* Translated by Catharine Misrahi, New York: Fordham University Press, 1982.

Lenker, Ursula. *Die westsächsische Evangelienversion und die Perikopenordnungen im angelsächsiscen England.* Munich: Fink, 1997.

———. "The West Saxon Gospels and the Gospel-Lectionary in Anglo-Saxon England: Manuscript Evidence and Liturgical Practice." *Anglo-Saxon England* 28 (1999): 141–78.

Letson, D. R. "The Poetic Content of the Revival Homily." In *The Old English Homily & Its Backgrounds,* 139–56. Edited by Paul E. Szarmach and Bernard F. Huppé. Albany: State University of New York Press, 1978.

Livingstone, Elizabeth A., ed. *The Concise Oxford Dictionary of the Christian Church.* Oxford: Oxford University Press, 1977.

Luz, Ulrich. *Matthew 1–7: A Continental Commentary.* Translated by Wilhelm C. Linss. Hermeneia. Minneapolis, MN: Fortress Press, 1992.

———. *Matthew 8–20: A Commentary on the Gospel of Matthew.* Translated by James E. Crouch. Hermeneia. Minneapolis, MN: Fortress Press, 2001.

———. *Matthew 21–28.* Translated by James E. Crouch. Hermeneia. Minneapolis, MN: Fortress Press, 2005.

Magennis, Hugh and Mary Swan, eds. *A Companion to Ælfric.* Leiden: Brill, 2009.

McKenzie, Steven L. and Stephen R. Haynes, eds. *To Each Its Own Meaning: Biblical Criticisms and Their Applications.* Rev. ed. Louisville, KY: Westminster John Knox, 1999.

Millful, Inge B. *Hymns of the Anglo-Saxon Church.* Cambridge: Cambridge University Press, 1997.

Nokes, Richard S. and Kathryn Laity, eds. *Curing Elf-Shot and Other Mysterious Maladies: New Scholarship on Old English Charms.* University Park, PA: Penn State University Press, 2009.

Orchard, Nicholas, ed., *The Leofric Missal.* 2 vols. Henry Bradshaw Society 113 and 114. Rochester, NY: Boydell, 2002.

Patrologia Latina. Edited by Jean-Paul Migne. 217 vols. Paris, 1844–1864.

Peifer, Claude. "The Rule in History." In *RB 1980: The Rule of St. Benedict in English and Latin with Notes*, 113–51. Edited by Timothy Fry, et al. Collegeville, MN: Liturgical Press, 1980.

———. "The Rule of St. Benedict." In *RB 1980: The Rule of St. Benedict in English and Latin with Notes*, 65–112. Edited by Timothy Fry, et al. Collegeville, MN: Liturgical Press, 1980.

Pfaff, Richard W. *The Liturgy in Medieval England: A History*. Cambridge: Cambridge University Press, 2009.

Pope, John C. *Homilies of Ælfric: A Supplementary Collection*. 2 vols. Early English Text Society 259, 260. London: Oxford University Press, 1967–1968.

The Sayings of the Desert Fathers: The Alphabetical Collection. Translated by Benedicta Ward. Cistercian Studies 59. Rev. ed. Kalamazoo, MI: Cistercian, 1984.

Skeat, Walter W. *Ælfric's Lives of Saints*. 4 vols. Early English Text Society 76, 82, 94, 114. London: Oxford University Press, 1881–1900. Reprinted in 2 vols., 1966.

Smalley, Beryl. *Study of the Bible in the Middle Ages*. 3rd ed. Notre Dame, IN: University of Notre Dame Press, 1964.

Smetana, Cyril. "Ælfric and the Homiliary of Haymo of Halberstadt." *Traditio* 17 (1961): 457–69.

———. "Ælfric and the Early Medieval Homiliary." *Traditio* 15 (1959): 163–204.

———. "Paul the Deacon's Patristic Anthology." In *The Old English Homily & Its Backgrounds*, 75–97. Edited by Paul E. Szarmach and Bernard F. Huppé. Albany: State University of New York Press, 1978.

Stanton, Graham N. "Matthew, Gospel of." In the *Dictionary of Biblical Interpretation*, 136–41. vol. 2. Edited by John H. Hayes. Nashville, TN: Abingdon, 1999.

Steinmetz, David C. "The Superiority of Pre-Modern Exegesis." *Theology Today* 37 (1980): 1, 27–38.

Swain, Larry. "Ælfric of Eynsham's Letter to Sigeweard: An Edition, Commentary, and Translation." PhD diss., University of Chicago, 2008.

Symons, Thomas. *Regularis Concordia Anglicae Nationis Monachorum Sanctimonialiumque. The Monastic Agreement of the Monks and Nuns of the English Nation*. London: Nelson, 1953.

Szarmach, Paul E. "Ælfric as Exegete: Approaches and Examples in the Study of the *Sermones Catholici*." In *Hermeneutics and Medieval Culture*, 237–47. Edited by H. Damico and P. Gallacher. Albany: State University of New York Press, 1989.

————. "Anglo-Saxon Letters in the Eleventh Century." In *The Eleventh Century*, 1–14. Edited by Stanley Ferber and Sandro Sticca. Acta 1. Binghamton, NY: CEMERS, 1974.

Szarmach, Paul E. and Bernard F. Huppé, eds. *The Old English Homily & Its Backgrounds.* Albany: State University of New York Press, 1978.

The Vercelli Book Homilies. Edited by Paul Szarmach. Translated by Jean Anne Strebinger. Toronto Old English Series, 5. Toronto: University of Toronto Press, 1981.

Vogel, Cyrille. *Medieval Liturgy: An Introduction to the Sources.* Translated and revised by William Storey and Niels Rasmussen. Portland, OR: Pastoral, 1986.

Wilcox, Jonathan. *Ælfric's Prefaces.* Durham Medieval Texts 9. Durham: University of Durham, 1995.

Index of Names and Topics

Index of Liturgical Forms and Homilies

Index of Scripture References